Landmarks in linguistic thought III
The Arabic linguistic tradition

Landmarks in Linguistic Thought III: The Arabic Linguistic Tradition is devoted to the main linguistic tradition of the Middle East, namely that of Arabic linguistics.

The reader is introduced to the major issues and themes that have determined the development of the Arabic linguistic tradition. Each chapter contains a short extract from a translated "landmark" text followed by a commentary which places the text in its social and intellectual context. The chosen texts frequently offer scope for comparison with the Western tradition. The book highlights the characteristics of a tradition outside the Western mainstream with an independent approach to the phenomenon of language and thus stimulates new ideas about the history of linguistics.

This book presumes no prior knowledge of Arabo-Islamic culture and Arabic language, and is invaluable to anyone with an interest in the History of Linguistics.

Kees Versteegh is currently Professor of Arabic and Islam at the Middle East Institute of the University of Nijmegen, the Netherlands. His publications include Zajjaji's *Explanation of Linguistic Causes* (1995), (ed.) *Arabic Outside the Arab World* (1994).

ROUTLEDGE HISTORY OF LINGUISTIC THOUGHT SERIES

Consultant Editor: Talbot J. Taylor
College of William and Mary, Williamsburg, Virginia

Landmarks in Linguistic Thought I:
The Western Tradition from Socrates to Saussure
Roy Harris and Talbot J. Taylor

Landmarks in Linguistic Thought II:
The Western Tradition in the 20th century
Roy Harris, Nigel Love and Talbot J. Taylor
Forthcoming

Landmarks in Linguistic Thought III:
The Arabic Linguistic Tradition
Kees Versteegh

Language, Saussure, and Wittgenstein: How to Play Games with Words
Roy Harris

Ideology and Linguistic Theory: Noam Chomsky and the Deep Structure Debates
Geoffrey J. Huck and John A. Goldsmith

Linguistics, Anthropology and Philosophy in the French Enlightenment: A Contribution to the History of the Relationship between Language Theory and Ideology
Ulrich Ricken, translated by Robert Norton

Linguistics in America 1769–1924: A Critical History
Julie Tetel Andersen

Generative Linguistics: A historical perspective
Frederick J. Newmeyer

Landmarks in linguistic thought III

The Arabic linguistic tradition

Kees Versteegh

ROUTLEDGE
London and New York

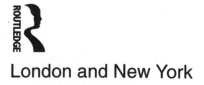

First published 1997
by Routledge
11 New Fetter Lane, London EC4P 4EE

Simultaneously published in the USA and Canada
by Routledge
29 West 35th Street, New York, NY 10001

Typeset in Times by Keystroke, Jacaranda Lodge, Wolverhampton
Printed and bound in Great Britain by T.J. International Ltd, Padstow, Cornwall

British Library Cataloguing in Publication Data
A catalogue record for this book is available from the British Library

Library of Congress Cataloging in Publication Data
Versteegh, Kees.
Landmarks in linguistic thought : the Arabic linguistic tradition / Kees Versteegh.
p. cm. — (History of linguistic thought)
Includes bibliographical references.
1. Arabic language—History. 2. Arabic language—Grammar—Theory, etc. 3. Arabic language—Grammar—Study and teaching—History.
I. Title. II. Series.
PJ6053.V47 1997
492′.7′09—dc20 96–36345
CIP

ISBN 0–415–14062–5 (hbk)
ISBN 0–415–15757–9 (pbk)

Contents

Introduction

Most studies on the history of linguistics concentrate on the history of mainstream Western theories of language and grammar. The present volume is devoted to a tradition outside this mainstream, the Arabic tradition. In various cultures in the Near East, such as Akkadian, Old Egyptian, Syriac, and Hebrew, some form of linguistic speculation was developed. But the main linguistic tradition was that of the Arabs, starting in the seventh century CE and ending in the nineteenth/twentieth centuries with the reception of Western linguistics in the Middle East.

In 632 the Prophet of Islam, Muḥammad, died in the city of Mecca in the Arabian peninsula. He had founded a community that had adopted the religious doctrine of Islam, as it was laid down in the revealed book, the *Qur'ân*. His successors as political leaders of the community, the caliphs, started a series of military expeditions into the world outside the Arabian peninsula; very soon these turned into real campaigns that led to the conquest of a large part of that world. Within a few decades Persia, Mesopotamia, Syria, Egypt and North Africa had become provinces of a new Islamic empire, which supplanted the Persian empire and became the most important rival of the Byzantine empire. In 711 the Muslim armies crossed the Strait of Gibraltar and conquered the Iberian peninsula. Their advance was stopped in France with the battle of Poitiers (732). In the Western Mediterranean Malta and Sicily were incorporated in the empire, and in the East parts of Central Asia soon became provinces as well.

The Arab armies brought to the inhabitants of the conquered territories not only their religion, but to an even larger degree the Arabic language. Until then it had been the language of Bedouin tribes roaming the deserts of the Arabian peninsula, but now it became the language of a large empire, in which it functioned as the language of religion, culture, and administration. The languages that were spoken in these areas at the time of the conquests were either supplanted by Arabic or marginalized. Some of them, such as Coptic and Syriac, eventually disappeared as living languages and lingered on in the limited function of ritual language for Christian groups. The Berber language remained the vernacular of a sizeable minority in North Africa until today. After having been reduced to the status of a regional language without much influence, Persian later went through a renaissance and turned into a major cultural language for the Islamic peoples, not only in Persia, but also in those areas to which Islam was brought in Asia, such as India and Malaysia. From the tenth century onwards Turkic-speaking peoples invaded the Islamic provinces from Central Asia and eventually became the new political masters of most of the Middle East and Egypt. After the fall of Constantinople (1453) and the demise of the Byzantine empire they founded the Ottoman empire, which became the major political power in the Eastern Mediterranean. At the other extreme of the empire Islamic Spain (*al-'Andalus*) remained Arabic and Islamic until the end of the Reconquest of the peninsula by Christians, which was completed in 1492 with the fall of Granada. After the fifteenth century the Arab provinces with the exception of Morocco became part of the Ottoman empire, and Arabic was replaced by Turkic as a political and administrative language until the twentieth century, after the end of the colonial period when the Arab provinces gained their political independence and reinstated Arabic as the national language of the new countries. In those countries where Islam had been accepted as the majority religion, such as Turkey, Iran, Indonesia and Pakistan, the role of Arabic as a religious language and the language of the Qur'ânic revelation is still gaining in strength.

The introduction of Arabic into the conquered provinces after the death of the Prophet had profound linguistic effects on the language itself. During the initial stages of the conquests Arabic became the dominant language, which everybody had to learn. Details about the process of arabization and acquisition are unknown, but the result of this process was the emergence of a new type of Arabic, a spoken language that existed alongside the old language of the Bedouin and the *Qur'ân*, compared to which it had a reduced structure. The coexistence of the two varieties of the language led to a diglossia, in which the Classical Arabic standard language functioned as the high variety (called by the Arabs *al-lugha al-fuṣḥâ* "the eloquent, correct language"), and the vernacular of the spoken language constituted the low variety (called *al-'âmmiyya* "the language of the people").

The Arabic tradition preserves the memory of this process in the form of many anecdotes in which the speech of the new inhabitants of the empire and the new Muslims was satirized. According to many reports the "pure" Arabs were shocked by the errors made by the neophytes and attempted to stem the tide of what they regarded as corruption of the language by codifying the norms of correct linguistic usage. One story has the governor of Iraq, Ziyâd ibn 'Abîhi, requesting the assistance of a well-known scholar, 'Abû l-'Aswad ad-Du'alî, who probably died around the year 688, for this job. At first 'Abû l-'Aswad refused, since he felt unworthy to the task and was afraid to lay down rules for the language of the divine revelation, but when he heard people making mistakes in the use of the declensional endings, he acquiesced and wrote the first treatise of Arabic grammar.

> According to one account Ziyâd ibn 'Abîhi sent for 'Abû l-'Aswad and said to him: "O 'Abû l-'Aswad, these foreigners have multiplied and corrupted the tongues of the Arabs. Couldn't you compose something to correct their language and give God's Book its proper declension?" 'Abû l-'Aswad refused and did not want to comply with his request. Then, Ziyâd sent for somebody and said to him: "Go and sit down in the road near to 'Abû l-'Aswad, and when he passes by you recite something from the *Qur'ân*, but make sure to make some mistake". The man did this and when 'Abû l-'Aswad passed by he recited "God keeps clear from the unbelievers and from His Prophet" [with genitive, instead of "God keeps clear from the unbelievers and so does His Prophet", with nominative]. 'Abû l-'Aswad was shocked. He returned immediately to Ziyâd and said to him: "I'd like to comply with what you asked me to do and I think it would be best to start with the declension of the *Qur'ân*".
>
> (Ibn al-'Anbârî, *Nuzhat al-'alibbâ'*, ed. by Attia Amer, Stockholm, 1962, p. 6)

This account of the origin of grammatical study is clearly a *topos*; in other linguistic traditions, too, the invention of grammar is connected with stories about grammatical mistakes, for instance in Sanskrit. In some versions of the story the central role in the foundation of grammar is assigned to the fourth Caliph, 'Alî ibn 'Abî Ṭâlib:

> The reason why 'Alî – may God have mercy on him! – founded this science is given by 'Abû l-'Aswad in the following story: I came to the Commander of the Believers 'Alî ibn 'Abî Ṭâlib – may God have mercy on him! – and saw in his hand a manuscript. I said to him: "What is this, Commander of the Believers?" He said: "I was reflecting on the language of the Arabs and noted that it had been corrupted by our mixing with these red persons -i.e., foreigners – and I wanted to make something for them on which they could fall back and on which they could rely". Then he handed me the manuscript, and I saw that it said: "Language is noun and verb and particle. The noun is what informs about a named object; the verb is that with which the information is given; and the particle is what comes for a meaning". He said to me: "Follow this direction (*unḥu hâdhâ n-naḥw*) and add to it what you find!"
>
> (Ibn al-'Anbârî, *Nuzha*, p. 4)

This story clearly has an etiological character: it attempts to explain the name of the discipline (*naḥw*) from a verb *naḥâ* "to take a direction" and it traces back to the venerable lineage of the fourth Caliph 'Alî the tripartition of the parts of speech into noun, verb, and particle, which was introduced in the first book on grammar, Sîbawayhi's *Kitâb* (cf. chapter 1, p. 36). Whatever the historical reality to the reports about 'Abû l-'Aswad, so much is certain that the origin of grammar was linked by the Arabic sources to the corruption of the Arabic language in the first centuries of the Islamic empire. A similar motive for the foundation of grammar is mentioned by Ibn Khaldûn in his historical account of the development of science in the Islamic world: grammar became necessary when the new Muslims threatened to corrupt the Arabic language by their mistakes (cf. below, chapter 12).

Probably, the figure of 'Abû l-'Aswad was used by later grammarians to serve as the eponym of their own school. There are alternative traditions in which other grammarians play the role of 'Abû l-'Aswad, and it can be shown that these accounts originated in other grammatical schools. The first written treatises stem from the end of the second century of the Islamic period (end of the eighth century CE), when al-Khalîl ibn 'Aḥmad wrote his dictionary of Arabic and Sîbawayhi his grammatical description of the language. Both worked and taught in the newly founded city of Basra. Earlier activities in the science of grammar had probably taken place in the rival city of Kufa, as well as in other cities such as Damascus, Mecca, and Medina. After the publication of Sîbawayhi's *Kitâb* the discipline of grammar was dominated by other grammarians from Basra, but the centre of their grammatical studies had shifted from Basra itself to the city of Baghdad, founded by the 'Abbâsid caliphs in 762 on the borders of the Tigris to serve as the new capital of the Islamic empire.

From the biographical literature we know the names of more than 4,500 grammarians and lexicographers who were active between 800 and 1500 CE. The only criterion for inclusion in the biographical dictionaries was whether one had actually taught grammatical texts to one's pupils. Being a teacher of grammar was not a profession in Islamic society: most grammarians had to work as lawyers, judges, booksellers, scribes or other jobs in order to earn money. Most of the grammarians mentioned in the sources are only names for us, and so are the titles of their works, but a considerable number of important writings have been preserved, from which the history of the discipline can be reconstructed with some degree of accuracy.

Several attempts have been made to link the origin of Arabic grammar to foreign linguistic traditions. We shall see below that in the ninth century the translation of Greek logical writings led to an influx of logical terminology in Arabic grammar. As for the formative period of the Arabic linguistic tradition, it has been claimed that the earliest writings exhibit some traces of foreign (Greek/Syriac) influence, in particular with regard to the classification of the parts of speech and in the terminology of the vowels and declensional endings. Yet, in its further development the Arabic linguistic tradition stayed remarkably clear of any foreign influence. As a result the Arabic grammarians operate within a system of linguistic thought that in many respects differs from the way Western scholars analyse the phenomenon of language.

The study of this tradition is worthwhile for several reasons. In the first place, the knowledge the Arab scholars had of their own language was vastly superior to our own, and a careful analysis of their ideas contributes to our own understanding of the structure of Classical Arabic. Many words, poetic quotations and grammatical phenomena are only known to us thanks to the grammarians' writings. Moreover, general historians of linguistics benefit from the acquaintance with an approach to the study of language that differs from the usual Western framework. The contrast between the two systems serves to highlight the characteristics of each tradition and thus to stimulate new ideas about the history of linguistics.

In the selection of the topics for the texts and chapters, preference has been given to those which allow a comparison with the Western tradition, for instance, the ideas about the origin of speech, the relationship of language and thought, the relationship of language and logic, the place of semantics in the theory of grammar. By necessity this selection misrepresents the character of the Arabic linguistic tradition: the average grammarian was concerned solely with the technical analysis of the language of the *Qur'ân*, the pre-Islamic poems, and the Bedouin, and could not be bothered with general speculations about the nature of language, the relationship between language and thought, the origin of speech, or the structure of other languages than Arabic. In our selection we have concentrated on the ideas some grammarians formulated about such topics, even though they were marginal for the mainstream tradition.

A special problem in dealing with non-Western linguistic traditions concerns the translation of technical terms. In Arabic theories on declension the case endings of the words are regarded as the effect of another word, called *'âmil* "governor", whose operative force is called *'amal* "governance"; lexically the verb *'amila* (*fî*) means "to act upon, to affect", and an *'âmil* is the governor of a province. Obviously, the choice of the words "governor" and "governance" in the translation of the Arabic terms conjures up the image of modern linguistics and specifically the government and binding model. This raises the question of the permissibility of such terms in translating Arabic grammatical theory. In fact, any translation of technical terms from another tradition poses a problem, since even terms such as "noun", "verb", "nominative", "accusative", "morphology", or "syntax" are closely connected with the Western grammatical tradition and therefore likely to distort the original meaning. Some scholars have concluded from this quandary that it is wisest always to use the Arabic terms (which makes a translation very difficult to follow for the non-Arabist). Another solution consists in using only neologisms, for instance, by calling the declensional endings a-case, u-case, i-case. This does not solve, however, the problem of the basic discrepancy between the Arabic approach and the approach of the dominant model in our society, that of Western school grammar and its various offshoots. Our solution will be different. Given the fact that the problems in analysing a language, if not the solutions, are basically identical for all civilizations and cultures, it may be surmised that the number of possible solutions is limited. In other words, it should be possible to find common ground between the various solutions, and even though they differ in their systematization and practical application, they are bound to share some theoretical presuppositions. The relationship between *'âmil* and *'i'râb* is formulated by the Arabic grammarians in terms that suggest a dependency between two constituents; as a provisional translation terms such as "government" and "declension" may, therefore, be retained. Whether or not this implies a basic relatedness with Western dependency grammar remains to be seen (cf. below, chapter 3, p. 45).

In chapter 1 the beginning of linguistic thinking in the Islamic world in the earliest commentaries on the *Qur'ân* (eighth century) is discussed in connection with the methods and the hermeneutic devices used in exegesis. The connection between exegesis and grammar constitutes the link with the next chapters. Chapter 2 deals with the role of al-Khalîl (d. 791) in the development of phonetics and lexicography. His observations on the phonetic structure of Arabic in the introduction to the famous *Kitâb al-'ayn*, the first Arabic dictionary, constituted the basis for all later lexicographical efforts in Arabic. We briefly sketch the system of lexicography used in the *Kitâb al-'ayn*, as well as the later developments in dictionary-making. Chapter 3 deals with the founder of Arabic grammar, Sîbawayhi (d. 793). He was the author of *al-Kitâb*, the first comprehensive analysis of language structure in the Arabic tradition, which remained both model and source throughout the centuries. The main topics of this chapter are the general principles of grammar presented by Sîbawayhi in the first sections of the *Kitâb* and the methodological aspects of his approach to linguistics (the idea of grammar as an explanatory system; synchronic analysis of language on the basis of a closed corpus; the status of the native speaker).

With the introduction of Greek logic and philosophy in the Arab world in the ninth century, a debate between philosophers and grammarians on the relationship between language and thought became inevitable. Chapter 4 deals with a discussion between a logician and a grammarian on the concept of "meaning", which epitomized the clash between the two disciplines. This confrontation with Greek logic profoundly influenced the development of Islamic thinking in general and did not fail to influence grammarians as well, in spite of their opposition to the logicians' claims. One of the most original authors of the tenth century, az-Zajjâjî, discussed the various levels on which linguistic explanations are formulated. His distinction of a didactic, an analogical, and a speculative level of linguistic reasoning represented one of the few attempts in the Arabic tradition to formulate an explicit metatheory of linguistics (chapter 5).

The exclusion of philosophy and logic from the discipline of grammar did not stop philosophers from elaborating their ideas on language and thought in their commentaries on Greek writings; al-Fârâbî's (tenth century) ideas on the relationship between language and thought and about philosophical grammar, based on the commentaries on Aristotle's writings, are discussed in chapter 6. Chapter 7 is dedicated to a group of scholars who occupy a special place in the development of Arabic thinking about language. The 'Ikhwân aṣ-Ṣafâ' (tenth century) compiled an encyclopaedia in which they combined Islamic and Greek wisdom and knowledge. One section in this encyclopaedia deals with the study of physical sound and its place in language, presenting a highly original theory of sound and communication.

From the ninth century onwards under the influence of the new ideas that had been imported from Greek philosophy, some Arabic grammarians who belonged to the Mu'tazilite school of theology began to occupy themselves with the question of the origin of speech. The "revelationists" advanced the thesis of a divine origin, whereas the "rationalists" attributed an important role to human intervention. In Ibn Jinnî's (d. 1002) work the two theories are discussed extensively and placed in a religious and linguistic context (chapter 8).

Although the general orientation of all Arab grammarians was formal/syntactic, some grammarians advocated the inclusion of semantic and pragmatic considerations in linguistic theory. Al-Jurjânî and as-Sakkâkî (elventh century) are the most important proponents of this trend, which was to have far-reaching effects on the later development of Arabic grammar. In chapter 9 we discuss some of the issues, for which they proposed a new approach, taking into account the semantic differences in language and the role of language in communication. From the tenth century onwards language and linguistics became an important issue in the study of the legal relevance of speech, in the discipline of the *'uṣûl al-fiqh*, the principles of law. Basing themselves on the Mu'tazilite view of language as a conventional and established system, they attempted to define the relationship between the linguistic sign and what it denoted. In his compendium of this science the Qur'ânic commentator ar-Râzî (eleventh century) discussed some of its principles (chapter 10).

Not all scholars remained within the general framework of the Arabic grammatical theories. Because of his theological beliefs the Andalusian grammarian Ibn Maḍâ' (twelfth century) rejected the entire rationalistic structure of Arabic linguistic theory, and demonstrated in detail that the theoretical constructions of the grammarians were unnecessary (chapter 11). His critique went unnoticed in the Arabic tradition, but in modern times his attempt to free grammar from theory was used in a plea for the modernization of linguistic education in Egypt.

We have seen above that the Arab conquests in the seventh century profoundly influenced the development of the Arabic language. The divergence between the standard language and the vernacular was the principal motivation for the emergence of grammar as an independent discipline. Most grammarians did not show any interest in the vernacular type of speech and concentrated entirely on the standard language, ignoring the language of the people. As a result there is no trace of a diachronic approach to language: the grammarians act as if there was no development in the Arabic language, which remained the same for all times. We have to turn to writers outside the discipline for an appraisal of the linguistic situation and the diachronic development. In his *Muqaddima* the famous historian Ibn Khaldûn (fourteenth century) developed a theory on the development of human society, in which he also discussed the role of language. In the text translated in chapter 12 he discusses the origin of the "corruption of speech", as well as the emergence of grammar as a weapon against linguistic change.

Partly because of their lack of interest in diachronic development, partly also because of their contempt for other languages than Arabic, Arabic grammarians as a rule did not occupy themselves with any other languages. A different situation obtained in the case of those Hebrew grammarians who wrote in Arabic. They were interested in the relationship between Arabic, Hebrew, and Aramaic and initiated the earliest comparative grammar of the Semitic languages. Among the Arabic grammarians there is one scholar who broke with the monopoly of Arabic as object of research. 'Abû Ḥayyân (d. 1344) wrote grammatical descriptions of Turkic, Mongolian, and Ethiopian, using the model of Arabic grammar to analyse these languages. The use of the Arabic model for other languages than Arabic, such as Hebrew and Turkic, is discussed in chapter 13.

Chapter 1

Linguistics and exegesis

Muqâtil on the explanation of the *Qur'ân*

Sufyân said: Someone who reads the *Qur'ân* and does not know its exegesis is like someone who upon receiving a book that is liked by many people, rejoices in it and begs someone to read it to him, since he cannot read himself, but finds no one. This is similar to someone who reads the *Qur'ân* and does not understand what is in it. Ibn 'Abbâs said: The *Qur'ân* has four aspects: exegesis, which is known to the scholars; Arabic language, which is known by the Arabs; allowed and forbidden things, which people cannot afford to ignore; and interpretation, which is only known to God Almighty. . . . Muqâtil said: The *Qur'ân* contains references to particular and to general things, particular references to Muslims and particular references to polytheists, general references to all people; it contains ambiguous and univocal passages, explained and unexplained passages; it contains deletions and explicit utterances; it contains connective items; abrogating and abrogated verses; it contains changes in the chronological order; it contains similar utterances with many different aspects; it contains passages that are continued in a different *sûra*; it contains accounts of earlier generations and accounts of what there is in Paradise and in Hell; it contains references to one particular polytheist; it contains commandments, laws, ordinances; it contains parables by which God Almighty refers to Himself, parables by which He refers to unbelievers and idols, and parables by which He refers to this world, to resurrection and to the world to come; it contains accounts of what is in the hearts of the believers and accounts of what is in the hearts of the unbelievers, polemics against the Arabian polytheists; and it contains explanations, and for each explanation there is an explanation

(Muqâtil, *Tafsîr al-Qur'ân*, I, 26–7, ed. by 'Abdallâh Maḥmûd Shiḥâta, 4 vols, Cairo: al-Hay'a al-Miṣriyya al-'Âmma li-l-Kitâb, 1979–87)

At first sight the text presented here in translation does not seem to be very linguistic in nature and its relevance to the development of linguistic studies might appear to be doubtful. None the less, on closer investigation it turns out that it contains the seeds of scholarly occupation with the text, from which later developments of a more linguistic nature were to spring. The passage has been taken from the introduction to one of the earliest commentaries on the *Qur'ân*, that of Muqâtil ibn Sulaymân, who died in 767. With this text we go back to the earliest written sources of Islam.

Muqâtil belongs to a generation of exegetes whose main purpose was to explain the text of the *Qur'ân* for the common believers, for whom the Holy Book was the main guide in their daily life. When the *Qur'ân* was revealed in Mecca to the Prophet Muḥammad around the turn of the sixth and the seventh century CE, it was a fragmented message, parts of which were memorized by the believers and by professional reciters. The fragments contained a large variety of subjects, from narratives to mystic experiences, from parables to instructions about the way of life of the Muslims. Especially in the latter half of his life, when he had migrated to Medina, some of the revelations the Prophet received consisted of highly technical instructions about inheritance, distribution of booty, food, marriage, and so on. After the death of the Prophet the earliest successors or caliphs took precautions to preserve the integrity of the text. They collected the written fragments, and under the third Caliph 'Uthmân an authoritative text was compiled, which became the basis for all later Qur'ânic codices. Codifying the *Qur'ân* involved a lot of philological work, such as the reform of the orthography, the sifting of variant readings, the elucidation of difficult forms, and the selection of dialectal variants. Even after the collection of the *Qur'ân*, professional readers continued to occupy themselves with those variant readings that survived the unifying efforts of the caliphs, each of them propagating his own readings.

Just like any other religious text the meaning of the *Qur'ân* is not always transparent. Right from the beginning specialists in the Muslim community must have assisted the common believers in understanding the text. Since some of the instructions contained in it are directly relevant for daily life in the community, such assistance was indispensable during the introduction of the new order, especially after the conquests when tens of thousands of neophytes had to reshape their lives according to the commandments of the new religion. Not much is known about the earliest beginnings of exegetical activities in Islam, but we do know that they all had in common a fundamental concern with the elucidation of the meaning of the text, rather than the study of its formal characteristics.

The names of dozens of commentators on the Qur'ânic text from the first two centuries of Islam are recorded in the biographical literature, but very few exegetical comments from them have been preserved. From the author of the quotation at the beginning of this chapter we have an entire commentary, which must have functioned as a unified text because it has an internal structure and contains many cross-references. Muqâtil had a bad reputation, for one thing because he was known as an anthropomorphist who had no qualms in assigning to God such human attributes as bodily parts, and for another because he was reputedly a fabricator of stories in his exegetical work. One anecdote presents him showing off about his personal acquaintance with scholars on whose authority he transmitted traditions from the Prophet, among them the famous Mujâhid ibn Jabr. Thereupon someone in the audience stands up and says: "I am Mujâhid, but I've never met you!". Without blinking an eye Muqâtil retorts: "That doesn't matter, what matters is the contents of the story". A third point of criticism is that he depended on Jewish sources (*'isrâ'îliyyât*) for his background information on the Qur'ânic narrations.

Yet, in spite of its bad reputation Muqâtil's *Tafsîr* on the Holy Book is one of the earliest complete commentaries and as such it presents an interesting picture of what exegesis may have been like in the first century of Islam. From commentaries such as the one by Muqâtil we can learn something about the methods used by the commentators. Their primary device of elucidation was the simple juxtaposition of text and paraphrase, sometimes introduced by explanatory notes such as "it means", "that is to say", "i.e.", "the intention is". In the following examples the

Qur'ânic text that is commented upon has been put between asterisks:

> *The example of those who disbelieve is like that of one who bleats* [Q. 2/171], this means: a sheep or a donkey (*Tafsîr* I, 155.12–13)
>
> *He is for you a manifest (*mubîn*) enemy* [Q. 2/168], this means: clear (*bayyin*) (*Tafsîr* I, 155.5)
>
> *For God is forgiving* [Q. 2/192] your idolatry (*Tafsîr* I, 168.7)
>
> *And the ones who were brought the Book* [Q. 2/144], this means the people of the Torah and they are the Jews (*Tafsîr* I, 147.4)

As these examples show, the explanation concerns all different levels of the text: sometimes lexical elements are explained, sometimes the meaning of a phrase, sometimes a factual remark is added, sometimes the paraphrase supplements words omitted in the verse. There is no single hermeneutic method, all Muqâtil does is follow the text and explain anything that might be unclear to the reader. Interspersed in the commentary are long stories about the Biblical background of the narratives told in the *Qur'ân*; in these stories he demonstrates his knowledge of the Jewish *Torah*. For his lexical explanations he must have had at his disposal a list of difficult words: these words are always explained in the same way at each and every occurrence. The word *mubîn* "manifest", for instance, is always paraphrased with *bayyin* "clear", apparently because the former (which derives from the same root) was no longer current at the time Muqâtil was writing. Likewise he always replaces the word *'alîm* "painful" with its synonym *wajî'*, the word *jannât* "gardens" with its synonym *basâtîn* and the archaic interrogative *'ayyân* "when?" with the more familiar word *matâ*.

At a very early stage there were also signs of a more linguistic interest in the text of the revelation. On several occasions Muqâtil adds remarks on some of the properties of the text that are of no immediate relevance for the understanding of the text and its functioning in daily life. He comments, for instance, on the provenance of words with a foreign etymology in the Qur'ânic lexicon or assigns certain lexical items in the text to pre-Islamic tribal dialects. He states, for instance, that the Qur'ânic word *qisṭâs* "path, road" derives from Greek (*Tafsîr* II, 530.12), which may be correct (some scholars believe that it comes from *dikastês* "judge") and points out the Persian origin of the word *'istabraq* "brocade" (*Tafsîr* II, 584.9), which is certainly correct. He refers to the tribal dialects of pre-Islamic Arabia in order to support his analysis of the meaning of idiomatic phrases, for instance when he explains the word *ghulâm* "young man" and adds that in the *kalâm al-'Arab* "language of the Bedouin" this word is used for every man whose beard has not yet grown (*Tafsîr* II, 598). Such information has little to do with the elucidation of the message and is of no conceivable help in applying the text to the exigencies of daily life.

In later times the question of foreign origin of Qur'ânic words became a controversial issue. For many grammarians and lexicographers it was a point of dogma that all words in the *Qur'ân* are Arabic; they spent a lot of effort on proving that words like *qisṭâs* and *'istabraq* belonged to an Arabic root, or, at the very least, that these words had already existed in pre-Islamic Arabic poetry. The *Qur'ân* had been revealed in the Arabic language so that the existing loanwords in the lexicon presented no problem. But as the *Qur'ân* is God's literal spoken word, it was impossible for orthodox believers to accept that the *Qur'ân* could contain any loanwords or neologisms, since that would imply a change in the divinity.

There is nothing to suggest that the early commentators were interested in the structure of the language of the revelation. Still they must have felt a certain degree of curiosity about the linguistic properties of the language; at least that is what transpires from their use of terminology. In the quotation at the beginning of this chapter Muqâtil presents a catalogue of subjects contained in the *Qur'ân*. The main categories in his list are:

- narrative (expository) parts, e.g., stories about earlier generations
- legal parts, e.g., laws and commandments
- instructive parts, e.g., parables and stories about Paradise and Hell

There are several things that are remarkable in his list, above all its heterogeneity: in between the three main categories of subjects there are various subjects that are not so easy to categorize. What are we to make of "deletions", "connections", and so on? These elements are the first components of a structural or formal analysis of the text of the *Qur'ân*, and therefore, from the point of view of the history of linguistics the most interesting parts. They demonstrate how within a purely semantic analysis of the text of the revelation a linguistic analysis could originate. The difference between the primitive analysis in the early commentaries and the analysis in later commentaries is that the early commentators had almost no technical apparatus at their disposal. The fact that they remarked on certain phenomena in the text at all demonstrates, however, that they were aware of formal features of the text.

Take for instance the device of *taqdîm*, literally "preposing". This term is used for three things, in the first place for a *hysteron proteron*, a change in the logical order of events, for instance when the *Qur'ân* says (Q. 3/55) *yâ 'îsâ 'innî mutawaffîka wa-râfi'uka 'ilayya* "O Jesus, I am the One who will let you die and raise you towards Me". The commentator adds that this is *taqdîm* (*Tafsîr* I, 279.1), because, as he explains, according to Islamic doctrine the act of raising towards God precedes Jesus's natural death during the apocalypse. In the second place it is used for prolepsis, when the result of an action is presented as coexisting with it, for instance in the case of the expression "clothes of fire" (Q. 22/19), which according to Muqâtil is *taqdîm*, because the phrase means "clothes that are made of copper which has been set afire" (*Tafsîr* III, 120.10). In the third place, it indicates the occurrence of syntactic hyperbaton, a change in word order, for instance in Q. 15/61 *fa-lammâ jâ'a 'alâ lûṭin al-mursalûna* "when to Lot came the people who had been sent". In this case the meaning of the verse is perfectly clear, but still the commentator feels compelled to add "there is *taqdîm* here, this means: when the people who had been sent came to Lot" (*Tafsîr* II, 432.11). Apparently he felt that this verse does not have the canonical word order of Arabic and found it worthwhile to point this out for his readers. The varying use of the term *taqdîm* is also interesting because it demonstrates how at this early stage the commentators did not yet distinguish between purely linguistic and semantic analysis of the text. In its syntactic sense, the term *taqdîm* could, of course, develop in a linguistic direction: in later grammar we find it used exclusively for the syntactic phenomenon of fronting, for instance, of the object of a sentence, as in *zaydan ḍarabtu* "Zayd [accusative] I hit".

In connection with the linguistic aspects of the commentary two other phenomena listed in Muqâtil's introduction need to be mentioned here, the deletions and the connections. In twelve passages in the commentary Muqâtil uses the term *'iḍmâr*, literally "hiding", to refer to something in the message that remains implicit, that has been deleted. As examples we may mention the following two passages:

> *Do not tell your vision to your brothers*: or else they might become jealous of you, deletion *or else they might plot against you* [Q. 12/5] (*Tafsîr* II, 318.13)

> *those who emigrated with you* [Q. 33/50]: to Medina, deletion (*Tafsîr* III, 501.2)

In both examples the commentator apparently feels that something is missing in the actual phrase: in the first example he believes that the result of the telling of the vision is not immediately the plotting of the brothers, since first they have to become jealous of Joseph; this intermediary step has been deleted in the actual Qur'ânic verse. In the second example the adverbial clause "to Medina" is felt to be indispensable for the understanding of the text. Both examples (and the same applies to the other occurrences in the commentary) are semantic in nature, and the term *'iḍmâr* is used as an exegetical device. In the earliest grammatical treatises we find the same term, but in the more restricted sense of "deletion" with syntactic results.

The second term is *ṣilât fî l-kalâm* "connections in speech". This term is applied by Muqâtil eleven times to syntactic cases of redundancy as in:

> **li-yaghfira lakum min dhunûbikum* "so that He may forgive you your sins"* [Q. 14/10]: *min* is here a connection (*Tafsîr* II, 399.18)

In this verse the verb "to forgive", which normally has a direct object, is "connected" with its object by the preposition *min*, probably used here in a partitive sense. The term *ṣila* literally means "link, connection", but the connotation is that the preposition is redundant. In later grammar the same term is used by the grammarians of Kufa in the sense of "redundant element", where the grammarians of Basra used the term *ziyâda* "addition". The survival of the term in Kufan grammar suggests a connection between the Kufan tradition and the work of the early exegetes. The development of the term illustrates the transition from a non-technical use to a technical term in linguistic theory.

Within the body of Muqâtil's commentary there are other instances of terms that refer in a non-technical way to syntactic or textual phenomena. He distinguishes between a number of text types that are defined partly by the contents of the message, but partly also by its form. One of these types is that of attributive clauses in which an attribute is presented of a person or persons mentioned in the preceding verse. Such clauses are very often introduced by the commentator with expressions such as "and then He describes them as follows" (*thumma na'atahum*), e.g., in the following passage:

> *for those who fear their Lord there are chambers, on top of which there are chambers* then He describes the chambers and says *built* [Q. 39/20) (*Tafsîr* III, 674.5)

Here the word *na'ata* introduces an attribute in the form of a passive participle "built" to the preceding noun "chambers". Elsewhere relative clauses or adjectives are introduced in the same way, for instance:

> *He guides to Himself those who repent* then He describes them and says *who believe* [Q. 13/27–28] (*Tafsîr* II, 377.2)

In these and many other examples the verb *na'ata* is used in a general sense of "describing". In later grammar *na't* became one of the technical terms for "attribute", especially in the Kufan tradition.

Another example of a text type, mentioned in the list at the beginning of this chapter, is that of *khabar* "account, story". In the body of the commentary Muqâtil often introduces a narrative about a subject that has already been mentioned with the phrase "and then He tells about them and says . . . " (*thumma 'akhbara 'anhum fa-qâla* . . .), for instance:

> *do you reckon that the Companions of the Cave were one of Our wonders?* then he tells about them and says *at the time when . . . * [Q. 18/9] (*Tafsîr* II, 576.6)

The narrative parts introduced in this way have in common that they contain a story about a preceding subject; their syntactic form varies widely. None the less, because of the peculiarities of Qur'ânic style in introducing narratives, the term *'akhbara* is often used with specific phrases, for instance those beginning with the particle *wa-'idhâ* "and lo". In later grammar the term *khabar* was used as a technical term for the predicate of the sentence, and we may safely conclude that there exists a connection with the non-technical use in the commentaries.

A third example is that of the exceptive phrases. Whenever a Qur'ânic verse contains the conjunction *'illâ* "unless", Muqâtil never fails to remark "and then He makes an exception to this" (*thumma istathnâ*). In itself this addition is redundant since the conjunction by itself clearly indicates the nature of the following clause. But apparently Muqâtil felt a need to distinguish this type of sentences, too, precisely because they were formally marked. In later grammar exceptive clauses are called *istithnâ'*. These examples prove that in a rudimentary form and on the basis of semantic features Muqâtil was aware of certain textual types that were not necessarily but frequently connected with formal characteristics.

In addition to the terms referring to textual types and phenomena of word order and deletion the commentators had at their disposal a few phonetic/orthographic terms that were needed to distinguish between otherwise homographic lexical items (e.g., *mushaddad* "geminate"). Of particular interest are the terms for the three short vowels of Arabic, /u/, /i/, and /a/, which are not found in Muqâtil's commentary, but are used by another commentator, Muḥammad al-Kalbî (d. 763). In Arabic the three vowels also serve as the three case endings of the singular noun, as in:

al-kitâb-u "the book [nominative]"
al-kitâb-i "the book [genitive]"
al-kitâb-a "the book [accusative]"

Yet, the commentator does not distinguish between the vowels of the declensional endings and those that occur within the word: in both functions the vowels receive the same names. He uses, for instance, the term *khafḍ*, which later in Kufan grammar indicated the genitive ending, indiscriminately for the vowel /i/ within the word (as in *mukhliṣîna*) and for the case ending (as in *thulth-i-hi*). As we shall see below (chapter 3) one of the major achievements of Sîbawayhi was to introduce a distinction between non-declensional and declensional vowels, on which he built all of his syntactic investigations on the relations between the constituents of the sentence.

Because of the small number of semi-technical terms and their infrequent and arbitrary use it would be an exaggeration to say that the commentators had at their disposal a technical apparatus for the description of the text. But very early on there must have been scholars whose interest focused on the language of the text, rather than its contents. We know that in the second half of the second century of Islam some scholars in Basra became interested in the structure of language as opposed to the structure of the text. They were still active as specialists of Qur'ânic exegesis, but extended their investigations to general phenomena of language. This development culminated in the first book on Arabic grammar, Sîbawayhi's (d. 793) *Kitâb*.

At the same time exegetical activities in Kufa were continued in a much more conventional way. A contemporary of Sîbawayhi at the end of the second century of Islam, al-Farrâ' (d. 822) wrote a large commentary on the *Qur'ân*, entitled *Ma'ânî l-Qur'ân* "Meanings of the *Qur'ân*", in which he commented on many of the linguistic properties of the Qur'ânic style, following the order of the text rather than presenting the grammatical facts in a structured way. The *Ma'ânî l-Qur'ân* have only recently become the focus of research and much about the Kufan theory of grammar is still unknown. But so much is certain that in Kufan grammar the link with exegesis was much stronger than in Basra. Qur'ânic commentators and readers of the *Qur'ân* were held in respect in Kufa, whereas in Basra there was a tendency to ridicule them because of their lack of insight in linguistic matters. There are many Basran reports about Qur'ânic readers making mistakes in their grammatical analysis of the *Qur'ân*, and there must have been a general feeling in circles of Basran grammarians that they themselves represented a new approach to the study of speech. The close link between exegesis and Kufan grammar is also visible in a number of technical terms that became current in the Kufan tradition and that seem to be derived from earlier exegetical practice. We already mentioned the case of the term *ṣila* in the sense of 'redundant element', that of *khafḍ* for "genitive" instead of the regular Basran term *jarr*, that of *na't* "attribute" instead of the current Basran term *ṣifa*, and the use of *'iḍmâr* in the sense of "textual deletion", rather than "linguistic deletion". Later treatises on the differences between Kufan and Basran grammarians never fail to point out such terminological differences, so that we may be certain that such differences really existed.

We shall see below (chapter 3) that the existing local traditions of Basra and Kufa were blown up by later generations into real schools. This development took place at a time when the representatives of the two local traditions started to meet each other much more frequently in the newly founded capital of the 'Abbâsid empire in Baghdad and felt the need to define their own group. At that time the representatives of the Basran tradition had reached such an advance on their competitors in the development of technical grammar that the latter did not stand a chance. Consequently, the exegetical approach to linguistics was abandoned by all grammarians and, eventually, the Basran approach won the day.

In spite of the low reputation of the commentators in Basra, grammarians working there also took over some of the terms current in the exegetical tradition, while modifying their technical application. Thus, for instance, *'iḍmâr* became one of the key terms of Basran linguistic theory. Building on the use of *'iḍmâr* in the commentaries, the Basran grammarians distinguished between the actual realization of the linguistic message by the speaker and the underlying level of the message. In this framework *'iḍmâr* represented the speaker's deletion of parts of the message, which had to be reconstructed by the linguist, not for the elucidation of the text, as in the commentaries, but for the syntactic explanation of the linguistic structure. We shall see in chapter 3 that the Basran grammarian Sîbawayhi, the founder of the grammatical system as we know it, departed from the approach of the exegetical works by concentrating wholly on the syntactic form of the message. The text of the *Qur'ân* remained one of the most important components of the linguistic corpus on which the grammarians relied, but it was no longer its textual character, but its linguistic form that was studied by the grammarian.

There is one other aspect in which the exegetical studies of the early commentators influenced the later development, that of lexicography. We shall see below (chapter 2) that in Islam the science of lexicography was kept separate from the science of grammar under the name of *'ilm al-lugha* "science of speech". In the earliest dictionary, that of al-Khalîl (d. 791), which will be discussed in chapter 2, an effort was made to include all lexical roots of the Arabic language. But al-Khalîl's dictionary had predecessors in specialized word lists that found their origin in exegesis. We have seen above that Muqâtil already had a list of difficult words, which he replaced in his commentary (e.g., *mubîn* was replaced by *bayyin*). Somewhat later scholars made lists in which they explained the strange or unusual words of the Qur'ânic text, under the name of *Kitâb al-gharîb* "Book of strange expressions". These were not dictionaries since they followed the order of the text of the *Qur'ân* and explained each word as it occurred. But they concentrated on the meaning of words and in this sense heralded the rise of lexicography. Likewise, some commentators felt the need to explain the etymology of the foreign words occurring in the *Qur'ân*. Others noted the occurrence of words with special features, such as homonyms, or words with two antonymous meanings, the so-called *'aḍdâd*. From there it was only one step to vocabularies that specialized in the collection of words in one semantic domain, such as the lexicon of the horse, the camel, or the human body.

The science of Qur'ânic exegesis (*tafsîr*) proper remained one of the pillars of the Islamic sciences. In later commentaries we still find linguistic remarks on the text of the *Qur'ân*, but these no longer represent an independent development within exegesis. Commentators received an extensive linguistic training at the hands of professional grammarians and it was from them that they borrowed their technical apparatus for the description of Qur'ânic usage. Exegesis went into various directions without losing the connection with its earliest roots and its original aim, which was the elucidation of God's intention. Because of the accumulation of knowledge commentators usually specialized in one aspect of exegesis. Thus we find commentaries whose main purpose is the discussion of the textual variants, others concentrate on the grammatical and syntactic analysis or the analysis of the narrative parts of the text. Still other commentaries are mostly interested in the legal aspects of the text.

A special branch of Qur'ânic exegesis is that of the mystical interpretation, in which the text of the revelation gains a completely new dimension. For the mystics the *Qur'ân* as we have it is only the surface of the truth: beneath the text there are hidden meanings that only the initiated who are inspired by divine knowledge can understand. They operated with the two categories of *ẓâhir* "outer, manifest" and *bâṭin* "inner, hidden" and maintained that the common believers could understand only the manifest meaning of the text, whereas the initiated were able to penetrate into its symbolic, hidden meaning. Some of them went so far as to deny the validity of the surface text with its ritual prescriptions. When God commands the believers to pray five times a day and to fast during the month of Ramadan, this is an encrypted message for deeper meanings, which only the mystic can grasp.

Chapter 2

Al-Khalîl and the Arabic lexicon

This is what al-Khalîl ibn 'Aḥmad al-Baṣrî – may he rest in peace! – wrote about the consonants of the alphabet, which are used by the Arabs as the pivot of their speech and their words, no word being without them. What he meant was that the Arabs demonstrate this in their poems and their proverbs and their speeches, since none of it deviates from this. On reflection it seemed to him impossible to start his book with the first consonant of the alphabet, which is the *'alif*, because the *'alif* is a weak consonant. When the first consonant was out, he did not want to start with the second one – the *b* – unless there were strong arguments and pressing motives to do so. He reflected on all the consonants and tried them out, and then discovered that all speech comes from the throat. Therefore, he concluded, the most likely consonant to start with was the one produced deepest in the throat.

His way of trying out the consonants was that he opened his mouth pronouncing a glottal stop and then producing a consonant, for instance, *'ab*, *'at*, *'ah*, *'a'*, *'agh*. He concluded that the ' is produced deepest in the throat. Therefore, he assigned the first chapter to the ', followed by the nearest consonant, and so on successively until he reached the last consonant, which was the *m*.

If you are asked about a word and you wish to know its place, then look at the consonants of the word. You will find it in the chapter of the consonant that occurs first in the order of the chapters.

Al-Khalîl ordered the alphabet and placed the consonants according to their place of articulation in relation to the throat. This is the order: ', *ḥ*, *h*, *kh*, *gh* – *q*, *k* – *j*, *sh*, *ḍ* – *ṣ*, *s*, *z* – *ṭ*, *d*, *t* – *ẓ*, *th*, *dh* – *r*, *l*, *n* – *f*, *b*, *m* – *w*, *'alif*, *y* – '.

Al-Layth said: Al-Khalîl said: Know that the biradical root may be permutated in two ways, like *qad – daq*, *shad – dash*. The triradical root may be permutated in six ways; this is called "six-way variation", like *ḍaraba – ḍabara – baraḍa – baḍara – raḍaba – rabaḍa*. The quadriradical root may be permutated in twenty-four ways, because each of its four radicals may be combined with the six permutations of the triradical roots, making a total of twenty-four ways. Only those which are actually used are recorded, those which are not used are omitted.

(*Kitâb al-'ayn*, ed. by Mahdî al-Makhzûmî and 'Ibrâhîm as-Sâmarrâ'î, 8 vols, Beirut, 1988, I, pp. 47–8)

These are the introductory words of the first dictionary of the Arabic language, the famous *Kitâb al-'ayn* "Book of the letter *'ayn*". Usually this dictionary is attributed to the grammarian al-Khalîl ibn 'Aḥmad, but, as we see in the above quotation, the elaboration of the lexicographical system is reported about him, not by him. We shall see below that al-Khalîl's authorship was doubted already in Classical times, although everybody was convinced that he was somehow connected with the *Kitâb al-'ayn*. Al-Khalîl is one of the famous figures of the Arabic linguistic tradition, ranking second only to Sîbawayhi (chapter 3). He is generally credited with the invention of not only lexicography but also musicology and metrics, and regarded as Sîbawayhi's main teacher.

Al-Khalîl was born in Oman in 718, in the Bedouin tribe of 'Azd 'Umân; he is sometimes called al-Farâhîdî, after one of his ancestors who was called Furhûd "young lion". He was a second-generation Muslim, but is generally reported as having been a devout believer with a tendency to asceticism. At an early age he came to Basra, at that time the centre of grammatical studies, where he studied grammar, music, poetry, and Islamic law. The achievement most often mentioned by his biographers is his invention of a metrical system with which the pre-Islamic poems could be described, allegedly because he heard a blacksmith rhythmically beat out a piece of metal, which inspired him to invent the science of metrics. He died in 791 (other reports mention 786 or 776) as the result of his scholarly pursuits: when he entered the mosque one day, pondering a scientific problem, he ran into a pillar and lost his life. Biographers attribute to him treatises about rhythm, metrics, musical tones and diacritical signs, but apart from the *Kitâb al-'ayn* none of his books has been preserved.

One of the reasons for his fame in the history of Arabic grammar is his scholarly connection with Sîbawayhi. Probably he was the only real teacher Sîbawayhi ever had, and he is mentioned by name hundreds of times in the *Kitâb Sîbawayhi*; if we are to believe the biographers, Sîbawayhi also means al-Khalîl whenever he uses the phrase *sa'altuhu* "I asked him" without explicitly mentioning a name. There is no absolute guarantee that the doctrines attributed by Sîbawayhi to his teacher are actually his: because of the innovations that Sîbawayhi introduced into grammar we may be fairly certain that they are not necessarily identical with al-Khalîl's opinions. Actually, we know from a few other testimonies that in some respects at least his theories and terminology differed from that of his pupil. Either Sîbawayhi modified the statements he transmitted from his teacher, or al-Khalîl himself later developed other opinions which did not reach Sîbawayhi. Generally speaking, we may at the very least assume that al-Khalîl was active in the domains in which he is cited by Sîbawayhi – strangely enough, he is not quoted at all in the section on phonetics and phonology at the end of the *Kitâb*, so probably Sîbawayhi did not attend al-Khalîl's lectures on these topics.

Later generations remembered al-Khalîl above all as the inventor of metrics and lexicography. In the latter science his name is connected with the first real dictionary of the Arabic tradition, the *Kitâb al-'ayn*. Before the *Kitâb al-'ayn* commentators on the *Qur'ân* had naturally been interested in its vocabulary; we have seen above (chapter 1, p. 14) that the commentator Muqâtil probably had at his disposal a list of difficult words with their more familiar equivalents. Some commentators and philologists started to collect word lists of interesting or difficult words in the text of the *Qur'ân* or the traditions from the Prophet. Other scholars began to collect vocabularies of typically Bedouin words that were falling into disuse, but were indispensable for understanding pre-Islamic poetry. Some of the vocabularies were arranged thematically: a few lists have been preserved, containing, for instance, the names of the horse, the camel, man, and scores of titles of similar treatises are known. A typical entry in such a lexicon reads as follows (this particular list on the terminology of palm trees and grapevines is ascribed to al-'Aṣma'î, who died in 831 and counts as one of the earliest lexicographers):

> Young palm trees are called *jathîth*; they are the first that sprout from the mother tree. They are also called *wadiyy*, *hirâ'*, and *fasîl* "base, ignoble, offset". When the offset is still attached to the stump and has not yet rooted, it is called *khasîs an-nakhl* "the vile part of the palm tree". The Bedouin call it *râkib* "rider". When the young sprout is torn from the mother tree together with the stump of its branch, it is said to be *mun'ala* "shod". When it is planted, they dig a well for it and plant it there, then they fill it up all around with slime from the river and dung. This well is called *al-faqîr* "the poor". The expression is: *faqqarnâ li-l-wadiyya* "we dug a well for the offset", verbal noun *tafqîr*. Another name for a young palm tree is *'aša'*
>
> (al-'Aṣma'î, *Kitâb an-nakhl wa-l-karam*, ed. by August Haffner and Louis Cheikho, *Dix anciens traités de philologie arabe*, 2nd ed., Beirut, 1914, pp. 64–5)

The emphasis in such treatises was on the lore of the Bedouin, their expressions, customs, proverbs, and poetry; the lexicographers had a special interest in recondite terms. The *Kitâb al-'ayn* introduced a radically different concept of lexicography since it aimed at the collection of all roots in language, rather than just recording rare words from Bedouin poetry. This in itself is a break with the tradition. But the arrangement of these words in the *Kitâb al-'ayn* is also remarkable. In the first place, the words are ordered around the permutations of their radicals. In Arabic as in all Semitic languages the consonants of the word carry the semantic load, whereas the vowels and auxiliary consonants provide the information about derivational and declensional morphology. Thus for instance, the root *k-t-b* produces the lexical items *kataba* "he wrote", *yaktubu* "he writes", *kutiba* "it was written", *yuktabu* "it is written", *kâtib* "writer", *maktûb* "written", *kitâb* "book", plural *kutub* "books"; *mukâtaba* "correspondence", *'aktaba* "he made someone else write", *istaktaba* "he asked someone to write", *takâtaba* "he corresponded with someone", *maktaba* "library", and so on. In all of these words the radical consonants *k-t-b* convey the notion of 'writing', whereas the auxiliary consonants (*m*, *t*, *y*, etc.) indicate the morphological categories. To represent the pattern of a word the grammarians used a notational device in which the letter *f* indicated the first radical of a word, the letter ' the second, and the letter *l* the third: the pattern of *maktaba*, for instance, is *maf'ala*, that of *istaktaba* is *istaf'ala*, and so on.

Al-Khalîl's system first assembles words in roots, putting together all the derivates from the root *k-t-b*. But then all roots containing these same consonants are assembled in a higher hierarchy; the root *k-t-b* is entered in one section together with the roots *k-b-t*, *b-k-t*, *t-b-k*, and *b-t-k*. In spite of the assurance in the introduction that it is very easy to find a word, this is a cumbersome arrangement, although it is a step forward compared to the arrangement of the word lists, which either followed the order of the text they explained, or arranged words semantically. In such systems it was almost impossible to find a word, unless one was reading a text. In the *Kitâb al-'ayn* there was at least an ordering principle, although this did not mean that one could know in advance exactly where a word was to be found. There is no indication that al-Khalîl's system was intended to reflect a higher semantic unity between the permutated roots, although some later grammarians looked for such common meanings (cf. below, chapter 8).

The second remarkable feature of al-Khalîl's arrangement is the order of the consonants. As explained in the above quotation he did not use the normal alphabetical order of the Arabic alphabet, but applied a phonetic criterion and started with the guttural consonants, then the velars, and so on, until he reached the bilabials. The reason given for this order is his reluctance to start with the element *'alif*, because it is a weak consonant. Actually, in the phonological theory of Arabic grammar the *'alif* has a special status: it is a glide like /y/ and /w/, but unlike these it is never realized on the phonetic level and serves only as an abstract phonological element (represented here as /"/). The long vowels that we distinguish in Arabic were not acknowledged by the Arabic grammarians. They regarded long vowels as combinations of a vowel and a glide (/w/, /y/, /"/), i.e., /uw/, /iy/, /a"/, which are realized as [û], [î], [â]. The only difference between /w/, /y/, on the one hand, and *'alif*, on the other, is that the latter either disappears at the phonetic level, or is realized phonetically as a glottal stop /'/ or as one of the two other glides. It has sometimes – erroneously – been thought that the grammarians' analysis was based on the Arabic script, which indicates only the short vowels and represents the long vowels by the three letters *w*, *y*, *'alif*. But rather than the writing system it was the structure of the language that led them to this analysis: the identical pattern of words such as *ṣufr* "yellow [plural]" and *sûd* "black [plural]" is apparent only when they are written phonologically: /ṣufr/ versus /suwd/.

Al-Khalîl's introduction of a new phonetic order of the consonants was probably a spontaneous invention. It has sometimes been speculated that he borrowed for this arrangement the model of the Devanagari alphabet of Sanskrit, which also starts with the velars and then progresses to the labials. But it is unnecessary to assume a foreign model. In the first place, once a phonetic order is adopted there are only two alternatives: from the throat to the lips, or the other way around, so there is an even chance for either order to be adopted. One might even say that starting in the throat is more reasonable, since that is where the articulation starts. Most other examples of Indian influence that have been adduced have turned out to be spurious, so that it seems safe to conclude that the adoption of the phonetic order by al-Khalîl was, indeed, an autonomous development.

We already noted that al-Khalîl's authorship of the *Kitâb al-'ayn* was doubted even in Classical times, his pupil al-Layth ibn al-Muẓaffar often being mentioned as the real author. In the introduction to the *Tahdhîb al-lugha* the lexicographer al-'Azharî (d. 981) counts al-Layth among the unreliable lexicographers against whom he wishes to warn his readers:

> When al-Khalîl died, he had not yet finished his *Kitâb al-'ayn*; al-Layth wished to publish the book in its entirety and published his own words under the name of al-Khalîl. When you see in the *Kitâb al-'ayn* "I asked al-Khalîl ibn 'Aḥmad" or "al-Khalîl ibn 'Aḥmad told me" he means al-Khalîl himself. But when he says "al-Khalîl says" he means himself. The confusion in the *Kitâb al-'ayn* arises because of al-Layth's "Khalîl". . . . I myself say: I have read the *Kitâb al-'ayn* more than once and worked through it time after time. I was concerned to follow up on its errors and mistakes. I expunged them from the book, noticing the correct points and pointing out the mistakes.
>
> (al-'Azharî, *Tahdhîb al-lugha*, ed. by Muḥammad 'Abd as-Salâm Hârûn, 15 vols, Cairo, 1964–7, I, pp. 28–9)

Possibly the attribution of the *Kitâb al-'ayn* to a pupil of al-Khalîl by the later tradition was a strategy to blame someone else for the inevitable errors and omissions found in this dictionary. Rather than holding al-Khalîl himself responsible, it was less embarrassing to say that he had written only parts of the book. The name of al-Layth ibn al-Muẓaffar turns up indeed in all accounts about the history of the *Kitâb al-ayn*, and even if he did not actually compose the whole book, he may at least be regarded as the editor who gave the book its final shape.

To give an idea of the set-up of the *Kitâb al-'ayn* we shall quote one lemma, that of the root *'-sh-q* "to fall in love with". This root is dealt with in the section on the consonants /'/, /q/ and /sh/, together with the roots *q-'-sh*, *q-sh-'*, and *sh-q-'*:

> *'Ashiqa-hâ 'ashaqan* "he loved her passionately", and the noun is *'ishq* "passion". Ru'ba says: 'He refrained from showing her his love after courting her, and he did not lead her astray between loathing and passion (*'ashaq*)'. A man is *'ashîq* "in love" with a woman; a woman is *'ashîqatuhu* "his beloved". They are *'ushshâq* or *'ashâshîq* "in love" with a woman.
>
> (*'Ayn* I, 124)

The information given by the *Kitâb al-'ayn* usually includes some derivations of a root, sometimes illustrated with a quotation from a poem or the *Qur'ân* in which the word in question occurs. The intention of the dictionary was to include all current roots from each combination of radicals, not necessarily all words derived from these roots. Common words were supposed to be known by the native speaker, so that the lexicographer did not feel the need to elaborate on them. The main distinction is made between those roots that are *musta'mal* "used" and those that are *muhmal* "neglected", i.e., "not occurring in Arabic". When words derived from a root are mentioned, this solely serves the purpose of showing that the root actually exists in the language.

In later lexicographers the wish to include all Arabic words became increasingly more manifest. Usually they copied all available information from earlier lexicographers and then added their own observations on rare words they had found in other sources. In this way the dictionaries were continually expanded. In al-'Azharî's (d. 981) *Tahdhîb* the lemma *'-sh-q* is already much larger than the original lemma in the *Kitâb al-'ayn*; it is found in the chapter on the consonants /'/, /q/, /sh/ that contains the same roots as the *Kitâb al-'ayn* under this heading, with the addition of *'-q-sh* and *sh-q-'*:

> 'Abû l-'Abbâs 'Aḥmad ibn Yaḥyâ was asked whether love or passion is more praiseworthy. He said: "Love, because passion includes a degree of exaggeration". Ibn al-'A'râbî said: "*'Ushuq* are the men who trim the sets of sweet-smelling plants; when

said of a camel *'ushuq* means one that keeps to its mate and does not desire any other". He said: "*'Ashaq* is the lablab-tree; its singular is *'ashaqa*". He said: "*'Ashaq* is also the arak-tree. An *'âshiq* 'lover' is called thus because he withers from the intensity of his passion in the same way as the *'ashaqa* 'lablab-tree' when it is cut."

'Abû 'Ubayd said: "*Imra'a 'âshiq* 'a woman in love', without the feminine ending *-a*, and likewise *rajul 'âshiq* 'a man in love'". I say: The Arabs delete the feminine ending from the feminine attribute in many words, e.g. [in the expression] "you regard her as stupid, since she is *bâkhis* 'deficient'". They also say *imra'a bâligh* "a nubile woman" when she has reached puberty, and they call a female slave *khâdim* "servant". In these words the masculine form is the same.

Al-Layth said: "The expression is *'ashiqa*, [imperfect] *ya'shaqu*, [verbal noun] *'ishq* 'to love'". This is what he said, but *'ashaq* is the verbal noun and *'ishq* is the noun. Ru'ba said in describing a male and female ass: "and he did not lead her astray between loathing and passion".

(*Tahdhîb* I, p. 170)

This lemma shows the development of lexicography in the two hundred years between al-Khalîl and al-'Azharî: many more sources were available, attempts were made at etymologizing, quotations from famous authorities were included, and there was room for criticism of the older dictionaries. In the quotation above the passage from the *Kitâb al-'ayn* that formed the starting point for al-'Azharî's treatment of the lemma *'-sh-q* is attributed to al-Layth, because, as we have seen, al-'Azharî did not wish to hold al-Khalîl responsible for what he regarded as errors in the text. He himself claimed that he had been able to avoid such mistakes because of his forced stay with a group of Bedouin. In the introduction he tells us that he was kidnapped by a Bedouin tribe, the Qarmatians:

I was taken captive the year the Qarmatians attacked the pilgrimage in Habîr. The people in whose hands I fell were Bedouin, most of them from the tribe of the Hawâzin, with some parties from Tamîm and 'Asad in Habîr, who had grown up in the desert. They followed the rains while foraging, and returned to the wells, pasturing their flocks and living from their milk. They spoke according to their Bedouin nature and their native instinct, hardly ever making any mistake or error in their speech.

> I stayed in their company for a long time.... From speaking to them and hearing their conversation among themselves I learned a large quantity of expressions and many rare words.
>
> (*Tahdhîb* I, p. 7)

In one respect, al-'Azharî did not go beyond the *Kitâb al-'ayn*. In spite of the disadvantages of its system of arrangement, al-'Azharî stuck to the permutations of the roots. Other lexicographers, such as Ibn Durayd (d. 934) in his *Jamharat al-lugha*, had improved on the system by reverting to the normal order of the Arabic alphabet, but al-'Azharî did not take over this innovation. The reluctance of the Arabic lexicographers to abandon al-Khalîl's arrangement is even more remarkable because in the meantime a better system had been introduced, that of the rhyming principle in which the words were arranged alphabetically according to their last radical, then the first and then the second. The motives for the rhyming ordering are unclear; perhaps they had to do with the need for writers to find rhyming words when writing poems or rhymed prose, or they were the effect of the grammarians' constant occupation with poetry in which the final consonants of words were essential for the rhyme. There may also have been a linguistic reason, in that the end of a word is less often affected in Arabic by morphological additions than the beginning.

The rhyming order was introduced by the grammarian al-Jawharî (d. before 1007) in his *Tâj al-lugha wa-ṣaḥâḥ al-'arabiyya* "The crown of the language and the correct part of Arabic", commonly known under the name *aṣ-Ṣaḥâḥ* (or *aṣ-Ṣiḥâḥ*). Al-Jawharî, a pupil of the grammarian as-Sîrâfî (cf. below, chapter 4), boasted that his system was unprecedented and that its innovations made it much easier to consult his dictionary. Apart from his new arrangement al-Jawharî also introduced a system of notation for vowels and diacritical signs, by writing them out in full with the names of the vowels. In the indication of morphological patterns he started from the principle of canonical patterns that needed no further indication, so that only irregular or less common patterns had to be indicated explicitly (e.g., for the verbal noun the pattern *fa'l* is taken to be canonical, *fa'al* is indicated with the term *muḥarrak* "vowelled"). The root *'-sh-q* is found in the chapter of the letter *q* and reads as follows:

> *Al-'ishq*: excess of love; *'ashiqa-hu*, [verbal noun] *'ishq*, pattern of *'alima-hu*, [verbal noun] *'ilm*; also *'ashaq*; on the authority of al-Farrâ'.

> Ru'ba says: "and he did not lead her astray between loathing and passion (*'ashaq*)".
>
> Ibn as-Sarrâj says: "He used only a second vowel in *'ashaq* for metrical reasons; he did use an *i* because of the adjacent '; apparently he did not want to combine two *i*'s, for that would be unusual in a noun".
>
> *Rajul 'ishshîq* "a man passionately in love", pattern of *fissîq*, i.e., "having much passion"; on the authority of Ya'qûb. . . .
>
> Al-Farrâ' says: 'They say *imra'a muḥibb li-zawjihâ wa-'âshiq* [without the feminine ending] "a woman who loves her husband and is in love with him"'. . . .
>
> (al-Jawharî, *Ṣiḥâḥ*, ed. by 'Abd al-Ghaffâr 'Aṭṭâr, 6 vols, 3rd ed., Beirut, 1984, IV, p. 1525)

The success of al-Jawharî's lexicon was considerable. For most scholars the *Ṣiḥâḥ* became the lexicographical authority *par excellence*; it was not superseded until the large compilations appeared, which constituted the final victory for the rhyming order. Unlike their predecessors, who had been more or less biased towards rare and interesting words, the compilers aimed at the inclusion of the entire lexicon. Ibn Manẓûr, a North African lexicographer who died in 1311, is the author of the famous *Lisân al-'Arab* "Language of the Arabs". His main sources are the above mentioned dictionaries, above all the *Tahdhîb* and the *Ṣiḥâḥ*, which he supplemented with data from other collections, quotations from poetry and other texts, and his own personal observations. The total number of entries is eighty thousand roots; under each root all derived nouns and verbs are treated in a free order. The lemma *'-sh-q* is found under the letter *q*:

> *'Ishq*: excess of love; it is also said that it is the admiration of the lover for the beloved, which can manifest itself both in self-restraint and immorality; *'ashiqa-hu* "he loved him", [imperfect] *ya'shaqu-hu*, [verbal noun] *'ishq*, *'ashaq*; and *ta'ashshaqa-hu* [same meaning]; but it is also said that *ta'ashshaqa* means "to pretend passion"; it is also said: *'ishq* is the noun and *'ashaq* is the verbal noun. Ru'ba says: "and he did not lead her astray between loathing and passion (*'ashaq*)".
>
> A man is *'âshiq* "in love", belonging to the group of *'ushshâq*. *'Ishshîq* pattern *fissîq*, i.e., "having much passion". A woman is *'âshiq* "in love", without the feminine ending, and *'âshiqa*. *'Ashaq* and *'asaq* with *sh* and *s*: sticking to a thing without

abandoning it. . . . *Ma'shaq* is the same as *'ishq*. Al-'A'shâ says: "There is no disease in me, and no passion (*ma'shaq*)".

'Abû l-'Abbâs 'Aḥmad ibn Yaḥyâ was asked which of the two is more praiseworthy, love or passion. He said: "Love, because passion has an element of exaggeration". A lover is called *'âshiq* because he withers from the intensity of his love, just as the *'ashaqa* withers, when it is cut. *'Ashaqa*: a tree that is green, but then it breaks and becomes yellow; on the authority of az-Zajjâj. It is asserted that the etymology of *'âshiq* is from this word. Kirâ' said: "New speakers of Arabic use it for the lablab-tree; its plural is *'ashaq*". *'Ashaq* is also the arak-tree. Ibn al-'A'râbî: "*'Ushuq* are the men who trim the sets of sweet-smelling plants". He also says: "When said of a camel it means one who keeps to its mate and does not desire any other". . . .

(Ibn Manẓûr, *Lisân al-'Arab*, ed. Cairo, 20 vols, X, pp. 251–2)

Ibn Manẓûr's *Lisân al-'Arab* has become without any doubt the most popular dictionary ever to be written in the Arab world: no library is complete without it, and the number of abbreviated versions, extracts, additions, appendices, and revisions is enormous. An even grander scheme was originally followed by the Persian lexicographer al-Fîrûzâbâdî (d. 1414) in his *al-Qâmûs al-muḥîṭ* "The all-embracing ocean". Originally, al-Fîrûzâbâdî wanted to write a dictionary in sixty volumes in which the entire language was recorded, but in the end he limited himself to two volumes, which still contained the respectable number of sixty thousand entries. He was able to cram all these entries into such a small space by being extremely economical in his definitions and by introducing a series of abbreviations in his dictionary, such as *m* (for *ma'rûf* "known") to indicate words of common usage that needed no further lexicographical description; or *j* (for *jam'* "plural"). Some of these abbreviations are still in use in modern dictionaries of Arabic. The *Qâmûs* became a very popular dictionary for private use, to such an extent that the word *qâmûs*, literally "ocean", has become the current word for "dictionary" in Arabic.

The last great compiler was Murtaḍâ az-Zabîdî (d. 1791) who brought together from all existing dictionaries no fewer than 120,000 entries in his *Tâj al-'arûs* "The bride's crown". Together with the other two compilations his work constituted the main source in the nineteenth century, when scholars in the Levant attempted to revive Arabic studies, for instance Buṭrus al-Bustânî, whose large dictionary *Muḥîṭ al-muḥîṭ* in its title recalls the *Muḥîṭ* of al-Fîrûzâbâdî. One can trace the definitions and examples in Classical dictionaries of Arabic through the nineteenth-century lexicographers to the dictionaries of the modern Arabic world.

In the West the first Orientalists, too, copied the Classical dictionaries, from the period of Jacobus Golius (d. 1667) to that of Georg Wilhelm Freytag (d. 1861), both of whom wrote a *Lexicon Arabico-Latinum*. All Western dictionaries of Arabic were superseded with Edward William Lane's (d. 1876) *Arabic–English Lexicon, derived from the best and the most copious Eastern sources; comprising a very large collection of words and significations omitted in the Ḳámoos, with supplements to its abridged and defective explanations, ample grammatical and critical comments, and examples in prose and verse*. In the title he indicated clearly that he regarded himself as heir to the "Eastern" dictionaries for most of his data, but at the same time he attempted to sift this mass of data critically with the instruments at his disposal. In the first book he intended to include "all the Classical words and significations commonly known to the learned among the Arabs"; the second book (containing "those that are of rare occurrence and not commonly known" never appeared). The first book was completed until the letter *qâf*; it is usually printed in eight volumes, of which the last contains notes for the rest of the alphabet. The lemma on *'-sh-q* that we quoted from al-Khalîl, al-'Azharî and the *Lisân al-'Arab* begins as follows in Lane's dictionary (V, p. 2054):

> 'shq
> 1. *'ashiqa*, aor. a (Ṣ, O, Mṣb, Ḳ, [accord. to the TA, said in the Mṣb to be like *ḍaraba*, but in my copy of the Mṣb it is correctly said to be of the class of *ta'iba*,]) inf. n. *'ishqun* and *'ashaqun*, (Ṣ, O, Ḳ,) the latter mentioned by Fr, and said by Ibn-Es-Sarráj to be thus by poetic license, and with two fet-ḥahs because two kesrehs are rare in nouns, (Ṣ, O,) or the former is a simple subst., and the latter is the inf. n., (Mṣb,) [and app. *ma'shaqun* also,] *He loved* (another, Ṣ, O, Ḳ) *excessively*; (IF, Ṣ, O, Mṣb, Ḳ;) [or *passionately*; or *with amorous desire*; or, agreeably with explanations of *'ishqun* below, *admiringly*; or *with blindness to defects in the object of his love*; or *with a disease of the nature of melancholia*;] and → *ta'ashshaqa* as trans. or *syn. with 'ashiqa* as such. (TA.) [See also *'âshiqun*.]

This is approximately one-sixth of the entire lemma; Lane repeats almost all information contained in the indigenous dictionaries. The abbreviations refer to the sources used by him (for instance, Ḳ = the *Qâmûs*; Ṣ = the *Ṣiḥâḥ*; and TA = the *Tâj al-'arûs*). Most of his sources are quoted through the *Tâj al-'arûs* or the *Lisân al-'Arab*.

Lane's dictionary is still used as one of the basic tools in Arabic philology because it enables one to consult all Arabic sources at one glance. Since he died before he could finish his dictionary, the Deutsche Morgenländische Gesellschaft started their Arabic–German dictionary with the letter *kâf* to serve as a sequel to Lane. This new project, of which the first fascicle appeared in 1957 and which in the meantime has progressed to the letter *m*, still uses the data from the Arabic sources, but in a different manner: the entries in this dictionary are based on an independent and systematic perusal of a large corpus of Classical texts. Likewise, the best Western dictionary of Modern Standard Arabic, Hans Wehr's *Wörterbuch der arabischen Sprache*, which appeared for the first time in 1952 and was soon translated into English, did not simply copy the data from the existing dictionaries, but selected its entries from an extensive corpus of Arabic literary and journalistic texts.

Chapter 3

Sîbawayhi and the beginnings of Arabic grammar

Chapter on the knowledge of the words in Arabic

The words are noun, verb, and particle which brings a meaning that is neither noun nor verb. Noun is *rajul* "man", *faras* "horse". Verbs are patterns derived from the expression of the events of the nouns; they have forms to indicate what is past; and what will be but has not yet happened; and what is being and has not yet been interrupted. The form of that which is past is *dhahaba* "he went away", *sami'a* "he heard", *makutha* "he stayed". The form of that which has not yet happened is, when you order something, *idhhab* "go away!", *uqtul* "kill!", *iḍrib* "hit!"; and when you predicate something *yaqtulu* "he will kill", *yadhhabu* "he will go away", *yaḍribu* "he will hit", *yuqtalu* "he will be killed", *yuḍrabu* "he will be hit". The form of that which has not yet been interrupted and continues to exist is the same, when you are predicating something. These patterns are derived from the expression of the events of the nouns; they have many different forms which will be explained, God willing. The events are like *aḍ-ḍarbu* "the hitting", *al-qatlu* "the killing", *al-ḥamdu* "the praising". As for those words that bring a meaning that is neither noun nor verb, they are like *thumma* "then", *sawfa* [particle of the future], the *w* used in oaths, the *l* used in annexion, etc.

Chapter on the course of the endings of the words in Arabic

These endings follow eight courses: accusative (*naṣb*), genitive (*jarr*), nominative (*raf'*), apocopate (*jazm*), a-vowel (*fatḥ*), i-vowel (*kasr*), u-vowel (*ḍamm*), zero-vowel (*waqf*). The eight endings are arranged formally into four pairs: the accusative and the /a/ are one pair formally, the genitive and the /i/ are one pair formally, likewise the nominative and the /u/, and the apocopate and the zero-ending. The reason I call them eight endings is to distinguish between, on the one hand, those words that receive one member of these pairs because it is produced by a governor; those endings are never permanent with the word; and, on the other hand, those words whose last consonant has a permanent ending that never disappears as the result of the action of a governor. Each of the governors has its own formal effect on the last consonant of the word, and this consonant is called the consonant of the declension. The accusative, the genitive, the nominative, and the apocopate occur on the consonants of the declension.

The consonants of the declension belong to the fully declinable nouns and to those verbs that resemble the participles. Such verbs have one of the four prefixes, /'/, /t/, /y/, /n/, as for instance in *'af'alu* "I do", *taf'alu* "you do, she does", *yaf'alu* "he does", *naf'alu* "we do". The accusative in the nouns is as in *ra'aytu zayd-an* "I saw Zayd"; the genitive is as in *marartu bi-zayd-in* "I passed by Zayd"; and the nominative is as in *hâdhâ zayd-un* "this is Zayd". There is no apocopate in the nouns because of their full declinability and because they receive the ending /n/ [which indicates indefiniteness]. When the ending /n/ disappears they [sc., the Arabs] do not wish to combine this disappearance with the disappearance of the vowel [in the apocopate].

The accusative in the verb is like *lan yaf'al-a* "he will not do", the nominative is like *sa-yaf'al-u* "he will do", and the apocopate like *lam yaf'al* "he did not do". There is no genitive in the resembling verbs, just as there is no apocopate in the nouns, because a word in the genitive ending is construed with another noun to which it is annexed and in which it prevents the nunation; this is impossible in these verbs. The reason they resemble the participles is that you say *'inna 'abdallâhi la-yaf'alu* "indeed, 'Abdallâh really does", which means the same as when you say *'inna 'abdallâhi la-fâ'ilun* "indeed, 'Abdallâh is really doing". You attach *la-* to this verb as you attach it to the noun, but you cannot attach it to [the perfect verb] *fa'ala*. You also say *sa-yaf'alu*, *sawfa yaf'alu* "he will do", attaching these two particles to the verb in order to convey a meaning, just as you attach the article to the noun to indicate definiteness. They are, however, not nouns, as shown by the fact that it is not allowed to use them in all constructions in which you can use a noun. Don't you see that if you said *'*inna yaḍriba ya'tînâ* "*indeed, will hit is coming to us", and similar things, it is not speech. The only reason they resemble the participles is their sharing the same meaning, as we shall demonstrate in its proper place, and the fact that they both receive the particle *la-*, as in God's words *'inna rabbaka la-yaḥkumu baynahum* "indeed, your Lord judges between them", i.e., *['inna rabbaka la-] ḥâkimun [baynahum]* "[indeed, your Lord] is judging [between them]", and the fact that they receive the particles *sa-*, *sawfa*, just as the nouns receive the article to indicate definiteness.

The /a/, /i/, /u/ and the zero-ending belong to those nouns that are not fully declinable in their speech and that resemble those words that are neither noun nor verb, but are only used to indicate a meaning, as for instance *sawfa* and *qad*. [They also belong] to the verbs that do not follow the course of the resembling verbs, and to the particles that are neither nouns nor verbs and that serve only to indicate a meaning. The /a/ in the nouns is as in *ḥaytha* "where [relative]", *kayfa* "how?", *'ayna* "where?". The /i/ in them is for instance in *'ulâ'i* "those", *ḥadhâri* "careful!", *ruwaydi* "careful!". The /u/ is for instance in *ḥaythu* "where [relative]", *qablu* "before", *ba'du* "after". The zero-ending is for instance in *man* "who?", *kam* "how much?", *qaṭ* "only, ever", *'idh* "since".

The /a/ in the verbs that do not follow the course of the resembling verbs is for instance in *ḍaraba* "he hit", and any other pattern that has the meaning of *fa'ala*. The last consonant of these verbs is not vowelless, because they share some features with the resembling verbs. You say *hâdhâ rajulun ḍarabanâ* "this is a man who hit us", using the verb as an attribute to an indefinite word, so that it has the same position as *ḍârib* "hitting", when you say *hâdhâ rajulun ḍâribun* "this is a man hitting". Moreover, you say *'in fa'ala fa'altu* "if he does, I do", which has the same meaning as *'in yaf'al 'af'al*. These verbs are verbs just as the resembling verbs are verbs: they may be used instead of them and they may be used as attributes instead of a noun, just as the resembling verbs may be used as an attribute. Therefore, they [sc., the Arabs] did not make their ending vowelless.

(Sîbawayhi, *Kitâb*, ed. Bûlâq, 2 vols, 1316 AH; repr., Baghdad, Muthanna Library, n.d., I, pp. 2–4)

The long quotation we have given here is from the first pages of the most famous book in the Arabic linguistic tradition, known as the *Kitâb Sîbawayhi*, the "Book of Sîbawayhi". Its place in the Arabic linguistic tradition is unrivalled, and the respect it has gained in this tradition is demonstrated by the name it received from one biographer, who called it *Qur'ân an-naḥw* "the *Qur'ân* of grammar", just as Sîbawayhi was sometimes called *'imâm an-nuḥât* "the imam of the grammarians". Without exaggeration one could say that the entire linguistic tradition in Arabic is nothing but a huge commentary on the *Kitâb Sîbawayhi.* In this respect the Sanskrit and the Arabic tradition resemble each other: at the beginning of both traditions stands an almost mythical figure whose work dominates the entire tradition.

In spite of the reputation of the *Kitâb* we know surprisingly little about Sîbawayhi's life. The few facts that are reported by the biographers can be told quickly. His full name was 'Abû Bishr 'Amr ibn 'Uthmân ibn Qanbar; he was born somewhere around 750 in Persia and received the nickname of Sîbawayhi, which in Persian means "smell of apples", according to some sources because he had a sweet breath. His father had not been a Muslim and when he converted to Islam he became a client of the Arab tribe of the Banû l-Ḥârith ibn Ka'b. His mother tongue was Persian and he never completely lost his Persian accent in Arabic. On arriving in Basra his original intention was to study Islamic law, but when he was ridiculed by some people for the grammatical mistakes he made he decided to study grammar instead.

Later biographers mention as many as six or seven teachers of Sîbawayhi. The problem is that they wished his biography to conform to the model of later biographies, which obligatorily contained a paragraph about a grammarian's teachers. Accordingly, every grammarian mentioned by Sîbawayhi in his *Kitâb* was elevated to the rank of teacher. If we go by the quotations in the text, of which there are hundreds, we would have to say that al-Khalîl ibn 'Aḥmad (cf. chapter 2), whom he quotes by far the most frequently, was his principal teacher. The phrasing of some of these quotations implies that he was personally in touch with al-Khalîl and often asked him for his opinion about grammatical problems. He must have met other grammarians, since he quotes their opinions in the *Kitâb*, but it is not clear in how far these were really his teachers.

All biographers mention the fact that he left Basra around the year 793 to return to his birth country, where he died soon after, probably at the age of forty. They link his departure to an incident that took place at the caliphal court in Baghdad. According to this story Sîbawayhi was challenged by a grammarian from Kufa, al-Kisâ'î (d. 799), to pronounce himself on an abstruse question: if you say in Arabic "I used to think that a scorpion's sting hurts more than that of a hornet, but they were the same", do you say *qad kuntu 'aẓunnu 'anna l-'aqraba 'ashaddu las'atan min az-zunbûr fa-'idhâ huwa hiya*, with both pronouns in the nominative, or *fa-idhâ huwa 'iyyâhâ*, with the second pronoun in the accusative? When Sîbawayhi declared that only the first alternative was correct, some Bedouin who were conveniently standing at the door but had actually been bribed by al-Kisâ'î, were brought in and announced that a true Bedouin would say only the second alternative. This humiliation caused Sîbawayhi, so the story goes, to leave Baghdad for his native Persia never to come back. Not surprisingly, only a few pupils of his are mentioned by the biographers, since he died before he had had the time to assemble a circle of pupils around him.

The book Sîbawayhi left to later generations was unique in several respects. In the first place it was the first coherent description of the entire system of the Arabic language. In the second place it was one of the first real publications in Arabic literature in any discipline. In the early period of Islamic civilization it was highly unusual for scholars to publish their teachings. Though this was not an exclusively oral civilization, since most scholars used to record their thoughts in writing, extemporized teaching was highly appreciated. Their pupils made notes and sometimes even published them, but not in the form of a completed book. Sîbawayhi, however, made his description of Arabic into a book, with a beginning and an end, and with cross-references, so that it could be read from cover to cover. Its uniqueness in this respect is borne out by the "title" it received, *Kitâb Sîbawayhi* "The Book of Sîbawayhi", i.e., the written publication of Sîbawayhi.

In spite of its unique features the Book was not an immediate success. After Sîbawayhi's death it was well known but also criticized by contemporaries. It was not until it came to play a role in the establishment of the Basran grammatical school that the *Kitâb Sîbawayhi* gained its special place in the history of Arabic linguistics. In the process of reception of the *Kitâb* a later grammarian, al-Mubarrad (d. 898), played a central role; he was also involved in establishing its definitive text. Al-Mubarrad was the pupil of a pupil of Sîbawayhi. He studied and taught in Basra, but spent most of his life in Baghdad where he became the rival of other grammarians, some of them from Kufa, who had gained entrance at the caliphal court. Partly because of this competition the grammarians from Basra tried to enhance their reputation by tracing back their own scholarly genealogy to a venerable past, in the first place to the mythical founder of Arabic linguistics, 'Abû l-'Aswad ad-Du'alî (cf. above, introduction, p. 3), and in the second place to Sîbawayhi, whom they connected with 'Abû l-'Aswad through a continuous line of scholars. In this search for a tradition of a Basran "school" Sîbawayhi's Book took up an important position and eventually was acclaimed as the *Qur'ân an-naḥw*.

According to the biographers, when he was young, al-Mubarrad rejected a great many teachings of Sîbawayhi and even published a book, entitled *ar-Radd 'alâ Kitâb Sîbawayhi* "The refutation of Sîbawayhi's *Kitâb*". But later he repented and withdrew the book (which is known only through a critique on it by an Egyptian grammarian, Ibn al-Wallâd). Instead, al-Mubarrad wrote a new book, *al-Muqtaḍab*, which served as a simpler version of the *Kitâb*, more accessible to the students than the *Kitâb Sîbawayhi*. He also took it upon himself to edit the *Kitâb Sîbawayhi*; as a result almost all manuscript copies of the *Kitâb* that have been preserved depend in one way or another on his recension. Henceforth, Sîbawayhi's authority was uncontested; one hardly ever finds explicit criticisms of his teachings in later grammatical literature.

What was the purpose of his book? As a Persian Sîbawayhi may have been struck by the differences between his own language and that of the Arabs which he learnt as a second language. Maybe this prompted him to write about the structure of speech in an innovative way. He calls the language he describes *lughat al-'Arab* or *al-'arabiyya* "the Arabic language"; the *'Arab* being the pure Arabic-speaking Bedouin, who had not yet been affected and contaminated by sedentary speech. For Sîbawayhi it was obvious that Arabic could be only the language and the poetry of the Bedouin, the *Qur'ân* being the prime example of this language. At the same time, in a city like Basra with its multilingual population and its patois, he must have been aware that not everybody spoke pure Arabic. In his references to the native speakers of Arabic he calls them "they": "they say", "they do not like this or that". But he also uses the "you" of the reader who is addressed: "if you say this, you mean . . . "; "this is as when you say"; or even "we": "this is as in our expression". In principle the language belonged to a well-defined group of people, the *fuṣaḥâ'*, whose Arabic was by definition correct. But through a process of idealization, not uncommon in a speech community in which there is diglossia, this language is also regarded as the mother tongue of all members of the community who have received an education and make an effort to speak correctly. Thus, on the one hand, the corpus used by the grammarians was closed, being limited to the text of the *Qur'ân* and the pre-Islamic poetry, but, on the other hand, the grammarians upheld the fiction of native speakers whose judgment could be trusted. In the early centuries of Islam there were certainly Bedouin who could be and were used as informants. But in the course of the centuries there were no longer any pure Arabic-speaking Bedouin around, and the native speaker, the pure Bedouin, became a fictional figure, although the grammarians continued to talk about "their language".

Since by definition the speakers of Arabic could not make mistakes, the purpose of linguistics was not a prescriptive one. Later grammarians, especially in the Islamic West, sometimes wrote treatises about the mistakes people made when they tried to write Classical Arabic, but in technical grammar this aspect of linguistics was hardly ever mentioned. There are no references to common mistakes in the books of the grammarians, nor is there any awareness of the changes the language had undergone (cf. also below, chapter 13). Arabic linguistics was, however, not purely descriptive either: for grammarians such as Sîbawayhi it was not enough simply to describe the language as it was used or spoken. Their aim was much more ambitious: since language is part of God's creation and since Arabic was the language selected by God for his final revelation to humankind, it was bound to be a perfect language without deviations or exceptions. Every single part of the Arabic language must exhibit this perfection and it was the self-appointed task of the grammarian to show in the tiniest detail of the linguistic structure that this was indeed a system in which every element was in its place, in which every phenomenon was explicable.

At the stage of grammar at which Sîbawayhi wrote, explanations could be crude and *ad hoc*: it sufficed to point at a superficial resemblance to explain a connection or a similar linguistic behaviour of two elements. For instance, in the quotation above Sîbawayhi points out that there is a construction in which one category of verbs may be used with the same meaning as a noun (participle), "'Abdallâh is doing" and "'Abdallâh does". He calls this category of verbs "resembling verbs" (*'af'âl muḍâri'a*; in Western terminology they are called "imperfect verbs") and explains the fact that the resembling verbs have the same endings as the noun by this shared construction. At a later stage of the discipline much more complicated and theoretical explanations were needed, as we shall see below in the work of az-Zajjâjî (chapter 5).

It is not easy to describe the contents of the *Kitâb*. Its arrangement differs from that of grammars in the Latin school tradition. After the general introduction from which we have quoted extensively above, Sîbawayhi first deals with syntactic questions, then there is a large section on all kinds of processes that have to do with derivational morphology; finally, phonological processes are treated that determine the actual surface form of the word. The terms used traditionally in the Arabic tradition to denote these sections need some explanation. The general term for grammar is *naḥw*; but this term also indicates the section of grammar dealing with the relations between constituents in the sentence, i.e., syntax including the treatment of the declensional endings. Morphology is called *ṣarf*; this includes derivational morphology and morphonology, i.e., those changes in words that are not connected with syntactic relations. These two terms divide grammar into two large parts, dealt with together in the *Kitâb Sîbawayhi*, but later also treated separately. Phonology was regarded as ancillary to morphology: those phonological processes that were relevant to morphology, such as the *'imâla* (fronting of /a/ in certain environments), changes involving glides, and assimilation, were added as an appendix to the grammatical treatises. Phonetics, i.e., changes in words that were completely independent of morphology, was dealt with briefly (Sîbawayhi has a section in which he mentions the places of articulation of the consonants), but only because without a minimal knowledge of phonetic terminology and classification it is impossible to deal with morphological questions. Phonetics as the science of the correct realization of linguistic sounds was dealt with in other disciplines, for instance in treatises on recitation. Acoustics and the science of sound were completely excluded from linguistics, but found a place in the treatises of the physical philosophers (cf. below the encyclopaedia of the 'Ikhwân aṣ-Ṣafâ', chapter 7). Lexicology was a separate discipline (*'ilm al-lugha*); most grammarians also received a lexicographical training, and most lexicographers also studied grammar, but it was perfectly well possible to say of a scholar that he was excellent in grammar, but lagged behind in lexicography, which shows that the two disciplines were really regarded as separate domains.

The quotation at the beginning of this chapter was taken from the introductory section of the *Kitâb*, in which elementary notions are dealt with, such as the parts of speech, the nature of declension, the constituents of the sentence. It has been surmised that in this part of the book Sîbawayhi introduced those innovations which he himself had brought to the discipline. It is, indeed, remarkable that in this section he quotes no other grammarians, whereas in the rest of the *Kitâb* grammarians are quoted on every page. If this is true, the introductory part, which was known in the Classical period as

Table 3.1 Contents of the *Kitâb*

Chapter	*Contents*
1–18	general notions
19–60	the object of the verb
61–99	infinitive as object
100–131	attributes
132–140	topic of the sentence
141–144	accusative with the particle *kam* "how much?"
145	accusative in exclamations
146–174	accusative in vocative clause
175–184	negation
185–202	accusative in exceptive clause
203–221	pronouns
222–232	interrogation
233–284	particles and their governance
285–317	diptotic declension of the noun
318–342	formation of the relational adjective
343–358	formation of dual and plural
359–396	formation of the diminutive
397–411	phonological matters (nunation, gemination, glottal stop)
412–415	numerals
416–431	broken plurals
432–476	morphonology of the verb
477–507	vowels
508–558	morphonology of the noun
559–574	phonetic matters (places of articulation, assimilation)

an independent part of the book under the name of *ar-Risâla* "The treatise", contains those points in which Sîbawayhi deliberately stepped away from the existing tradition. This means that it may be regarded as an introduction to his own system.

The most essential innovation Sîbawayhi introduced appears to have been the systematization of the declensional system. We have seen above that in the old commentaries on the *Qur'ân* no distinction was made between declensional vowels and other vowels (chapter 1, p. 19). This means that the first /u/ in the word *yaktub-u* had the same status and was given the same name as the second /u/, although the latter is the declensional ending of the nominative. Likewise, the end /u/ of *yaktub-u* was treated the same way as the end /u/ in the undeclinable word *ḥaythu*. In the *Kitâb* the treatment of the endings of words is given a prominent position at the beginning of the introduction, underlining the innovatory character of this treatment. Apparently Sîbawayhi rejected the old method of calling all vowels by the same terms, whether they were declensional or not, which is why he made a careful distinction between those endings that were produced by the action of another word in the sentence, a governor (*'âmil*), and those words in which the ending was invariable (Table 3.2).

The status of the declension is thus directly connected with the important principle of *'amal*, governance. The relationship between governor (*'âmil*) and declension (*'i'râb*) is formulated by the Arabic grammarians in terms that suggest a dependency between two constituents. Just like Western dependency-type grammars the Arabic grammarians explicitly specify that within each syntactic structure all elements, except one, depend on another element, but never directly on more than one. One of the strictest rules in Arabic syntactic theory is precisely that there can never be more than one governor (*'âmil*) for a governed element, although one governor may govern more than one element at the same time.

Table 3.2 The endings of the words

	with governor	*without governor*
/a/	*naṣb*	*fatḥ*
/i/	*jarr*	*kasr*
/u/	*raf'*	*ḍamm*
zero	*jazm*	*waqf*

The Arabic theory of governance (*'amal*) is often formulated in terms of another important metaprinciple in their grammatical system, that of the hierarchy in speech. Each element has its own status and therefore its own rights. All elements, whether phonological, morphological, or syntactic, are assigned their own place on a scale from light to heavy. In the case of phonological elements these terms refer to the degree of sonority: vowels are lighter than glides, which in their turn are lighter than full consonants. Within the group of the vowels /a/ is the lightest vowel, then /i/, then /u/. The degree of weight an element has determines its behaviour in both phonology and morphology. In verbs containing a glide as one of their radicals, for instance, the combination of the glide with vowels frequently leads to a change: /awa/ becomes /a"/, which is realized as [a:], e.g., /da'awa/ → [da'a:] (for the representation of the long vowels see above, chapter 2, p. 27). A combination such as */CiCuC/ is impossible in Arabic, because, as the grammarians assert, this would mean that the speaker has to go from a light to a heavy element; /CuCiC/ on the other hand is a permitted combination.

In syntax, too, the hierarchy of elements from light to heavy plays an important role, but in a somewhat different sense than in phonology. In syntax the lightness of an element means that it is more flexible in its syntactic behaviour and more variable in its form. Nouns are lighter than verbs, for instance, because they can be used in more syntactic slots than the verbs, and their morphological form (declension and the inflection for number and gender) varies according to their syntactic role. The lighter an element is, the weaker its force to govern another element. Thus, verbs are heavy (i.e., less flexible in their syntactic behaviour) and at the same time stronger (i.e., able to govern other elements in the sentence). In this way each element is assigned its own specific place within the system of language, and according to this place it is entitled to certain "rights", for instance, the right to be declined.

The hierarchy set up by the grammarian of the linguistic elements is not a static one. Within the grammatical system the relations between elements are dynamic and susceptible to modification and change. The grammarians developed an extensive vocabulary to indicate the place, role, position, function, rank, status, and category of elements within the system and with the help of this vocabulary they were able to define also under which circumstances an element could replace another element, i.e., when it could be used in the syntactic function that belonged to another element. Such an element came to resemble the element it replaced and, according to the status of that element, it either gained or lost some of its own rights. Thus, the resemblance between elements became an important explanatory principle in grammatical theory. The case of the imperfect verb was mentioned above: through its resemblance to the noun it gained a partial right to the nominal declensional endings, *yaktub-u*, *yaktub-a*, *yaktub*. In Western grammars of Arabic these endings of the imperfect verb are called modal endings, which receive the names of verbal moods: "indicative", "subjunctive", and "jussive". For the Arabic grammarians the endings of the imperfect verb are not merely similar to those of the nouns, they are identical with them. Thus, the imperfect verb is said to have a nominative, an accusative and a special verbal case-ending that does not occur in the nouns, the apocopate (*jazm* "cutting off"). Such examples show that from the perspective of the grammarians the linguistic system was a formal system, conditioned by formal properties of the elements involved, by their resemblances to each other. This is reflected in the terms they assign to many linguistic categories: the imperfect verb, for instance, is not called after its semantic properties but because of its resemblance to another syntactic category it is called "resembling verb" (*fi'l muḍâri'*).

The comparison between the status of various elements within the system is called by the grammarians *qiyâs*, from the verb *qâsa* "to measure", usually translated in English by "analogy". Yet, the *qiyâs* of the Arabic grammarians represents a totally different concept: it is a method to explain apparent deviations from the rules in certain phenomena by referring to their resemblance to other phenomena. The result is an increased regularity because the rules are applied to as many phenomena as possible. This kind of analogical reasoning is different from the concept of "analogy" in Western linguistics, which serves as an instrument to explain irregularities by showing how they developed by interference from other phenomena. In Arabic philosophical terminology the same term *qiyâs* translated the concept of the Aristotelian syllogism, but the grammatical *qiyâs* has nothing to do with this logical method, either. Since linguistic analogy (*qiyâs*) is a post-factum explanation of linguistic phenomena, it does not operate as a method to produce linguistic forms. Before Sîbawayhi some of his predecessors did try to introduce new, more correct forms on the basis of analogy and to correct the text of the *Qur'ân* accordingly. This method is criticized explicitly by Sîbawayhi. The ultimate criterion of linguistic correctness is what is "heard" (*samâ'*), i.e., what can be attested in actual usage. The grammarian's *qiyâs* is secondary in the sense that it can be applied only to phenomena that actually occur.

The last theoretical principle to be mentioned here is that of the relationship between the surface level and the underlying level in speech. We have seen above (chapter 1) that the oldest Qur'ânic commentaries already demonstrate an awareness of the incongruence between what people say and what they intend to say or mean. Since the commentators were only interested in finding out what God actually meant in the *Qur'ân*, their approach to such discrepancies was to provide a semantic paraphrase of the text, in which the underlying intention was made explicit. The grammarians dealt with the relationship between realization and underlying level from a different perspective. Since the grammarians' task was to explain all relations in grammar, they were frequently forced to explain expressions that did not conform to the rule system they had set up. They had no alternative but to have recourse to an underlying level on which the regularity sought after was restored. Speakers tend to "hide" elements in their utterances (this is the principle of *'iḍmâr* we have met with above in the old commentaries), which obscures the actual relations in the sentence. Imagine for instance someone asking someone else "who is standing there?". The answer to such a question might be simply "Zayd", without a predicate, because the speakers of Arabic strive after conciseness. The grammarian then restores the underlying level by reinstating the understood predicate: "Zayd is standing". The problem becomes more acute when we take an Arabic utterance of someone exclaiming *al-kilâba* "the dogs! [accusative]". This sentence is harder to explain since there is no overt governor for the accusative ending. By applying the principle of restoration to this sentence the grammarian may then reconstruct the underlying level as *'arsil al-kilâba* "send the dogs!", with the understood imperative *'arsil* serving as governor. In this context the restitution of an underlying level serves as an explanation of the syntactic relations between the constituents of the actual sentence.

In some instances the analysis of the grammarians forced them to posit zero-elements in the surface structure whose presence was necessary for a satisfactory explanation of the syntactic relationships. They distinguished between two basic types of sentences: the nominal sentence, headed by a noun, and the verbal sentence, headed by a verb. The verbal sentence starts with a verb (*fi'l*), followed by the agent (*fâ'il*) and by the object (*maf'ûl*), e.g.:

ḍaraba *zaydun* *'amran*
fi'l *fâ'il* *maf'ûl*
"Zayd hit 'Amr"

In the nominal sentence there are two sentential constituents, the topic (*mubtada'*, literally "the word with which the sentence starts") and the predicate (*khabar*), which may be a noun as in the following example:

zaydun *'akhû-ka*
mubtada' *khabar*
"Zayd is your brother"

or a verbal sentence, as in the following example

zaydun *ḍaraba* *'amran*
mubtada' *khabar*
fi'l fâ'il maf'ûl
"Zayd hit 'Amr"

In this sentence the verb *ḍaraba* "hit" needs an agent, since the word *zaydun* is already occupied as topic of the sentence. According to Arabic grammatical analysis the agent in this case is a zero-element. In Western grammars of Arabic this type of sentence is usually regarded as a stylistic alternative for the canonical *ḍaraba zaydun 'amran*; for the Arabic grammarians it is a fundamentally different type of sentence. Sîbawayhi's main argument for this distinction is the fact that in the verbal sentence *ḍaraba zaydun 'amran* verb and agent show agreement, whereas in the nominal sentence *zaydun ḍaraba 'amran* there is no agreement between the topic and the verb. This difference becomes visible when the two sentences are put in the plural:

ḍaraba z-zaydûna 'amran/az-zaydûna ḍarabû 'amran
"the Zayds hit 'Amr"

In the nominal sentence, the form *ḍarabû* is analysed by Sîbawayhi as the verb *ḍaraba* + the pronominal element *-û*, which functions as its agent. In this way he explains the difference in agreement between the two sentence types, which remains inexplicable in most Western grammars of Arabic. We may note here that Sîbawayhi's main reason for the distinction is a formal one; later grammarians, such as al-Jurjânî, blamed him for this exclusive interest in the formal aspects of syntax and proposed a semantic distinction between the two sentence types instead (cf. below, chapter 9).

In the terminology of the grammarians the underlying level is often referred to as *'aṣl* "principle, origin" or *ma'nâ* "meaning, intention". In Sîbawayhi's *Kitâb* the operation by which the grammarian links actual sentences with an underlying level is called *tamthîl* "exemplification", but in later terminology the current term is *taqdîr* "assigning to something its status". Sîbawayhi very often uses the word *ma'nâ*, usually translated with "meaning". Yet, he barely touches upon the semantic aspect of speech. We have seen above that the lexical meaning of words was dealt with in a separate discipline: Sîbawayhi hardly ever provides explanatory glosses for rare words in his many quotations from poetry. "Meaning" is used by him in two different ways. In many places *ma'nâ* indicates the intention of the speaker, which is different from the underlying level reconstructed by the grammarian for syntactic reasons, but has more to do with the pragmatic aspect of speech. Speech is used for a purpose and this purpose is acknowledged and recognized by the native speakers. Therefore, the grammarian may refer to this intention in order to distinguish between variant constructions. In the second place, *ma'nâ* is used for the functions of elements of speech. The function of the morpheme *-t-*, for instance, is to denote feminine gender, both in nouns (*kabîr-at-un* "large [feminine]") and in verbs (*kataba-t* "she wrote"). Likewise, the function of the particle *'a* is to denote interrogation as in *'a-kataba* "did he write?". This functional meaning is more or less taken for granted by Sîbawayhi: he does not provide an extensive analysis of its semantic contents but simply states that these are the functions of the elements. In this respect, linguistics has moved away completely from the semantic approach of the early commentaries on the *Qur'ân*. In the case of the declensional endings, for instance, it is the function that determines their "meaning", and they do not possess a meaning of their own. In Arabic grammar the names of the declensional endings do not indicate any semantic content, as in Greco-Latin grammar ("nominative", "genitive", "accusative", or in the case of the verbal moods, "indicative", "subjunctive", "optative"), but refer to their phonological shape. We have referred above (p. 6) to the problem of finding the right equivalents for the Arabic terms in translating: part of this difficulty lies in the fact that all Greco-Latin terms are semantically oriented, whereas the Arabic terms refer to the form or rank of elements.

Sîbawayhi's *Kitâb* remained the authority for all later grammarians, many of whom wrote commentaries on its text, for instance as-Sîrâfî (cf. below, chapter 4). For some time it also remained the model for the order in which many grammatical writings treated their material: syntax, morphology, phonology. The arrangement in itself was not regarded as sacrosanct, and in the course of the centuries several changes were introduced. One of Sîbawayhi's immediate successors, al-Mâzinî (d. 863), wrote a treatise exclusively about morphology, and this new trend was followed by other authors. In the ninth/tenth centuries grammarians began to write shorter introductions to linguistics that were explicitly meant for beginning students. Such works as, for instance, az-Zajjâjî's very popular *Kitâb al-jumal* and Ibn Jinnî's *Kitâb al-luma'* contain a minimum of controversial issues and limit themselves to a straightforward treatment of the basic rules of grammar. Probably for didactic reasons, too, the grammarian az-Zamakhsharî (d. 1144) introduced an entirely new arrangement of the grammatical material in his *Kitâb al-mufaṣṣal*: after a section on the basic notions of grammar he divides his book into three sections, each of which is dedicated to the functions of one declensional case (nominative, accusative, genitive). Since in this volume we concentrate on the general ideas about language rather than the technical aspects of grammar, we shall not go into the technical innovations that were introduced by grammarians throughout the tradition. What must be pointed out is the fundamental unity of Arabic linguistic theory: after seven or eight centuries grammarians continued to quote Sîbawayhi's *Kitâb* as an authoritative source and even when they disagreed with him, they tried to preserve as much as possible the way he formulated solutions to grammatical problems.

Chapter 4

The debate between logic and grammar

[On the request of the vizier Ibn al-Furât the grammarian 'Abû Sa'îd as-Sîrâfî takes it upon himself to refute the opinions of 'Abû Bishr Mattâ ibn Yûnus, the logician, who had claimed that the only way to distinguish truth from falsity was by the science of logic. As-Sîrâfî says to Mattâ:] "Tell me what you mean by logic! For when we understand what you mean by it, our discussion with you about which parts of it may be accepted as correct, and which parts have to be rejected because they are false, will take place in a satisfying manner and by an acknowledged method." Mattâ answered: "I mean by 'logic' a linguistic tool by which correct speech can be distinguished from incorrect, and false meaning from true, like a balance. With its help I distinguish between what weighs more and what weighs less, between what is superior and what is inferior." 'Abû Sa'îd said: "You are wrong, because correct speech is distinguished from wrong speech by the ordering of its composition and by the correctness of its declension, when it is Arabic we are speaking. False meaning is recognized by reason, when it is by reason that we are investigating. . . . Besides, since logic has been established by a Greek in the language of his people, according to their convention and their agreement on its rules and forms, why do the Turks and Indians and Persians and Arabs need to study it and adopt it as their judge and arbiter, accepting everything it asserts and rejecting everything it denies?" Mattâ retorted: "They need to do that because logic investigates those intentions that can be understood and those meanings that can be grasped, by studying the impulses of the mind and the motions of the soul. In the intelligible things all people are alike. Don't you see that 'four plus four equals eight' and similar statements are alike for all nations?"

[As-Sîrâfî objects to the use of such facile examples in the discussion and asserts that the only way to reach the intelligibles is through language. He says:] "This means that you do not invite us to study logic, but to learn Greek, while you yourself do not know the language of the Greeks. So why do you invite us to study a language you do not know yourself, since it has disappeared a long time ago, its speakers have perished, and the people who communicated in it and used it in their daily intercourse have become extinct? Besides, you transmit it through Syriac. What can you say about meanings that have been distorted by the translation from one language, Greek, into another language, Syriac, and from that into yet another language, Arabic?"

[Mattâ stresses the special achievements of the Greeks in philosophy and wisdom, but as-Sîrâfî rejects this claim: knowledge and wisdom are distributed equally among all nations. It would be better for Mattâ to learn to speak Arabic correctly, since that is the language he uses, or attempts to use, in the debate. Perhaps then he would realize that he had no need for the language and meanings of the Greeks. As a final test he asks him about the meanings, i.e., functions, of the Arabic word *wa-* "and". To this challenge Mattâ answers:] "That is grammar, and grammar is something I have not studied, because a logician does not need it, whereas the grammarian needs logic very much: logic investigates the meaning, and grammar investigates the expression. If the logician comes across the expression, it is by accident, and if the grammarian stumbles upon the meaning, that too is by accident. Meaning is nobler than expression and expression is humbler than meaning."

[This is the central statement of the entire discussion. As-Sîrâfî rises to the challenge by turning it completely around:] "Grammar is logic, but isolated from the Arabic language, and logic is grammar, but understood within language. The only difference between expression and meaning is that the expression is natural, whereas the meaning is rational."

[He continues by stressing the fact that the Greek language has disappeared completely, and that Mattâ is in need of Arabic words in order to express the meanings he wishes to express:] "This is why the expression disappears with time, since time effaces the traces of nature and replaces them with other traces. This is also why the meaning is permanent in time, because the receptacle of meaning is the mind, and the mind is divine: the matter of the expression is earthly, and all earthly things wither away."

[Mattâ answers that the only thing he needs to know about Arabic is that it consists of noun, verb, and particle, which lays him wide open to further scorn by as-Sîrâfî, who says:] "You are more in need of knowledge of the Arabic language than knowledge of the Greek meanings! Meanings are not Greek or Indian, but languages are Persian or Arabic or Turkic. Yet, you claim that the meanings occur by reason, investigation and reflection; the only thing that remains to learn are the rules of the language. Why then do you revile the Arabic language, while you explain the books of Aristotle in that language, although you ignore its essence?"

('Abû Ḥayyân at-Tawḥîdî, *Kitâb al-'imtâ' wa-l-mu'ânasa*, ed. by 'Aḥmad 'Amîn and 'Aḥmad az-Zayn, 3 vols, Beirut, 1953, I, pp. 108–28)

In 932 a debate took place in the 'Abbâsid capital of Baghdad that epitomized the discussions that were raging between representatives of conventional Arabic scholarship and supporters of the innovations introduced by the *'ulûm yûnâniyya* "Greek sciences". The participants in the debate were the aged Mattâ ibn Yûnus (d. 940), an enthusiastic partizan of Greek logic and philosophy, and the young 'Abû Sa'îd as-Sîrâfî (d. 979), a paragon of all the Arab virtues, a connoisseur of Arabic poetry and grammar, and an accomplished debater in the style of the Arabic *majâlis*, public discussions between scholars. Mattâ was a Syrian Christian, whereas as-Sîrâfî claimed to be defending Islam. Although as-Sîrâfî was no more than forty years old at the time of the debate, he had already made himself a name with his commentatorial work on the *Kitâb Sîbawayhi*; his commentary was regarded for centuries as the best way to study the *Kitâb*. He had studied with the grammarian Ibn as-Sarrâj (d. 928), and among his pupils was at-Tawḥîdî, the author of the report from which we have quoted above. Before we go into the altercation itself we shall sketch the changes that were taking place in Arabo-Islamic society as the result of the translation of Greek writings.

After the Arab conquests of the seventh century the Arab tribes were faced with the necessity of administering an empire that stretched from Islamic Spain in the West to Transoxania in the East. The civilizations in this empire had long traditions of scholarship and learning and in the beginning they viewed the uncouth barbarians that were their new masters with disdain. The Arab armies had to rely on administrators from the conquered peoples to keep the records of the tax registers and to do most of their writing, in Greek, Syriac, Coptic or Persian. Syria, Persia, and Egypt had been parts of a large Hellenistic cultural area, and especially in Syria there had been a long tradition of education in schools and universities.

The Arabs' feeling of military and religious superiority helped them impose their language and religion on the conquered peoples in a relatively short period of time, yet they were forced to acknowledge the superior knowledge and experience of the Syrians and Copts in disciplines they knew nothing about, particularly in the practical sciences of medicine and astrology/astronomy. During the dynasty of the Umayyads, who reigned as the successors of the first caliphs in the capital of Damascus from 661 to 750, the first translations of Persian and Greek writings were made at the request of the court. Some of the Umayyad caliphs commissioned translations of astrological and medical books and established court libraries, where such translations were deposited.

Most of the translators were Christians and Jews, often speakers of Syriac, whose second language became Arabic. They acted as intermediaries between the two cultures. Most works were first translated from Greek into Syriac, after which other translators took care of the translation from Syriac into Arabic. Only a few of the early translations have survived; later generations of translators judged these early efforts to be incompetent, inasmuch as they aimed at a word-by-word transposition of the Greek text into Syriac and Arabic, so that the result was often incomprehensible. The early translators simply transliterated Greek technical terms, which increased the obscurity of these texts. Probably knowledge about the Greek sciences remained limited to a very small group of people at court, and there was no public domain for these disciplines, let alone an educational system in which they could be taught.

The breakthrough of Greek knowledge took place in the reign of the early 'Abbâsid caliphs who came to power in 750 and reigned the vast Islamic empire from the newly founded capital of Baghdad. The Caliph al-Ma'mûn, who reigned from 813 to 833, was one of the chief patrons of the work of the translators and a warm advocate of Greek science. According to the Arabic tradition the immediate cause of the introduction of Greek writings was a dream in which al-Ma'mûn saw an old man sitting on his own throne:

> Al-Ma'mûn said: I saw in a dream an old man sitting on the throne in my own audience chamber. I wondered about him and paid him my respect. When I asked people about him, they told me he was Aristotle. I said, let me ask him something and I asked him: "What is the good?" He said: "What reason regards as good". I said: "What else?" He said: "What the people regard as good". I said: "What else?" He said: "What the law regards as good". I said: "What else?" He said: "Nothing else!" This dream was the direct cause for bringing out the books.
>
> (Ibn 'Abî 'Uṣaybi'a, *'Uyûn al-'anbâ'*, ed. by August Müller, repr. Westmead, 1972, pp. 186–7)

The implication of the story of this dream is that Greek knowledge ("the books") implies a rational approach to science: the first criterion for all knowledge is reason. Such an approach, applied in this anecdote to ethical issues, fitted in perfectly well with the development of Islamic theology at this period of time. Al-Ma'mûn was sympathetic towards the movement of the Mu'tazilite theologians, who proclaimed the primacy of reason before revelation and demanded the establishment of the truth of the *Qur'ân* by rational means first, since the act of belief has to be preceded by the force of reason. The accumulated knowledge of Greek philosophy and the tools of Greek logic were welcomed by these theologians, who used these to build up their own philosophical system (cf. below, chapter 8 and chapter 10 on the role of the Mu'tazila in linguistics). Since al-Ma'mûn sympathized with the theologians of the Mu'tazilite school, it is not surprising that he enthusiastically endorsed the translation of the Greek writings.

Whatever the historical foundation for the story of al-Ma'mûn's dream, it is true that in his reign the translation movement started to flourish as it had never before. Al-Ma'mûn founded a special academy for translators, called the *Bayt al-Ḥikma* "House of Wisdom", and engaged dozens of translators to translate all the Greek and Syriac manuscripts he had acquired from the Byzantine area. For the Arabs there was a large difference between the contemporary Byzantine empire, their arch-enemy, and the Classical Greek culture, even in the names they gave them. The Byzantines were called *ar-Rûm*, i.e., the Rhomaeans, the successors of the Roman empire, a name the Byzantines themselves also used, and the Classical Greeks were called *al-Yûnân*, i.e., the Ionians. Whereas the Arabs freely admired the knowledge and experience of the Classical Greeks whose writings they translated and learned to love, they despised the Byzantines, whom they regarded as a debased form of Greeks, who had no proper respect for their own heritage. The Arabs felt that the burden and responsibility to preserve this heritage had fallen on their own shoulders, since the Byzantines could no longer be trusted to take care of it.

The first writings to be translated were mostly medical writings by Galen and Hippocrates. But because of the intimate connection between philosophy and medicine in Greek antiquity, very soon introductory treatises on philosophy were translated as well, soon to be followed by the most important Aristotelian writings as well as commentaries by Peripatetic philosophers such as Ammonios. One of the most famous translators, Ḥunayn ibn 'Isḥâq (d. 873), has left us a list of the more than a hundred treatises he personally translated. He must have been a remarkable scholar, with a profound knowledge of Greek, Syriac, Persian, and Arabic. In his list he laid down the rules for editing and translating Greek manuscripts. About Galen's *Book on the medical schools* he explains, for instance, that he first collected all surviving Greek manuscripts and then collated them in order to obtain a correct text; he then translated this text into Syriac and compared it with the existing Syriac translation before translating it into Arabic; he concludes by saying that this is the way he always works. Although the Arabic tradition did not elaborate a formal theory of translation, later sources praise Ḥunayn's innovating approach to translating, which concentrated on the meaning of the text rather than providing a word-by-word paraphrase.

The influx of Greek writings thoroughly affected Islamic society. We have already mentioned that the Mu'tazilite theologians needed Greek logic and philosophy in order to carry out their programme of rationalist theology. But in other disciplines, too, the exigencies of modern scholarship made themselves felt. Very soon, no respectable scholar could fail to use at least some superficial notions of philosophy and logic in his work, for instance by properly defining the notions with which they operated, by carefully circumscribing their own scientific domain, by classifying the subject matter of their writings according to logical rules, and by providing their treatises with an introduction in which they presented their material in an orderly fashion. Commentators of Sîbawayhi's *Kitâb*, such as Mattâ's opponent as-Sîrâfî, were embarrassed by what they felt to be Sîbawayhi's insufficient definitions of the basic notions of linguistics. In the first pages of the *Kitâb* (cf. above, p. 36) Sîbawayhi "defines" the noun by giving two examples of nouns, and the verb by providing an ambiguous description that could be applied to physical actions as well as to grammatical verbs (both are called in Arabic *fi'l*). The commentators hastened to explain why Sîbawayhi had neglected this important aspect of scholarly discourse; one of the reasons given by az-Zajjâjî was that he regarded the definitions as self-evident and therefore omitted them.

Since even as-Sîrâfî was fully convinced of the need to use logical notions in analysing language, his manifest irritation vis-à-vis the representatives of the new science, as shown in the debate with Mattâ, was not directed against logic *per se*, but must have a different background. The immediate cause of the debate was Mattâ's claim about the function of logic as a tool to distinguish between truth and falsity. The implication of this claim was that the logician was more qualified to judge about the correctness of meanings than the grammarian, who should occupy himself solely with the correct expression of those meanings in a particular language. If such a claim were to be accepted by the Islamic community, it was feared by many scholars, this would mean the total submission to the representatives of a foreign, heathen culture. It was, therefore, imperative, for as-Sîrâfî to demonstrate the inherent falsity of Mattâ's claims and those of his colleagues.

The simple scheme of Mattâ, as reproduced in the text of the debate, was that expressions belong to the level of speech and are accidental, whereas the meanings belong to a higher level. They are universal for all nations, only the languages of the nations differ in their surface rules for the expression of the meanings. "Meanings" (*ma'ânî*) in this context refers to the logical operations of the mind (as in Mattâ's example of the arithmetic truth of a simple addition) and may be equated with "concepts" as far as the simple meanings are concerned, and with "propositions" as far as the compound meanings are concerned. For the grammarians, however, "meaning" referred to an inherently linguistic entity, the semantic aspect of a phonetic expression. According to as-Sîrâfî meaning in this sense is not universal at all: each language has its own meanings (in one passage he says that meanings are the same for all people, but there he is making a hypothetical statement for the sake of argument). In this use of the word "meaning" as-Sîrâfî is simply following the current linguistic usage of this term. Most grammarians (cf. above, p. 50) use *ma'nâ* in one of three meanings: the lexical meaning of words (as discussed by the lexicographers); the intention of the speaker (as discussed by the exegetes); and the meaning or function of a word, which is what the grammarians are concerned with.

Seen from this perspective it is obvious that as-Sîrâfî could never accept Mattâ's statements and did not challenge him purely for the sake of argument. Anyone wishing to explain Aristotle's thoughts in Arabic should first of all obtain a thorough knowledge of the language. Otherwise one risks losing sight of the specific properties of each language and the differences between languages, thereby obscuring what one wishes to explain. The example of the conjunction *wa-* "and" and, at a later stage of the discussion, that of the preposition *fî* "in" demonstrate the need for native-like command of the language before one dare even think of saying something in Arabic. Concerning *fî* as-Sîrâfî quotes the logicians against themselves:

> I have heard you say that the grammarians do not know the proper constructions of *fî*, because they only say that it is used for contents, just as they say that *bi-* is used to express companionship. *Fî* [you claim] is used for several things, since one can say "something is in a container", "the container is in a place", "the leader is in leadership", "leadership is in the leader". But all this dissection stems from the minds of the Greeks on the basis of their language, and it cannot be understood by the minds of Indians, Turks, or Arabs.
>
> ('*Imtâ'*, p. 117)

At this point in the discussion the vizier asks as-Sîrâfî to enlighten the audience concerning the true meanings of *fî* and *wa-*, which he does with great expertise and brilliance. The rest of the "dialogue" consists in as-Sîrâfî's heaping scorn on Mattâ and bombarding him with questions to which he either does not know the answer or, when he tries to answer, he is immediately shut up by the victorious grammarian. An easy butt for his attacks are the terms commonly used by the logicians, such as the many abstract substantives that are loan translations from Greek (e.g., *kayfiyya* "quality", *laysiyya* "not-being", *'ayniyya* "locality") and their use of incomprehensible formulas such as "there is no A in B, C is in some B; therefore A is not in C".

In view of the composition of the audience during this debate it is not surprising that the logician stood no chance and was thoroughly defeated. All spectators were Arab intellectuals, who rejoiced in the humiliation of an exponent of the foreign sciences at the hands of a young grammarian playing to the public for all his worth and correcting Mattâ's mistakes against Arabic grammar whenever given a chance. Besides, the account wc have of the debate was made by an admirer and pupil of as-Sîrâfî's, at-Tawḥîdî. But it was not just a matter of xenophobic mistrust of anything foreign. The essence of Arabic culture and grammar was at stake. The propagandists of Greek science claimed a universal validity for logic that undermined the uniqueness of Arabic culture. If, as Mattâ claimed, the meaning of Arabic and Greek words was the same, then it could easily be defended that these meanings fell under the competence of the logicians. In that case the grammarian would become a simple schoolmaster whose only job was to teach children how the meaning established by the logician was represented in a particular language by a particular word. To counter such preposterous claims the grammarians defended the view that meanings were language-specific, and since the only meanings Arabic grammarians were interested in belonged to the Arabic language, their position was that all meanings fell within the domain of Arabic grammar.

Fortunately, the grammarians are not our only source on this controversy. A Christian philosopher, Yaḥyâ ibn 'Adî (d. 974), wrote a small treatise in which he summarized the issue of the difference between logic and grammar. Yaḥyâ was a pupil of Mattâ and al-Fârâbî (cf. below, chapter 6); he translated a number of Aristotelian writings and wrote on logic, physics, and mathematics, as well as on Christian theological issues such as the trinity and the nature of Christ. The treatise, entitled *Tabyîn al-faṣl bayna ṣinâ'atay al-manṭiq al-falsafî wa-n-naḥw al-'arabî* "Explanation of the difference between the arts of philosophical logic and Arabic grammar", presents the issue in a dispassionate way, outside the heated atmosphere of the debate between as-Sîrâfî and Mattâ.

Yaḥyâ begins by unambiguously declaring that both grammar and logic are an art (*ṣinâ'a*), i.e., a science in their own right. This means that each must have its own specific subject and aim, and it is in these respects that they differ from each other. Apparently he believes that by applying neat logical distinctions the matter may be solved to everyone's satisfaction. It is obvious what the subject of grammar is:

> When the subject of an art is that on which it acts, the subject of the art of grammar must be that on which grammar acts. Clearly, its action consists in providing words with an ending /u/, /a/, or /i/, or in general, in inserting vowels or omitting them in accordance with what the Arabs do. Since the action of grammar consists in inserting or omitting vowels, and since this takes place in words, these must be the subject of grammar.
>
> (Yaḥyâ ibn *'Adî*, *Tabyîn al-faṣl*, ed. by Gerhard Endress, *Journal for the History of Arabic Science* 2 (1978), pp. 181–93, p. 189)

Yaḥyâ then explains that the vowel endings occur in accordance with the meanings of the words, but this does not mean that the grammarian has any competence in the study of meanings. His argumentation betrays the subtle semantic shift the term *ma'ânî* "meanings" has undergone: in the quotation above the term is used for the functions a word has within the sentence, e.g., agent or object. But when Yaḥyâ says that the *ma'ânî* cannot be the subject or the aim of the discipline of grammar, he has in mind the objects that are signified by the words. About these objects he can safely say that they are not affected by the vowel endings provided by the grammarians: even when a sentence is pronounced without declensional endings, its meaning is quite clear, and conversely, when a sentence is ambiguous, it does not help to supply the correct declensional endings.

Yaḥyâ's conclusion is identical to Mattâ's, although it is formulated a bit more cleverly. The study of meanings is the monopoly of the logician. When grammarians occupy themselves with the meaning of an expression, they do so not as grammarians but as ordinary native speakers who wish to express their thoughts. The discipline of logic, on the other hand, deals with the subject of signifying expressions, rather than with expressions *per se*, and only with those expressions that signify universal matters, rather than particular matters. Its aim is to combine these expressions in such a way that they correspond to the truth (or to reality). The aim of grammar is then to provide these true expressions with the correct vowel endings according to the rules of the Arabic language. As we can see from this conclusion, in spite of his moderate formulation substantially Yaḥyâ draws the same lines between the two disciplines as Mattâ did.

After the uneasy start of the relationship between logic and grammar some kind of truce was reached. Logical methods were incorporated in linguistics; even those grammarians who like as-Sîrâfî resisted these claims had no objections to the introduction of new notions and definitions in their own discipline. In his commentary on the *Kitâb* as-Sîrâfî himself put logical terminology to good use, not by borrowing it wholesale but by carefully selecting the notions he needed for his linguistic analysis. He does not criticize the *Kitâb*'s lack of formal definitions, but simply remarks that Sîbawayhi did not feel the need to define, for instance, the noun (cf. above, p. 58), and then adds his own definition:

> With respect to the noun, Sîbawayhi did not give a definition to set it apart from other words and to distinguish it from the verb and the particle, but simply said "The noun is *rajul* and *faras*". . . . If someone asks about the definition of the noun, the answer is: "Any word whose form signifies a meaning that is not connected with an accidental time is a noun".
>
> (as-Sîrâfî, *Sharḥ Kitâb Sîbawayhi*, ed. by Ramaḍân ʿAbd at-Tawwâb and Maḥmûd Fahmî Ḥigâzî, Cairo, 1986, I, p. 53)

In this definition the notion of "connection with time", which distinguishes the verb from the noun, is borrowed from logical writings, as it is in the various definitions that are discussed by az-Zajjâjî in his *'Îḍâḥ* (d. 949; cf. below, chapter 5). Az-Zajjâjî demonstrates his intimate acquaintance with logical definitions, while carefully differentiating between the aims of the two disciplines of logic and grammar. Almost all grammarians of this period acted in the same way: many of them belonged to the Muʿtazila and had no problems with Greek logical methods, as long as they could use them for their own purposes without being swallowed by them. Some grammarians apparently went too far for the taste of most grammarians in their attempt to change the discipline of linguistics by organizing it according to logical standards. Such an approach could lead to an accusation of mixing the two disciplines, as happened to ar-Rummânî (d. 994), a Muʿtazilite grammarian who had studied with Ibn as-Sarrâj (cf. below, p. 70). Of him the biographer says: "He used to mix his speech with logic so that 'Abû ʿAlî al-Fârisî said: "If grammar is the way 'Abû l-Ḥasan ar-Rummânî talks, we have no part in it; but if it is the way we talk, he has no part in it!'" (Ibn al-'Anbârî, *Nuzha*, ed. by Attia Amer, Stockholm, 1963, p. 189).

At the logicians' end, after things had calmed down, scholars quietly went on with the synthesis of foreign and Islamic elements. This is the approach we find in al-Fârâbî (d. 950; cf. below, chapter 6) and later on in al-Ghazzâlî (d. 1111), who completed the edifice of what we have come to know as Islamic philosophy. The ultimate effect in grammar was slight. In most cases the influence of logic made itself felt solely in the form of the presentation. Grammatical treatises no longer started in *medias res*, but took care of presenting each new notion in the form of a definition. Some of the definitions of the verb and the noun have unmistakably been borrowed from Arabic translations of Aristotelian writings, but at the end of the day Arabic grammar remained what it had been before, an Arabo-Islamic discipline without foreign influence.

Chapter 5

The development of linguistic theory

Az-Zajjâjî on linguistic explanation

We distinguish three categories of grammatical causes: didactic causes; analogous causes; dialectic and speculative causes.

The didactic causes are those which enable you to learn the Arabic language. For we do not hear – nobody does – the whole of the language, every single word, but only part of it. From this part we deduce the corresponding expressions. For instance, when we hear *qâma zaydun wa-huwa qâ'imun* "Zayd stood up and he is standing", and *rakiba zaydun wa-huwa râkibun* "Zayd rode and he is riding", we recognize the active participle and we say *dhahaba wa-huwa dhâhibun* "he went out and he is going out", and so on.

As for the analogous causes: if someone explains that in the example *'inna zaydan qâ'imun* "verily, Zayd is standing" *zayd* is put in the accusative on account of *'inna*, and you ask him: "But why should *'inna* cause an accusative in the noun?", the answer is: "Because *'inna* and cognate words bear a resemblance to transitive verbs with one object. They are, therefore, compared to them and, because of their resemblance, receive the same governance. A word in the accusative bears a formal resemblance to the object, and a word in the nominative to the agent, so that [the whole construction] resembles a verb with the object placed before the agent, as in *ḍaraba 'akhâka muḥammadun* "Muḥammad hit your brother", and so on."

The dialectic and speculative causes are relevant for further questions about *'inna*. One could ask, for instance: "In what way do these particles resemble the verbs, and to which verbs do you compare them, to the past or to the future or to the present? Or to the durative or to the punctual? And when you compare them to verbs, why are they given the same treatment as those verbs which have their object placed before their agent – as in *ḍaraba zaydan ʿamrun* "ʿAmr hit Zayd" – and why not the same treatment as those verbs which have the agent before the object? The latter category is the principle, and the former only a secondary derivation!"

(az-Zajjâjî, *'Îḍâḥ*, ed. by Mâzin al-Mubârak, Cairo, 1959, pp. 64–5)

In the preface to the *Kitâb al-'îḍâḥ fî ʿilal an-naḥw* "The book of the explanation of the linguistic causes", from which the above text is taken, the grammarian az-Zajjâjî states that he was the first to deal with the topic of the *ʿilal an-naḥw*, the linguistic causes, and throughout his book it becomes clear that his approach to the study of language is indeed innovative. In this chapter we shall see how in the fourth century of Islam, roughly the tenth century of the common era, linguists tried to get a grip on the methodological bases of their discipline.

Az-Zajjâjî was born between 860 and 870 near Hamadhan in present-day Iran and he probably died in 949 in Ṭabariyya (modern Tiberias). His chief fame rests on a compendium of Arabic grammar, the *Kitâb al-Jumal*, which throughout the centuries has remained one of the most popular introductions to the science of language. It is a traditional grammar, in which the entire structure of the language is dealt with, but it differs from other summaries by its didactic qualities. The number of commentaries on this work is staggering: according to one source there were more than 120 commentaries in North Africa alone, and we have the titles of at least forty-nine commentaries, some of which have been published. Up till our time the *Kitâb al-Jumal* has remained in use as a handbook of Arabic in traditional universities in the Islamic world. Among his other writings are books on particles, collections of grammatical discussions, lexicographical treatises, and a few commentaries on the writings of other grammarians. In this chapter we shall be concerned mainly with the contents of the *Kitâb al-'îḍâḥ*.

We know hardly anything about az-Zajjâjî's life, but we do know something about his intellectual background because he himself tells us about his teachers in one of the chapters of his book. He says, for instance, that the arguments mentioned in his book are of three kinds:

> Some of them are mentioned in the books of the Basrans and the Kufans, but in a language so complicated and difficult that I have interpreted [their arguments] in terms that are easier to understand for those who study this book. . . . A second group is constituted by those arguments which I was able to elicit from the rules [of the language] of the people. I have formulated them inasmuch as I discovered that language was dependent on them, and that they formed the basis of analogy. Finally, there are those arguments which I transmitted from the teachers whom I met and whose classes I used to attend. . . . In most cases I have translated in Basran terms those arguments of the Kufans which I mention.
>
> (*'Îḍâḥ*, p. 78)

This autobiographical sketch is quite interesting for a number of reasons. In the first place, it shows what kind of sources a grammarian such as az-Zajjâjî used in his research: books, independent research, and lectures by other grammarians. In the second place, it shows his dependence from grammarians belonging to both the school of Basra and that of Kufa. Throughout the book it is obvious that he strives at a certain measure of impartiality by mentioning arguments for and against each group. According to the Arabic historiography of the grammatical tradition (see above, chapter 3), when the centre of culture and scholarship was transferred to Baghdad the old distinction between two schools lost its significance, and they merged into one school of Baghdad. Western accounts of the history of the Arabic grammatical tradition, on the other hand, tend to ascribe the distinction of two schools precisely to this period. According to this view, the grammarians attempted to legitimize their own theories by projecting them back on to an earlier period, using the names of grammarians who had lived one or two centuries before them as eponyms for their own "school".

Az-Zajjâjî's testimony shows that at least for some scholars the old tradition was still alive, even though their adherence to one school or the other may have been dictated by ulterior motives, such as the wish to irritate an opponent. But az-Zajjâjî's last remark in the quotation given here also shows that people at his time were fully aware of the terminological differences between the two schools. Many grammarians explicitly tell us, for instance, that the Kufan terms for "genitive" (*khafḍ*) or "particle" (*'adâ*) differ from the Basran equivalents (*jarr* and *ḥarf*, respectively).

Apart from the changed relationship between the Basran and Kufan school, there is one factor that was of decisive influence in the formation of a new intellectual atmosphere in Baghdad in the ninth/tenth centuries and that brought about a novel approach to the study of language. In chapter 4 we have seen that the introduction of Greek logical doctrines in the Arabo-Islamic world led to a confrontation between logicians and linguists, both of whom tried to affirm their hegemony in the study of language. In the end the representatives of the imported knowledge of logic had to give in, and grammar remained the domain of the specialists of the Arabic language. But the grammarians who came after this period could not escape the influence of the Greek doctrines: even the grammarian as-Sîrâfî, who, as we have seen, was a staunch defender of the Arabic language, uses a lot of logical terms in his work and strives at a presentation of his theories and comments in a way that satisfies the requirements of logic. As-Sîrâfî was a contemporary of az-Zajjâjî, and they appear to have known each other. Many other grammarians who had engaged in the debate between logic and grammar, such as Ibn as-Sarrâj were among his teachers. We have seen above (cf. p. 62) that some of these teachers were actually accused of mixing logic with grammar.

Az-Zajjâjî himself repeatedly declares that he is a grammarian and does not wish to talk about language in the same categories as the logicians do. In the discussion about the definition of the noun, for instance, he says that there is one definition according to which a noun is "an invented sound with a conventional meaning, not specified by time" (*'Îḍâḥ*, p. 48). This is, of course, a version of the Aristotelian definition of *ónoma*, and az-Zajjâjî introduces this definition by saying that "the logicians and some grammarians have given a definition which exceeds the limits of grammar". He adds that "according to logical requirements and logical theory, it is correct, indeed, but their objective is not the same as ours, nor do we have the same purpose". He himself prefers another definition of the noun: "A noun in the language of the Arabs is something active or something passive or something which replaces something active or passive". It may be mentioned in passing that there is some evidence that this latter definition also betrays some traces of Greek influence. In Greek (Stoic) philosophy bodies or substances were defined as things that either act or are being acted upon, and this may have been the origin of az-Zajjâjî's use of the criterium of activity/passivity in his definition of "noun".

The fact alone that he devotes an entire chapter to the problems connected with establishing a correct definition and another chapter to a detailed discussion of all the existing definitions of the parts of speech shows that he knew the "proper" fashion to write a scholarly introduction to a treatise on language. His work is full of references to logical doctrine, which by his time had become part and parcel of the intellectual framework of scholars in almost every discipline. This is not to say that the grammarians regarded themselves as logicians. They opposed the influx of logical theories and, as az-Zajjâjî did, explicitly proclaimed their independence from logic. In the next chapter we shall see that in logic itself the Aristotelian tradition developed largely in isolation from other disciplines.

The influence of the logical approach to language can be seen even more clearly in the selection of topics in the *Kitâb al-'îḍâḥ*. In his other publications az-Zajjâjî deals with the normal topics of grammar, such as are found in the writings of every grammarian: syntactic problems in which the correct declensional endings are explained, morphological problems in which complicated morphological patterns are analysed, and phonological problems in which the phonotactics of Arabic are treated. But the titles of the chapters of the *'Îḍâḥ* show a different preoccupation: which of the three parts of speech has priority over the others, which of the three verbal tenses has priority over the others, why are nouns lighter than verbs, why is the nominative of the dual in Arabic formed with an *â*, why is the nominative of the singular formed with a *u*?

These and similar problems are situated on a different level than the normal rules of grammar, the "principles" (*'uṣûl*) as az-Zajjâjî calls them. These rules or principles correspond more or less with the first category of linguistic causes in the translated text above. In Arabic they are called *'ilal ta'lîmiyya*, i.e., causes that have to do with teaching the language. At this level you learn that the agent in Arabic receives a nominative ending *u*, that the active participle has the pattern *fâ'il*, or that the dual of substantives is formed with *â* in the nominative and with *ay* in the genitive/accusative. The leading principle here is the simple analogy of similar forms. When you hear from the verb *ḍaraba* "to hit" the active participle *ḍârib*, you assume that from the verb *kataba* the active participle is *kâtib*. Similarly, when in one sentence the agent is indicated with the nominative ending, you assume that in all other sentences of the same type the agent likewise has to receive the nominative ending.

But the problems with which az-Zajjâjî deals in the *'Îḍâḥ* go beyond this level. From the very beginning grammarians had not limited themselves to the description of Arabic, but they had aimed at explanations of a higher level. We have seen above that Sîbawayhi frequently had recourse to methodical principles such as resemblance, for instance in the case of the imperfect verb. Throughout Sîbawayhi's *Kitâb* the facts of language are incorporated in a hierarchical system in which words and categories have certain rights and functions, and in which some words are weaker than others. This level might be called the level of "analogical causes", because the grammarian applies the method of linguistic analogy to find out why words behave in a certain way. The imperfect verb is a case in point. The speakers of the language "know" that nouns are declined, whereas verbs and particles are undeclinable. Within the category of the verbs there is, however, one category that does receive endings that are similar to those of the nouns. At the second level of linguistic argumentation these endings are explained by the "resemblance" of the imperfect verb to the noun. The imperfect verb resembles the noun in a number of aspects (which is why it is called in Arabic *muḍâri'* "resembling"; cf. above p. 43). In Sîbawayhi the main resemblance is the fact that the imperfect verb may replace a noun, in this case an active participle, in certain constructions, e.g.:

'inna zaydan la-ḍâribun/'inna zaydan la-yaḍribu
"Zayd is really hitting"/"Zayd really hits"

Since these sentences mean the same thing, so the argument goes, the imperfect verb resembles the nominal forms and thereby earns the right to be declined. In the same way the partial loss of declension in a category of nouns (the so-called diptotic nouns) is explained by reference to their resemblance to the verbs. Later grammarians add a host of other aspects, among them the phonological pattern of the imperfect verb which is similar to that of the active participle:

/yaḍrib-u/	/ḍa"rib-u/
CvCCvC	CvCCvC

Arguments or analogies of this kind clearly belong to a higher level than the simple analogy of the learner of the language. They explain the linguistic facts by referring to a relative ordering of the categories with varying degrees of resemblance. Obviously, this is something the learners of the language do not need, and for them the first level of grammatical rules is quite sufficient.

Before az-Zajjâjî one of his teachers, Ibn as-Sarrâj (d. 928), had been concerned with the establishment of a linguistic methodology. According to him linguistic reasoning and argumentation uses *'ilal* to explain the phenomena of speech. His first level is the ordinary *'illa* "cause", that corresponds with az-Zajjâjî's *'illa ta'lîmiyya*. Beyond this cause there is, however, another cause, which he calls quite appropriately the "cause of the cause" (*'illat al-'illa*), and which explains the rules of grammar within a system of analogy and hierarchy. According to the grammarian Ibn Jinnî such a reasoning leads to nothing, however, since for each cause one would have to find a higher-level cause: "If someone were to try and find an answer to such questions, the number of causes would multiply. This would lead to defective arguments and weakness of mind in those who advance them" (Ibn Jinnî, *Khaṣâ'iṣ*, ed. by Muḥammad 'Alî an-Najjâr, 3 vols, Cairo, 1952–6, I, p. 173).

Az-Zajjâjî's innovation is that he prevents the chain of causation to go on *ad infinitum* by setting up a third level of argumentation, on which the causes that are adduced by linguists to explain the rules of grammar are explained in their turn by extra-linguistic arguments. This is the level of the *'ilal jadaliyya wa-naẓariyya*, the speculative and theoretical causes. On this level the linguistic arguments are supported with outside evidence. As an example let us go back to the vowel of the nominative, which is *u*. On the first level of argumentation the learners come to recognize the use of this vowel for the agent or the topic of the sentence, e.g.:

ḍaraba zayd-u-n 'amr-a-n "Zayd hit 'Amr"
zayd-u-n rajul-u-n "Zayd is a man"

With the help of these and other examples the learners will be able to use the same ending in similar sentences in which there is an agent or a topic. On the second level of argumentation an explanation is sought for the fact that agent and topic share the same ending. Such an explanation may be given, for instance, in terms of the common element of predication in both sentences. Although they have a different syntactic structure (cf. above, chapter 3, p. 49) both agent and topic are constituents about which something is said by a predicate, be it a verbal or a nominal one, and in this respect they resemble each other. Such an analogy between the two functions satisfies the requirements of the second level.

On the third level, that of speculative theory, the choice of the vowel *u* is called into question. Why has this particular vowel been selected to express these syntactic functions? At this point the grammarian has recourse to an extra-linguistic, physiological argument: the *u* is the heaviest vowel, i.e., the vowel that is hardest to pronounce (which phonetically speaking is true since its pronunciation involves raising the back of the tongue which costs more in terms of physical energy than raising its middle part). This is why it was selected to indicate the agent and the topic: since the accusative in Arabic has more than one function (object, adverbial adjunct of time and place, circumstantial accusative, accusative of cause, and so on) and the nominative only one (topic and agent being counted as one), it is reasonable to assign the heaviest vowel, the *u*, to the nominative, and the lighter *a* to the accusative. An alternative explanation states that the nominative is the first of the nominal cases, which makes it the most suitable candidate for the vowel *u*, which is the first of the vowels.

Considered in isolation, the above explanations look very much like *ad hoc* arguments and it is true that the grammarians were most inventive in finding explanations for the given facts of language. One must not forget, however, that the whole of grammar was regarded by the grammarian as a coherent structure, in which arguments could be applied across categories and elements. In other words, a resemblance in one part of the structure could very well serve as an explanation in another part, and a defect in one element could be compensated by assigning additional rights to another. Besides – and this applies to the whole of Islamic scholarship – since the entire creation is a coherent structure, there is no objection to borrowing arguments from physical science in order to explain linguistic phenomena. After all, language is part of the creation and obeys, therefore, in principle the same laws as the rest of the creation.

Let us take another example of the tripartite explanation. In the translated text above the particle *'inna* is mentioned as an illustration of the three categories of arguments. The main function of the particle *'inna* is to serve as a topicalizer of the entire sentence. Take, for instance the sentence

ḍaraba zaydun ʻamran
"Zayd hit ʻAmr"

In this sentence, as we have seen in chapter 3, the agent may be topicalized and become the topic of the sentence, as in

zaydun ḍaraba ʻamran
"Zayd, he hit ʻAmr"

But it is also possible to emphasize the entire sentence, with the help of the particle *'inna*:

'inna zaydan ḍaraba ʻamran
"indeed, Zayd hit ʻAmr"

or, in a nominal sentence,

'inna zaydan 'akhûka
"indeed, Zayd is your brother"

The translation in this case is by necessity a bit awkward; traditional Western grammars translate *'inna* with "verily, indeed", but there is no adequate translation to cover all aspects of the meaning of the particle. The early grammarians were not overly interested in the semantic aspects of the particle *'inna*, but they were very much intrigued by its syntactic behaviour, since it puts the topic of the sentence in the accusative. It is the grammarian's task to explain why the particle is allowed to operate in this way. In the Arabic grammatical tradition *'inna* is a member of a group of particles that behave similarly; the group also includes particles such as *'anna* "that [conjunction]", *li-'anna* "because", *ka-'anna* "as if", which are known collectively as *'inna wa-'akhawâtuhâ* "*'inna* and its sisters".

In this case, the second tier of the argumentation consists in a formal analogy between verbal sentences with an object, on the one hand, and *'inna* with its construction, on the other:

'inna zayd-a-n rajul-u-n "indeed, Zayd is a man"
ḍaraba ʻamr-a-n zayd-u-n "Zayd hit ʻAmr"

Obviously, this resemblance is purely formal and has nothing to do with the function of the constituents on a semantico-syntactic level. The underlying structure of the sentence with *'inna* shows a topic/predicate relationship, in which *zayd-u-n* is the topic and *rajul-u-n* the predicate. But the grammarians reason that *'inna* resembles the verb in that it causes an accusative in one word and a nominative in another, just as the verb causes the accusative in the object and the nominative in the agent.

There is a further problem in that the normal word order in verbal sentences is verb–agent–object; the order in the sentence given here is a possible but highly marked one. Az-Zajjâjî quite rightly mentions as one of the possible objections to this analogy of the second level that in itself there is no reason why the construction with *'inna* should be compared to a secondary (i.e., marked) construction. But, he states, the answer to such a question belongs to the third level. In the *'Îḍâḥ* he himself does not provide any answers; he quotes this and similar questions only in order to illustrate the kind of objections that may be raised on the third level. But we know from other writings what kind of answers may be expected. They are always formulated in terms of the weakness/strength of the elements involved. In other words, arguments on the third level regard the structure of language from the outside and look upon it as a society of words in which strong elements compete with weak elements, just as in human society. Strength in the language system correlates with the rights an element has and with its power over other elements. The exact reasons for the additional rights *'inna* receives are perhaps not very relevant here, the main point being that it resembles the verb (e.g., by its undeclinable ending in *-a* just like the perfect verb).

In a similar fashion, the adjective's syntactic position is explained. According to the theory of the Arabic grammarians many adjectives can exercise some kind of governance on substantives, as in the following sentence:

ar-rajulu *ṭ-ṭawîlu l-wajhi*
the-man the-long the-face [genitive]
"the man with the long face"

In this sentence the adjective is said to operate on the following substantive, which results in its genitive ending. The adjective resembles the active participle, since both have a masculine/feminine and a singular/dual/plural distinction. The participle in its turn resembles the verb, since both express an action. This explains why the participle can have an object in the accusative, and why this power is partially assigned to the adjective as well, so that it can cause a genitive ending in a substantive. All of these analogies are formulated in terms of relative strength and power:

the stronger a word is, the more power it can exercise on another word. The third level of argumentation imposes, as it were, a hierarchical order on the society of words.

The distinction of levels of argumentation shows that the Arabic grammarians were very much aware of the difference between a purely descriptive grammar (corresponding to what az-Zajjâjî calls the *'uṣûl* "principles") and an explanatory grammar (corresponding to the *'ilal*). Ordinary speakers of the language have the principal rules at their disposal, but it is the task of the grammarian to explain these rules. At the end of his chapter on linguistic causes az-Zajjâjî tells a story about al-Khalîl (cf. above, chapter 2), who was asked one day if he had borrowed his explanations (or causes) from the Arabs or invented them himself. His answer was as follows:

> The Arabs speak according to their instinct and nature and they know the structure of their speech. In their minds there is a solid knowledge about its causes, but these are not transmitted from them. I regarded something as a cause, whenever I was convinced that it was the right cause for what I tried to explain with it. If I was right about this, well that is exactly what I aimed at! If there happens to be another cause, you could compare my situation to that of a judicious man who enters a house that is built with good proportions, a miracle of harmony and arrangement. Now, this man by reliable information or evident proof and manifest arguments is convinced of the sound judgment of its builder and whenever he sees some part of the house, he says: "He did this according to such-and-such a cause or because of this or that reason". He says so on account of a cause which occurs to him and which he believes might be the truth. It is possible that the wise builder of the house acted, indeed, according to the cause mentioned by the man who entered the house, but it is equally well possible that he acted according to some other cause. Nevertheless, what was mentioned by the man [who entered the house] could just as well have been the right cause. So, if someone has in mind another cause for grammar than the ones I mentioned, let him come forth with it!
> ('*Îḍâḥ*, p. 66)

With his three categories of linguistic "causes" or arguments az-Zajjâjî set up a model for the structuring of linguistic argumentation. He was certainly not alone in this respect: all grammarians of this period used similar arguments. But as he himself boasts in the introduction to his *Kitâb al-'îḍâḥ*, it is true that he was the first to present a formal theory of linguistic argumentation. Strangely enough, later grammarians do not seem to have developed this theory any further. We do not find any elaboration of this scheme until Ibn al-'Anbârî (d. 1181), who in his *Luma' al-'adilla* dealt with the criteria of knowledge as they were applied in the second- and third-level arguments. He proposed formal conditions for the application of linguistic analogy in order to avoid the kind of free-for-all that threatened the basis of linguistic reasoning. Grammarians felt free to set up all kinds of analogy to explain linguistic phenomena, and Ibn al-Anbârî felt it to be his duty to restrict the application of this instrument. In his treatise he discusses the relative value of linguistic criteria, the two most important of which are analogy (*qiyâs*) and the transmission of linguistic data from reliable sources of Arabic (*naql*). He concludes that conclusive evidence for the correctness of a linguistic phenomenon can consist only in the testimony from an authority (Classical poetry, the *Qur'ân*, or the language of the Bedouin, cf. above, chapter 3). The use of analogy by linguists can serve only as additional explanation or support in the selection of alternatives and must be carried out under strict conditions. It may be added that in his discussion of linguistic methods Ibn al-Anbârî borrowed almost the entire line of reasoning from a neighbouring discipline, that of legal science.

Az-Zajjâjî himself remained chiefly known for his books on grammatical principles rather than for his theory of linguistic argumentation. Ironically, he believed himself to have been an innovator in the discipline of the *'ilal*, but later generations remembered him as the author of the *Jumal*, *ṣâḥib al-jumal*, as he is often called by later biographers.

Chapter 6

The relationship between speech and thought

Al-Fârâbî on language

The meaningful words are divided into noun (*ism*), verb (*kalim*) – these are what the grammarians of the Arabic language call *fi'l* – and compound expressions. Nouns are for instance *zayd* "Zayd", *'amr* "'Amr", *rajul* "man", *ḥayawân* "animal", *bayâḍ* "whiteness", *sawâd* "blackness", *'adâla* "justice", *kitâba* "act of writing", *'âdil* "just", *kâtib* "writing", *qâ'im* "standing", *qâ'id* "sitting", *'abyaḍ* "white", *'aswad* "black". In general, a noun is a single word that signifies a meaning without signifying by itself the time of that meaning. Verbs are actions such as *mashâ* "he walked", *yamshî* "he walks", *sa-yamshî* "he will walk"; *ḍaraba* "he hit", *yaḍribu* "he hits", *sa-yaḍribu* "he will hit", and so on. In general, a verb is a single word that signifies a meaning as well as the time of that meaning. Some verbs signify a past time, like *kataba* "he wrote", *ḍaraba* "he hit", others a future time, like *sa-yaḍribu* "he will hit", still others a present time like *yaḍribu l-'âna* "he hits now". Compound expressions may be divided into those that consist of two nouns, like *zayd qâ'im* "Zayd is standing", *'amr 'insân* "'Amr is a man", *al-faras ḥayawân* "the horse is an animal"; and those that consist of a noun and a verb, like *zayd yamshî* "Zayd walks", *'amr kataba* "'Amr wrote", *khâlid sa-yadhhabu* "Khâlid will go away", and so on.

The meaningful words also include those words that the grammarians call *ḥarf* "particle", which are used to denote a meaning. These *ḥurûf* consist of many different categories, but to this day the scholars of the discipline of Arabic grammar are not accustomed to give each category its own distinctive name. In enumerating the categories of these words we shall, therefore, have to use the names we have learned from the grammarians of the Greek language, since they assigned to each category its own name. They call one category *khawâlif* "pronouns", another one *wâṣilât* "articles", another one *wâsiṭât* "prepositions", another one *ḥawâshî* "adverbs", another one *rawâbiṭ* "conjunctions". Some of these *ḥurûf* may be construed with nouns, others with verbs, still others with expressions that are combinations of the two. Each of the *ḥurûf* is construed with another expression, since they signify the fact that the meaning of this expression is in a certain state.

We must realize that some categories of terms that are current in the discipline of grammar are used by the general public in a certain sense, while they are used by the scholars in a different sense. Frequently the scholars in one discipline use the expressions in one sense, but the scholars in another discipline use them in a different sense. The discipline of grammar studies the categories of expressions according to the current signification in the general public rather than according to their signification among scholars. This is why the grammarians only recognize those significations that are current in the general public, but not those that are current with the scholars. In many cases the meanings of the expressions that are used by the general public are identical with those that are used by the scholars. But when we intend to define the significations of these expressions, we aim at the meanings these expressions signify for the logicians exclusively, since we have no need for any of the meanings of these expressions apart from those that are used by the scholars of this discipline.

(al-Fârâbî, *Kitâb al-'alfâẓ al-musta'mala fî l-manṭiq*, ed. by Muḥsin Mahdî, Beirut, 1968, pp. 41–3)

In the quotation translated here the philosopher al-Fârâbî, the second Aristotle as he was sometimes called by his biographers and admirers, expresses himself rather unfavourably on grammatical terminology: for the scientific and philosophical study of language Arabic grammarians use a terminology that is grossly insufficient to catch all the details and shades of meanings of words and expressions. He explicitly refers to the grammarians of the Greek language, who in his opinion had a much better idea of the intricacies of language and therefore invented a terminology that was much more suitable for the classification of expressions. His critical remarks on the terminology notwithstanding, al-Fârâbî's attitude towards grammar was not merely negative. Throughout his work he tried to reconcile grammar and logic: in his view of science both were disciplines in their own right, each having its own responsibilities and its own domain. In this respect his approach differed from that of logicians such as Mattâ ibn Yûnus, who more or less explicitly relegated grammar to a minor position in scientific thought (cf. above, chapter 4). A second characteristic of his work, which also sets him apart from logicians such as Mattâ, is his thorough knowledge of Arabic. Unlike most Muslim scholars, however, his acquaintance with Greek made him aware of the differences between languages, and he actively engaged in their comparison from the point of view of a logician: the meanings expressed by the various languages are universal, but the way each particular language expresses these meanings differs.

'Abû Naṣr al-Fârâbî was born in Transoxania, but came to Baghdad in order to train as a philosopher, i.e., to get acquainted with Greek philosophy and logic. At that time the teaching of philosophy and other Greek sciences in Baghdad was completely in the hand of Syrian Christians, who controlled the translation movement and thus the access to the Greek sources. It was at their hands that al-Fârâbî was trained, but unlike them he sought contact with Muslim scholars, with whom he as a Muslim wished to be associated. Al-Fârâbî spent most of his life in the 'Abbâsid capital, where he died in 950. It is very well possible that he heard of the debate between Mattâ ibn Yûnus and as-Sîrâfî about the universalist claims of the proponents of logic (chapter 4) since he was in Baghdad at that time and probably even knew the protagonists of the debate: Mattâ's pupil Yaḥyâ ibn 'Adî also studied with him, and he had an interesting scholarly relationship with as-Sîrâfî's teacher Ibn as-Sarrâj (d. 928; cf. p. 70). According to the biographers Ibn as-Sarrâj studied logic and music with al-Fârâbî, who in his turn studied grammar with Ibn as-Sarrâj. According to one source Ibn as-Sarrâj once made a mistake in a gathering of grammarians and was severely criticized by a colleague, whereupon he said: "You have taught me a lesson! I am going to abandon what I studied since I read this book, i.e., the *Kitâb Sîbawayhi*, because I have neglected it for the study of logic and music. But now I shall return to it" (*al-Fihrist*, ed. by R. al-Mâzdarânî, Beirut, 3rd ed., 1988, p. 68).

Whatever the truth to this story, there can be no doubt that the grammarians thought of grammar and logic in terms of an opposition, whereas al-Fârâbî sought to establish links between the two disciplines. In some respects his efforts were successful, since in Ibn as-Sarrâj's main work, the *Kitâb al-'uṣûl* "Book of the principles" there are many traces of the influence of logical doctrine and method. As for al-Fârâbî, his interest in linguistic matters and his knowledge of the grammatical system of Arabic are manifest in all of his writings.

For al-Fârâbî associating with Arabic grammarians was an essential part of his programme, which aimed at reconciling the two disciplines and avoiding the mistakes Mattâ had made in his debate with as-Sîrâfî. When the latter asked Mattâ about the meanings of the Arabic preposition *fî*, his ignorance of the various constructions in which *fî* is used in Arabic invalidated his claims about the universal validity of logic. Al-Fârâbî wished to show that the philosophers' claim was justified since their insight into the rules of expressions could even contribute to the study of Arabic. In order to build up this claim of the relevance of logic for the study of grammar he developed a theory about the origin and development of language from a logician's point of view, in which he demonstrated his awareness of the relevant differences between languages in general and between Greek and Arabic in particular. Unlike Mattâ, who wished to monopolize the field for the "new" knowledge of Greek provenance, al-Fârâbî's aim was to incorporate both disciplines on a higher level. This trait in al-Fârâbî's thinking was no doubt connected with his universalism and his conviction that logic has to deal with something that transcends the domain of any particular language and is common to all languages.

The point of departure for his studies was the traditional Alexandrian framework of the study of Aristotle's writings. Long before Islam the university of Alexandria had become a centre for the study of the Aristotelian corpus. The Alexandrian commentators had developed a practical curriculum for the study of philosophy, in which logic served as an introduction. At this university a fixed canon of Aristotelian writings was studied with the help of commentaries and introductions such as Porphyry's *Eisagôgê*. One characteristic of the canon was the inclusion of rhetoric and poetic, which completed the eight parts of logic (first the treatises on the elements of syllogistic arguments: *Categories, De Interpretatione, Analytica Priora*; then the treatises on dialectic reasoning: *Analytica Posteriora, Topica, Sophistici Elenchi*; and finally *Rhetorica* and *Poetica*).

The translators in Baghdad copied this curriculum in their own teachings and writings, and this was the curriculum al-Fârâbî followed in his classification of the sciences. He did not follow the Alexandrian scheme slavishly, but introduced innovations that set his work apart from the conventional philosophers and logicians of the early translation movement, in the first place by including his knowledge of Arabic grammar, and in the second place by incorporating elements from other Greek philosophers, for instance Platonicism in his theory of the Islamic state, and Neo-Platonicism in his theory of metaphysics. Al-Fârâbi did not stand alone in this kind of eclecticism; other Islamic philosophers, too, borrowed from other schools of thought whenever they deemed fit. The apogee of Islamic eclecticism was reached with the 'Ikhwân aṣ-Ṣafâ', whose theory of universal emanation contains elements from many different philosophical schools (chapter 7).

Many of al-Fârâbî's writings deal with Aristotle's logical writings, on which he wrote commentaries that continued to serve as an introduction to Greco-Islamic philosophy for later generations of scholars such as Ibn Sînâ. His commentary on *De Interpretatione* has been preserved, but his commentary on the *Categories* was lost. In these commentaries he developed the canonical theory of signification of Islamic philosophy within the framework of Aristotle's statement at the beginning of the *De Interpretatione*: sounds are symbols of thoughts and letters are symbols of sounds. He notes that the name of the science of logic in Arabic, *manṭiq*, may lead to ambiguity. Like the Greek original *lógos*, the word *manṭiq* is derived from a root meaning "speech" (*nuṭq*). Al-Fârâbî was aware of the confusion this might cause, since the word *manṭiq* is used both for speech and for reason. He distinguishes between three different uses of *nuṭq*: exterior speech, interior speech, and reason. The grammarian's domain is only exterior speech, but the logician has to deal with all three domains, which is why logic received its name.

Of more direct interest to the history of linguistics are some of al-Fârâbî's other treatises, in which he further developed his particular blend of linguistics and logic. The *Kitâb al-ḥurûf*, literally "Book of letters", deals with the subject matter of Aristotle's *Categories*, but also contains a number of other topics. He traces the origin and development of language from a logician's point of view, loosely basing himself on Aristotle's brief remarks about the nature of language as a conventional instrument of communicating thought. Al-Fârâbî sketches the development of language and culture in much detail and gives an elaborate version of the origin of speech. He starts by explaining that people in different regions are built differently, which is why their movements differ and why they move towards different things more easily than to others. These are the things they wish to point out to their fellow human beings, first by gestures, then by vocalizations (*taṣwît*). Since their articulatory organs differ, the vocalizations with which they indicate these objects differ, too, and as a result each region has a different language.

His sketch then turns to the institutionalization of language, which he attributes to a typically Greek figure, a name-giver: in each community there is an "important man" (*'insân muhimm*) whose example is always followed by the other members of the community. This leader of the community persists in giving names to objects until everything has a name, and he may, therefore, be regarded as the speech-giver (*wâḍi' al-lugha*), just as there is a law-giver in all communities. There is no room for the divine in this sketch of the origin of speech, the scenario includes only human beings acting out a convention among themselves. Al-Fârâbî does not express himself on the reasons why a certain word is selected for a certain object, probably because he regarded these as arbitrary: just as people instinctively move towards certain things, so they move their articulatory organs instinctively, each community in its own way.

After the giving of names to objects, the people of each community go on establishing names for actions, then to habits and qualities until everything has been named. It is here in particular that we see al-Fârâbî's linguistic preoccupation. In his scenario of the invention of speech the logical categories (substances, accidents, attributes) are assigned to linguistic classes of words (nouns, verbs, adjectives). Such a view of the development of speech may be a crude one, but it is completely unlike the purely logical concern of Aristotle. The intelligent people in the community take care to express the relationship between the *'alfâẓ* "expressions" and the *ma'ânî* "meanings" in the proper way, maintaining as much as possible the equivalence between the two, especially in the division into genera and species. Such people also observe that sometimes objects receive similar accidents and they express this by giving their expressions similar endings. In this original way al-Fârâbî sought to explain the origin of declensional endings: in Arabic these are often called *'aḥwâl* "states" because they indicate the states the substantive is in, in other words the accidents of the substances. In a similar way he explains the development of homonyms and synonyms, the combination of expressions in sentences, which express a combination of meanings, and the use of metaphors, which eventually leads to the use of rhetoric and poetics.

His sketch is rounded off by the conclusion that the expressions that are invented become habitual for the people in each community:

> This enables them to become accustomed to these expressions in their mind and their tongue in such a way that they do not recognize anything else, and their tongue becomes unable to pronounce any other expressions or any other form than the form these expressions have received in their community, or any other ordering than the order of the utterances to which they have become accustomed. Those expressions that have been established conventionally in their minds correspond to those they have received from their predecessors, who have received them in their turn from their predecessors; and these in their turn have taken them from the one who first established these expressions for them. . . . This is the eloquent and correct part of their expressions, and these constitute the language of that community. Those expressions that differ from it constitute the barbarisms and errors.
>
> (*Kitâb al-ḥurûf*, ed. by Muḥsin Mahdî, Beirut, 1970, pp. 141–2)

In this way language, just like law, becomes part of the natural and conventional development of society. Since the institution of language took place according to the natural instinct of the first name-givers, the correlation between the sounds and the objects indicated by them was a natural one – not in the sense that the sounds expressed the essence of the objects, but in the sense that the first speakers' natural constitution made them utter certain sounds rather than others. Epistemologically, the resulting names are arbitrary and it is impossible to use them as a means of gaining knowledge about the essence of the objects.

Al-Fârâbî's interest in the difference between languages is another sign of his linguistic approach towards logic. In accordance with his universalist attitude he does not grant any preferential treatment to Arabic. This may be illustrated by a long passage in the *Kitâb al-ḥurûf* in which he discusses the lack of a copula in Arabic. In dealing with the categories al-Fârâbî mentions the category *al-mawjûd* "being, existing" and then states:

> Since its earliest institution Arabic has not had an expression that could take the place of *hast* in Persian, or *estin* in Greek, or of equivalent expressions in all other languages. Yet, this is something that is needed in the speculative sciences and in the discipline of logic. When philosophy was imported to the Arabs, those philosophers who spoke Arabic, and started to translate the meanings of philosophy and logic into the language of the Arabs, felt the need for [a copula]. When they found that since its first origin Arabic had never possessed any expression which could translate those contexts where *estin* was used in Greek and *hast* in Persian, and which could replace the equivalent expressions in those passages in which all other nations used it, some of them believed that the word *huwa* could be used instead of Persian *hast* and Greek *estin*. This expression is used in Arabic as a pronoun, for instance in *huwa yaf'alu* "he does" and *huwa fa'ala* "he did". But sometimes *huwa* is used in Arabic in some of the constructions in which speakers of other languages used the above-mentioned expression, as for instance in *hâdhâ huwa zayd* "this <he> is Zayd". Here the expression *huwa* in Arabic is not at all used as a pronoun. Likewise *hâdhâ huwa dhâka lladhî ra'aytuhu* "this <he> is the one I saw" and *hâdhâ huwa l-mutakallim yawma kadhâ wa-kadhâ* "this <he> is the one who is speaking on such-and-such a day" and *hâdhâ huwa shâ'ir* "this <he> is a poet", and also *zayd huwa 'âdil* "Zayd <he> is just". They used *huwa* in Arabic instead of *hast* in Persian in all constructions in which the Persians used this word *hast*.
>
> (*Kitâb al-ḥurûf*, p. 112)

It must have been a shock for Arabic grammarians – if they bothered to listen at all to the words of a philosopher – to hear a native speaker of Arabic proclaim the superiority of all other languages to Arabic, which turned out to be the only language not to possess an expression for the copula. Instead, the philosophers had to have recourse to an auxiliary construction with the pronoun *huwa* in order to translate the equivalent Persian and Greek phrases. This was not the only example al-Fârâbî gave of differences between languages, and it was not the only example of a universal meaning which was expressed better in other languages than in Arabic. But the example of the copula was a striking one since it concerned a notion that was regarded as fundamental to any philosophical discussion, that of existence. Nobody could deny that there was a strange anomaly in Arabic in that "the teacher is just" was normally expressed without a copula (*al-mu'allim 'âdil*), whereas the same expression in the past or the future tense was expressed with a copula (*kâna l-mu'allim 'âdilan* "the teacher was just", *sa-yakûnu l-mu'allim 'âdilan* "the teacher will be just").

The need to treat Arabic as a normal language just like any other language, with its good and bad qualities, is a recurrent theme in al-Fârâbî's writings. In the quotation at the beginning of this chapter he concludes that the classification of the parts of speech by the Arabic grammarians, which he probably came to know through his teacher Ibn as-Sarrâj, was deficient, since it did not cover all necessary distinctions. At the beginning of the *Kitâb* Sîbawayhi explicitly categorizes all words that are not nouns or verbs as particles, and in this he was followed by all subsequent grammarians (see above, chapter 3). Yet, al-Fârâbî noted that this rest category included a number of very different word classes with different functions. Prepositions, for instance, are distinguished by him as a separate category (*wâsiṭât*) because of their special function as logical operators; in Arabic grammatical theory some local prepositions were classified as nouns (e.g., *fawqa* "upper part, on top of") or as particles (e.g., *li-* "for").

It must have been a humiliating conclusion for the Arabic grammarians that their classification was judged to be insufficient for the analysis of Arabic, since the arguments and examples al-Fârâbî used were derived from their own language and implied a failure on their part to take note of certain phenomena and distinctions in the language they were supposed to be experts in. In this respect al-Fârâbî was a more formidable opponent than Mattâ had been, since he was able to draw the attention of his audience to aspects of their own language they had not observed themselves. It is, however, doubtful that there ever was such a live confrontation between him and any grammarian: at least that is what transpires from the fact that no grammatical work quotes him by name.

The tendency to treat all languages and cultures on an equal footing is a pervasive trait in al-Fârâbî's writings. In one remarkable passage he discusses the origin of religions and the need for an expansion of the lexicon in communities to which a new religion is brought. We have seen in chapter 1 that the issue of loanwords was a controversial one, because it came dangerously close to the idea of a human authorship of the *Qur'ân*. Al-Fârâbî appears to take a positivist view of this matter: when a new religion is brought to a community, new words are needed to express the new notions this religion brings:

> When the bringer of the religion needs to make new words for it, he can either invent names that were unknown before his time in this community, or he can use the names of those things in the community that most closely resemble the new laws he has brought. If before this time the community had another religion, he often uses the names of the laws of that first religion and applies them to similar laws in his own religion. If his religion or part of it was borrowed from another community, he often uses the names of those laws that were borrowed to indicate them, after having changed their form so that their sound and pattern become like the sound and pattern of [the expressions in] his own community and are, therefore, easier to pronounce.
>
> (*Kitâb al-ḥurûf*, p. 157)

One might have expected that as a Muslim, even though he was a philosopher, al-Fârâbî would make allowances for the special character of Islam, but he simply extends his reasoning to all religions and does not seem to make any difference between the origin of Islam and that of other religions. His views on loanwords in religion are also applied by him to his own discipline, that of philosophy. The early translators simply transliterated the Greek terms in order to create a new vocabulary in Arabic. Al-Fârâbî clearly states that this is not the best method, even when the words have received an Arabic shape. He prefers the method of the later translators who used Arabic terms that were close in meaning to the notions that had been borrowed from Greek philosophy and logic, and explicitly states that this is more appropriate. As examples he cites the Arabic terms *'unṣur* "element" and *mâdda* "matter", which replaced the early translations *'usṭuquss* and *hayûlâ*, from Greek *stoicheĩon* and *húlê*.

The most systematic treatment of the relationship between logic and grammar is found in another work, the *'Iḥṣâ' al-'ulûm*

"Enumeration of sciences", in which al-Fârâbî positions grammar within the system of the sciences. In his view, grammar has an important role to fulfil, and it is perhaps not a coincidence that in his classification of the sciences it occupies the first place, followed by logic. Although he never hides his ideas about the universality of logic as against the particularity of grammar, al-Fârâbî does not make the mistake Mattâ ibn Yûnus made of belittling the role of grammar (and the grammarians). Both disciplines have their own place and both deal with rules that govern the use of words:

> This science [sc., logic] corresponds to the science of grammar, because the relationship of the science of logic to reason and the intelligibles equals the relationship of the science of grammar to language and the expressions. The rules that the science of grammar provides for the expressions are paralleled by the rules that the science of logic provides for the intelligibles. . . . It has in common with the science of grammar that it provides the rules for the expressions and it differs from the science of grammar in that the science of grammar only provides rules concerning the expressions of a particular nation, whereas the science of logic provides universal rules that are valid for the expressions of all nations.
>
> (al-Fârâbî, *Kitâb 'iḥṣâ' al-'ulûm*, ed. by Ángel Gonzalez Palencia, Madrid & Granada, 1953, 23.1–5; 33.4–7)

The material difference between grammar and logic from al-Fârâbî's perspective is clearly the same as that in Mattâ and Yaḥyâ ibn 'Adî. Unlike them, however, al-Fârâbî has a clear picture of the domain of grammar and he makes a serious effort to underline the importance of grammar as a science. In describing grammar he uses the terminology that was familiar to the grammarians, but the picture he gives is that of a Greek science and is undoubtedly based on Greek examples, possibly that of Dionysius Thrax' *Téchnê*. We have seen above that his terminology for the third part of speech is borrowed from Greek grammar, and so is his classification of the parts of grammar. When he states that in every nation grammar consist of seven parts, he must have had in mind something like the Dionysian classification of the parts of grammar: the science of the single words, the science of the compound words, the science of the rules of the single words, the science of the rules of the compound words, the rules of orthography, the rules of orthoepy, and the rules of poetry (*'Iḥṣâ'*

p. 12). The last three parts are never included in grammar by the Arabic grammarians. The classification of the first four parts probably aims at a distinction between morphology and syntax, but in a way that was foreign to the Arabic grammarians.

Similarly, in his syntactic analysis not only his choice of paradigms ("walking", "whiteness"), but also his approach to sentence structure were completely alien to the indigenous grammatical tradition. In the quotation at the beginning of this chapter we have seen that al-Fârâbî distinguishes between two sentence types, one consisting of two nouns ("the horse is an animal"), the other consisting of a noun and a verb ("Zayd is walking"). The latter type is presented by him in the form of a sentence, *zayd yamshî*, that would be classified by the grammarians as a nominal sentence, since it starts with a noun (cf. above, p. 49). In both sentence types al-Fârâbî distinguishes two constituents, a subject (*mawḍû'*) and a predicate (*maḥmûl*). Such an analysis, based on logical categories of propositions, was irreconcilable with the formal analysis of the Arabic grammarians.

Another typical example of the foreign flavour to al-Fârâbî's classification of grammar is when he discusses the verb. He says that from a quantitative point of view verbs are divided into those with three, four, or more radicals, and from a qualitative point of view into weak and sound verbs. This parallels the kind of classification in terms of the accidents of the parts of speech that is found in Greek grammatical treatises. The Arabic grammarians never regarded weak and sound verbs as two different conjugations: weak verbs contain a glide (/w/, /y/, /"/) and are subject to certain morphonological rules, but they are not a special kind of verbs. In such details al-Fârâbî betrays his foreign model and in spite of his efforts to find acceptance for his ideas with the grammarians, not only his own theories but also those of his pupils, such as Ibn as-Sarrâj, were rejected by the learned community of Islamic scholars.

Chapter 7

The 'Ikhwân aṣ-Ṣafâ' on the theory of sound and meaning

Know, O my brother, that speech is sound produced in consonants that are articulated and that signify intelligible meanings from different places of articulation. The lowest place of articulation of the consonants is the back of the throat, which is contiguous to the top of the chest. The sound comes from the lungs, the home of the air. Likewise in the macrocosm, which is like a large man, the origin of the sound is the air beyond the moon and the breath in the world of the stars. Therefore, in man, who is a microcosm, the meaning of that which is signified by the sounds is located in the lungs and in the strength of his breath. Similarly, the movements and sounds that are found beyond the moon are a likeness and symbol for those superior sounds and for the ordered vowels: the former are spirits and the latter are bodies.

The origin of the sounds is air in the lungs which ascends until it reaches the throat, and then it is turned around by the tongue according to their places of articulation. If it comes out in articulated and composed consonants, its meaning is recognized and its message is understood. If it comes out without consonants, it is not understood, but it is like the braying of an ass or the grumbling of a camel or coughing, or something like it. But if the tongue delivers it to its known place of articulation in intelligible consonants, it is called speech and talking, regardless of the form it receives in each people in accordance with convention and the help of nature. This depends on their flexibility of consonants and their freedom of behaviour in the places of articulation of their speech, and the lightness of their language in accordance with the temperament of their natures and the climate of their countries and their diet. [It also depends] on what the signs of their birth have imposed upon them and what the stars have ordained for them when the principle of language was instituted for them, at first conventionally and later according to rules, and what has branched off from this principle, and what further divisions it has undergone. . . .

Know further that people differ in their speech and their language in accordance with the difference in body and composition. The origin of the difference in language is the difference in places of articulation and the difference in the ability to convey what an eloquent speaker can convey. Some people assert that corruption of speech, too, is the result of a corruption of composition and temperament. But this assertion is incorrect: corruption of speech results from the difference in strength and weakness in articulating the consonants. It is a corruption in the tongue, which changes and removes the consonants from their places of articulation.

There are many different accidents that may happen to the tongue, and when they happen speech is corrupted. It is a paralysis that befalls one, like faltering, sputtering, stammering, being tongue-tied, mispronunciation, stuttering, lisping, and so on. When people have difficulty in speaking, it is said they have knot in their tongue; when some of the Arabic sounds are intermingled with some of the foreign sounds, it is said that they have a heavy accent; when they are unable to talk swiftly, they are said to falter. It is called stammering when someone's speech organs are unable to articulate the words so that the meaning can hardly be understood; this is close to the sounds of animals and mutes.

Meanings can be understood from those who pronounce correctly and from those who mispronounce alike; the only thing in which people differ is the degree of eloquence. Beautiful sound and sweet speech and pure language may be found in the common people and in the elite, as well as in women and children. But not everyone with a beautiful sound and pure speech is eloquent in conveying meanings, setting up arguments, reasoning, and removing ambiguity from the mind of the hearer, nor in waking the ignorant from his sleep and sobering up the drunk from his stupor with notes of warning and exhortation.

Those who have a melodious voice and pure speech often use these in songs and poems. The reason for this is the love for worldly pleasures and sensual passions, and for that which speech may contain in the way of frivolity and wantonness and the like. But there is no reality to their meanings. Their utterances are nothing more than making sounds and raving, similar to the sounds of animals and lunatics and drunks and children and women and imbeciles.

The principle of meanings is that they are those propositions whose validity in predication is demonstrated by the knowledge of their reality and the purpose of their form. The definition of meaning is that it is any utterance that signifies reality and guides towards an advantage; when they are predicated, they are true, and when they are used in a proposition, they correspond to reality. Predication is in four kinds: proposition, question, command, prohibition. Some people distinguish six categories, others ten. But the principle is these four. Three of them are not affected by truth or falsity, and one of them is affected by truth or falsity, namely the proposition, which includes negative and positive and possible and impossible statements.

('Ikhwân aṣ-Ṣafâ', *Rasâ'il*, ed. Beirut, 4 vols, III, pp. 114–20)

One of the most mysterious groups in the history of Islamic philosophy and scholarship is a group of scholars who called themselves 'Ikhwân aṣ-Ṣafâ', literally "Brethren of Purity". We know next to nothing about their identity, nor about their activities, nor even about the exact time when they were active. The only information we have is contained in the encyclopaedia they left behind, called *Rasâ'il* "Treatises" or "Letters" for short; the complete title is *Rasâ'il 'Ikhwân aṣ-ṣafâ' wa-khillân al-wafâ' wa-'ahl al-'adl wa-'abnâ' al-ḥamd* "The Epistles of the Brethren of Purity, the Friends of Loyalty, the People of Justice, and the Sons of Praise". It was probably composed in the tenth century by an anonymous group of people, who hid behind this name of 'Ikhwân aṣ-Ṣafâ'. Although contemporary authors sometimes mention the names of persons who allegedly were involved in the composition of the epistles, they admit their uncertainty about the real identity of the authors. Why the Brethren preferred to remain anonymous is unclear. Perhaps they were afraid of persecution because some of their doctrines could hardly be called orthodox. Another reason may have been that they thought the time had not yet come to realize their ideas, especially because their entire approach was elitist: only people with a pure soul and intellect were able to understand their ideas. They themselves say this about their anonymity:

> Know, my pious and merciful brother, that we do not hide our secrets from the people out of fear from the powers of the world, or to avoid inciting the masses. But we hide them to protect God Almighty's gifts to us, as the Messiah exhorted us: "Don't let the wisdom in the hands of those who do not deserve it, for that is an injustice to it, and don't withhold it from the people who deserve it, for that is an injustice to them."
>
> (*Rasâ'il* IV, p. 166)

In their work, which consists of fifty-two epistles, the Brethren aimed at a synthesis of all available knowledge about everything, "the study of all the sciences that are found in the world". The purpose of this exercise is never made explicit, but the 'Ikhwân frequently hint at the possibility for human beings to free themselves from the fetters of earthly existence and to purify their souls with the help of this knowledge. Men are "prisoners, strangers in the prison of nature and shipwrecks in the sea of matter" (*'asrâ ghurabâ' fî 'asr aṭ-ṭabî'a gharqâ fî baḥr al-hayûlâ, Rasâ'il* IV, 166), but there is salvation in a secret knowledge destined only for the initiated, and they exhort the reader to use this knowledge well: "Strive, O brother, after the purification of your soul and your effort may well overcome your desire for these earthly matters, which the Lord of the Worlds has condemned" (*Rasâ'il* I, 403).

The atmosphere of the encyclopaedia is that of a secret fraternity, organized in circles of increasing degrees of initiation. At the same time the Epistles breathe an atmosphere of tolerance and a willingness to derive knowledge from any source. In the approximate period in which they were active – the tenth century – such a combination of enlightenment and secretiveness was often associated with one or both of two things: gnostic knowledge as it was practised by the Shi'ites of the more extreme kind, and Greek philosophy of a Neo-Platonicist brand. It is therefore not surprising that their work was particularly popular in circles of the Isma'îlîs, a branch of Shi'ism. Later Isma'îlîs claimed the authorship of the Epistles for one of their own hidden imams, and although the 'Ikhwân are probably not to be regarded as Isma'îlîs themselves – they did not believe in the immaculate and infallible imam as the Shi'ites did – they may well have been influenced by the ideas of Shi'ism, which had always been a hospitable place for Neo-Platonicist theories of emanation.

The Brethren were certainly Muslims or at least they regarded themselves as Muslims, but at the same time they emphasized the value of other religions. Eclecticism, i.e., the wish to derive knowledge from any available source, and tolerance towards all existing doctrines are the leading principles of their philosophy: "Generally speaking, our brothers – may God help them! – should not turn away from any science, or shun any book, nor should they become partisans of any doctrine, because our opinion and our doctrine encompasses all doctrines and comprises all sciences" (*Rasâ'il* IV, 41–2). It is not surprising that their contemporary, more orthodox fellow Muslims regarded this enterprise with reservations, and in a simplification of the facts accused the Brethren of aiming at a syncretism of Islamic law with Greek philosophy.

Greek philosophy is certainly one of the main sources for the ideas of the Brethren, in particular the Neo-Platonicist variety of Plotinus. Like Plotinus, they believed in the fundamental unity of all nature because of its emanation from a creator. From the creator the Universal Active Intellect was the first emanation, from which the Universal Soul derived, as well as all further emanations, including the Primary Matter, from which all physical beings emanate. Although there were differences between Plotinus and the 'Ikhwân in the precise chain of emanations, they agreed on the general principle.

There must have been other sources for the philosophy of the 'Ikhwân; in some respects their doctrine resembles that of the Islamic mystics, but also that of the gnostic doctrines that were widespread in the Middle East. They knew about Pythagoras and although they did not follow his numerological ideas entirely they were influenced by his approach towards philosophy, according to which the entire universe is dominated by a sublime harmony of the spheres. Gnostic influence is apparent all over the treatises. In one passage about the creation of the world they say (*Rasâ'il* III, 112.18) that after having created Adam and Eve God inspired 'Uṭârid, the master of reason (*ṣâḥib al-manṭiq*) with speech. In this 'Uṭârid we recognize the figure of Mercury or Hermes, the protagonist of all wisdom literature.

The Epistles are divided into four sections: mathematical sciences (fourteen epistles about mathematics, geometry, music, ethics, logic); physical sciences (seventeen epistles about the cosmos in all its forms, the mineral, zoological and botanical world, the senses, humoral pathology, life and death); psychological and rational sciences (ten epistles about mind, love, numerology); religious sciences (eleven epistles about the nature of God, prophets, imamate, magic). The last epistle of the second part is entitled *fî 'ilal ikhtilâf al-lughât wa-rusûm al-khuṭûṭ wa-l-'ibârât* "about the causes of the difference between the languages and the scripts and the expressions". It deals with language, specifically with the relationship between sound and meaning, in the context of the hierarchy of all creation. But their preoccupation with the phenomenon of speech was rather different from that of the average linguist. They were not interested in the detailed rules of Arabic morphology and syntax, but attracted by the much larger picture of language as a means to obtain knowledge. In order to study this instrument they called in the help of Greek philosophy.

There is another passage in the Epistles in which they deal with the relationship between language and thought. There they present a synthesis of Aristotelian ideas about logic and language which adheres more to traditional Greek theories of logic as they are found for instance in the work of al-Fârâbî (cf. above, chapter 6), namely in the first part of the *Rasâ'il* in the epistle about the *Eisagôgê* (I, 390–403). Just as al-Fârâbî did, they derive the Arabic word *manṭiq* "logic" from *nuṭq* "speaking" and distinguish between exterior and interior (spiritual) speech. Exterior speech is studied by the linguists, but the science of logic is needed to determine the value of our reasoning.

In the seventeenth epistle a comprehensive theory about the entire process of speaking, not only from the point of view of the speaker but also from that of the listener, is given. This meant that they had to deal with the way speech reaches the hearer, i.e., by means of sound. Sound according to their definition is the striking of air (*qar' al-hawâ'*); this is identical with the Stoic definition of sound. The air originates in the lungs; it is forced out through the throat and is led by the tongue through various constrictions at the places of articulation. This is the process of striking the air. The air that has been struck starts to make a wave-like movement and this movement (*tamawwuj al-hawâ'*) reaches the ear, and goes from there first to the brain and then to the heart. The next step in the process is that hearers have to understand the speech that reaches their ears. The heart is the organ that distinguishes between intelligible (*mafhûm*) and unintelligible sounds; from the former it distils the meanings (*ma'ânî*): this is the process of knowledge.

But sound is only the medium through which language reaches us. Although it is indispensable for the transfer of the sensory information we need to form knowledge about the world, it belongs to the impure matter. Not all sounds are therefore relevant for the process of understanding: sounds of animals or material objects, and sounds of natural phenomena, do not contain any meaningful elements, but only those sounds that are emitted in certain combinations. Sound is the medium through which the meanings may reach our heart. This is possible only when speech is articulated in the correct way. In connection with this the Brethren formulate a theory of defects of speech, in which they point out that unlike corruption of language speech defects are not the result of a disturbance in the balance of the body, but a paralysis of the tongue that occurs by some external accident. Corruption of language, on the other hand, is caused by a disturbance of the balance of the body, which in principle can be cured. Since the difference between humans and animals is not the uttering of sounds but the conveying of meanings, corruption of language has to do with the higher faculties of the human mind.

The central notion of "meaning" in the Epistles is connected directly with their view of reality. Not all meanings are true, but only those that correspond to reality. Meanings are ranked according to their connection with reality (*ḥaqîqa*) and this reality is of course the reality of the Brethren's Neo-Platonicist world view. Speaking in a communicative way involves more than just correspondence with reality: not all sentences containing a true meaning are useful in communication. The Brethren develop a theory according to which the communicative value of language depends on the contribution an utterance makes towards our knowledge of reality. Thus, for instance, a tautological proposition, although it has a meaning, has no *fâ'ida* "communicative value", since it does not improve our knowledge, nor does it bring any new information. In accordance with their approach to philosophy the Brethren are clearly elitist in this respect, too. Just as only the initiated are able to understand the true meaning of philosophy, only the eloquent are able to speak truly. Eloquence (*balâgha*) in this context has nothing to do with the composition of poems or the ability to hold beautiful speeches but is directly linked with the relation between sound and meaning. Only the truly eloquent, i.e., the one who has been initiated in the secrets of the world, is able to convey this truth in such a way that his fellow human beings understand it and are persuaded by it. As the Brethren formulate it:

> If eloquence consisted solely in reaching the utmost boundaries of meanings, the whole world would be full of eloquent people, both among the elite and among the common people, because anyone who expresses what is on his mind, reaches his goal in making the hearer understand what he intends to say, according to his abilities and the assistance of his articulatory organs. But eloquence implies making one's meaning understood in the most concise words and the most eloquent speech, so that the hearer understands it in the easiest way and by the shortest path through clear explanation and truthful words.
>
> (*Rasâ'il* III, p. 121)

In an ideal communicational situation the eloquent person deals with an understanding person who understands correctly and efficiently what other people tell him. The process of assigning true meanings to sounds and extracting them again from the message in the heart is not an easy one to describe. According to the Brethren the meanings (*ma'ânî*) are formed in the soul and they adhere to the sounds throughout the process of production and perception. What their exact status is remains unclear. In some respects the meanings are dependent on the sounds, just as the pure form always needs matter in order to manifest itself, and therefore (*Rasâ'il* III, pp. 108–9) "there is no way to know a meaning that cannot be expressed by any sound in any language". On the other hand, the meanings in the higher spheres are directly perceptible without the sounds (*Rasâ'il* III, p. 117). This would seem to imply that they do have an independent status from the sounds and are related to the Platonic ideas that have an existence outside the material world. Yet, in other passages the Brethren use the term *ma'ânî* for conventional meanings of linguistic sounds, that can even be uttered by those who do not understand them themselves or who intended to express another meaning.

At the end of the epistle on language there are a few sections on topics that seem to be unrelated to the discussion on language: these deal with such things as hostility, disagreement, jealousy, competition. On closer view it turns out that in the system of the 'Ikhwân there is a close relationship between speaking and the relations between people in society. Only speech that corresponds with reality is worth its name. The source of all bad feelings and enmity between human beings is the result of inappropriate use of words, i.e., the use of words that do not correspond with reality. If only people would stop using "untrue" words, all enmity would disappear and there would no longer be any disagreement. This underscores the ethical dimension of the philosophy of the 'Ikhwân and the important role they assign to language:

> Know that there are two kinds of disagreement: praiseworthy and blameworthy. Praiseworthy disagreement is like the disagreement among readers of the Qur'ânic text or legal scholars, as long as they do not disagree about the meanings and do not distort the words and do not replace one word by another. . . . If they speak in the correct way, their disagreement is an advantage, because many Arabs disagree with each other in many things of the Arabic language. But blameworthy disagreement is what is found in sects and schools.
>
> (*Rasâ'il* III, p. 164)

In this way the Brethren were able to transpose their theory of emanations from the cosmos to the world of speech: the true meanings as reflections of the highest principles are emanated in the words, and just as the ideas with each successive emanation become more and more corrupted, the true meanings are partially disguised by the need to express them in imperfect words. The Brethren constantly refer to hidden secrets that are unattainable to normal people. In the sublunar world it is (almost) impossible to reach a state of perfection in the use of language. But in the higher spheres reigns perfect sound, to which all human beings aspire, which is why having a sweet voice and a beautiful sound is important since it symbolizes man's longing for perfection and unity with the higher spheres. The language of the higher spheres must, therefore, also be perfect. In our world one can reach a certain degree of insight, and therefore a certain degree of eloquent speech, i.e., meaningful, i.e., truthful speech. But only in the higher spheres is it possible to reach the ultimate truth, just as the people in Plato's cave could perceive only the shadows of the real objects, i.e., the Platonic ideas in the world above, the true meanings.

The meanings are the root, the origin (*'aṣl*), the sounds (or words) are the *húlê*, the matter in which they are poured. Another simile compares the meanings to the souls, and the words to the bodies. In both comparisons the sounds represent the impure, earthly matter that is never a perfect receptacle for the meanings, although one can do one's best, just as the artist strives after perfection in sculpting a statue, or the potter in shaping the clay. In the higher spheres the meanings are not even in need of ordinary words and sounds to express them, because there they can be perceived directly without the intermediary of corrupting and corrupted sounds.

> Know, O brother, that if men could communicate to each other the meanings that are in the thoughts of their souls without expressing them with their tongues, they would not need speech, which consists in audible sounds. Hearing the sounds and trying to understand them is a burden for the souls, because they have to learn languages and train their tongues in eloquence and elocution. But the souls of all human beings are fettered in the body and veiled by the darkness of the substance, so that none of them sees anything except the outer forms, which are the three-dimensional bodies. They do not know what knowledge others have except when people express what is in their soul to their fellow beings, which is only possible with the help of instruments and organs such as the tongue and the lips and the exhaling of air. . . . Therefore, we need exterior speech and we have to teach it and to study its laws, which take a long time to explain. The pure spirits that are not embodied do not need language and speech for the mutual understanding of the knowledge and the meanings that are in their thoughts. They are the spirits of the stars, because they have been cleansed from the filthiness of the bodily desires, and freed from the sea of matter and the prison of nature.
>
> (*Rasâ'il* I, p. 402)

The Brethren were not the only ones to articulate a theory about correspondences between the sounds of language and the world around us or above us. In the theories of Jâbir ibn Ḥayyân we find an entire system of such correspondences. Jâbir's name is connected with a large collection of writings on alchemy, medical science, and occult sciences; according to some scholars these were attributed to him by later authors. They wished to profit from his reputation as a great alchemist, which stretched even to medieval Europe where he was known as Geber. There has been a lot of controversy concerning the dating of these writings. The historical Jâbir may have lived at the end of the eighth century, but most of the writings that have been put out under his name probably originated somewhere around 900, possibly in the same period as the Epistles of the 'Ikhwân aṣ-Ṣafâ'.

Jâbir went much further than the 'Ikhwân did in establishing a correspondence between word and meaning. His speculations about this correspondence are based on what he calls the *mîzân al-ḥurûf* "balance of letters", which reflects the balance of nature in the theory of the four humours. According to this theory the four humours (yellow bile, black bile, blood, and phlegm) are characterized by the absence or presence of the four natures, i.e., heat, coldness, humidity, and dryness. In the *mîzân al-ḥurûf* the twenty-eight letters of the Arabic alphabet are arranged according to these four natures in four groups in the order of their numerical values. With the help of extremely complicated calculating tables this classification enables the alchemist to calculate how many measures of each nature are present in an object, usually a metal, as represented by the consonants in the name of that object. With the help of this method the nature of the metals is disclosed to the alchemist, who of course needs this knowledge to change it.

The theories about the correspondence between name and nature in Jâbir's writings clearly derive from Greek sources ranging from the numerical speculations of the Pythagoreans to Plato's dialogue *Kratylos*. In the dialogue the theory of correspondence is mentioned only to ridicule it, but it was probably popular in Plato's time in circles around the atomic philosopher Democritus. In the case of Jâbir the direct source for his ideas was probably Neo-Pythagorean philosophy, with an admixture of Neo-Platonicism, the same sources that are usually assigned to the Epistles of the 'Ikhwân aṣ-Ṣafâ'. In the chapter about the origin of speech (chapter 8) we shall see that there was one Mu'tazilite author who maintained that there was a *munâsaba ṭabî'iyya* between sound and meaning; similar ideas on a linguistic level are known from the work of Ibn Jinnî.

Although Jâbir's main interest was the investigation of the nature of physical elements, he often uses grammatical theory as a heuristic instrument: just as the grammarian applies his methods of *taṣrîf* "morphology" in order to determine their radicals, the alchemist or physical scientist dissects the objects in order to find out about their constituent elements. He even uses the same term to indicate these elements, *'aṣl*, i.e., "root, principle". Along the same lines the shape of the word may tell us something about the true nature of the object denoted by it. Thus, for instance, the name of *zîbaq* "mercury" (actually a loanword from Persian) is derived from its form, since it consists of the two words *ziyy* "exterior, appearance" and *labiq* "elegant".

If names are a representation of the true nature of the objects, as Jâbir asserts, then the difference of the names of the objects in different languages poses a serious problem. In his view language originated as an act of nature, not in the sense that names are arbitrary, as in Aristotelian philosophy, but because the nature of the objects is imprinted on the mind, which then enunciates the correct name, i.e., the name that corresponds to its nature. Apparently, Jâbir reflected a lot about the existence of different names and in his writings he lists these names. Ideally, each name should represent the true nature of the object, but this is a difficult thesis to uphold, since names vary widely. One solution that Jâbir seems to have considered seriously is the invention of a technical language for alchemy based on the values of the letters as they had been calculated by him. In this language the name of the object would correspond perfectly to the nature of the object. Unfortunately, we have no detailed information about this tantalizing suggestion that sounds particularly familiar to anyone acquainted with the history of linguistics in Western Europe.

We have seen above (chapter 1, p. 22) that in the mystical exegesis of the *Qur'ân* the leading principle of the explanation of the text was the idea of a hidden meaning (*bâṭin*) behind the veil of the actual text (*ẓâhir*). This kind of explanation is close to the approach of the 'Ikhwân aṣ-Ṣafâ', who claimed a special insight in the hidden truth, not because of any signs or indications in the text but because of the relationship of the pure soul with the higher spheres. In some branches of Islamic mysticism the explanation of the text concentrated on the correspondence between physical properties of the text and hidden secrets, in the spirit of Jâbir's investigations in the names of the metals. In these circles the physical sound or form, even though it was a corruption of the original meaning, was regarded as a guide or a channel to the truth that could be used as a legitimate instrument. One of the physical properties of the text was its written form: some commentators relate the form of the letters to the nature of the things designated by them. Since in the Arabic writing system letters have a numerical value, such speculations often take the form of numerological analysis (gematria): the value of the letters are used to calculate the truth arithmetically. The logical conclusion of such speculations is the use of letters in talismans and amulets, which became extremely popular in some forms of Islam.

Chapter 8

The origin of speech

Ibn Jinnî and the two alternatives

Is the origin of speech revelation or agreement? This is a subject that requires a lot of consideration, although there is a consensus among most speculative philosophers that the origin of speech is mutual agreement and convention rather than revelation and inspiration. On the other hand, 'Abû 'Alî [al-Fârisî] – may he rest in peace! – said to me one day: "It comes from God". He argued by referring to God's words "He taught Adam all names". But this verse does not put an end to the controversy, because it may be interpreted in the sense that He enabled Adam to give names. It is not impossible that this is the meaning of God's words, and if this is a possible interpretation, the evidence of the quotation disappears. 'Abû 'Alî himself used to argue like this in some of his lectures, and it is also the opinion of 'Abû l-Ḥasan [al-'Akhfash]. The latter left open the possibility of interpreting God's words as referring to an agreement, in the following way: God taught Adam the names of all created beings, in all languages, Arabic, Persian, Syriac, Hebrew, Greek, and so on. Adam and his children spoke these languages, then his children spread all over the world and each one of them became associated with one of these languages exclusively and forgot the other ones, because of their lack of familiarity with them.

[At the end of the chapter about the origin of speech, after lengthy arguments in favour of both opinions, Ibn Jinnî says:] Know that in the course of the years I have constantly investigated this subject and reflected about it. I find myself strongly attracted by the various motives and arguments that affect my thinking in different ways. This is because when I reflect on the state of this noble, excellent, subtle language, I find in it such a wisdom and subtlety and precision and elegance that it overwhelms me so that I am transfixed by fascination. My colleagues – may they rest in peace! – have reported the same thing, and I have followed their example. By following its lead I discovered the validity of the position they were inspired to take and the excellence of the insight which they received and which was made clear to them. In addition there are traditions that are transmitted from the Prophet about its [sc., language] deriving from God Almighty. Therefore, I became convinced that it was revealed by God – praised be He! – and inspired by Him. Then again, I recall the same objections that have occurred to me and my colleagues and that have drawn our attention. When I reflect on God's wonderful and brilliant wisdom I do not exclude the possibility that God Almighty may have created before us – even if this is beyond our grasp – people with better minds than ours and quicker wits and braver hearts. Thus, I stand dejected between the two scales of the balance. I try to weigh them, but I turn away in defeat. If afterwards some bright idea will occur to me which may tip the scale in favour of one position or the other, I shall adopt it. In God we trust!

(Ibn Jinnî, *Khaṣâ'iṣ*, ed. by Muḥammad 'Alî an-Najjâr, 3 vols, Cairo, 1952–6, I, pp. 40–1, 47)

Ibn Jinnî, or with his full name 'Abû l-Fatḥ 'Uthmân Ibn Jinnî, one of the most interesting grammarians of the Arabic linguistic tradition, was born in Mosul somewhere around 932, as the son of a Byzantine slave (possibly his name is derived from the Greek word *gennaĩos* "high-born"). He was a precocious boy and started lecturing on grammatical problems at the age of seventeen. During one of his lectures someone in the audience made a few comments and then introduced himself as 'Abû 'Alî al-Fârisî, a famous grammarian, whose reputation was widely acclaimed. According to the biographers 'Abû 'Alî drily remarked on the boy's activities "you have become a currant while still being a fresh grape" (as-Suyûṭî, *Bughya*, ed. by Muḥammad 'Abû l-Faḍl 'Ibrâhîm, 2 vols, Cairo, 1964–5, II, p. 132). Ibn Jinnî immediately vowed never to teach again until he had received a thorough training at the hands of 'Abû 'Alî, and indeed he did not resume teaching until the death of his master in 987. In the intervening period he followed 'Abû

'Alî on all of his travels, first living with him in Mosul, then travelling to Aleppo, the cultural and political centre of the Hamdanid emirate, hence to Baghdad, Shîrâz, and finally again to Baghdad, at that time the seat of the Buwayhid sultanate, where he died around 1002. The association with 'Abû 'Alî thus marked his entire career as a grammarian, and, although he also studied at the hands of other masters, the pages of his works testify to his profound respect for 'Abû 'Alî. The latter's work is known to us mainly from an introductory treatise on grammar, called *al-'Îḍâḥ*, and a series of collected problems discussed during his travels (called "the Aleppine questions", "the Shîrâzian questions", "the Baghdadian questions", and so on).

Ibn Jinnî's activities as a teacher were limited to a short period between the death of his master and his own death in 1002; consequently, he had only a few pupils. His numerous works, many of which have been preserved, present a complete picture of his grammatical doctrines. His interests exceeded those of the average grammarian. Apart from a large number of influential and highly respected grammatical treatises on almost every technical point of grammar he wrote a book called *al-Khaṣâ'iṣ* "The special features", a veritable encyclopaedia of all conceivable topics of interest to the linguist. Some of the topics covered by this remarkable book are: the origin of speech; criteria of correctness of speech; regularity and analogy in language; metatheoretical principles of linguistics; pre-Islamic dialects; metrical phenomena; etymology and word derivation; the relationship between sound and meaning; homonymy and synonymy; phonological rules; phonetic processes; elision and deletion; metonymy; linguistic errors, and so on.

In this chapter we have started with a quotation from one of the first chapters of the *Khaṣâ'iṣ*, about the theories on the origin of speech. Ibn Jinnî is one of the very few grammarians to discuss this subject, not surprisingly in view of his interest in the relationship between sound and meaning and his Mu'tazilite leanings. Like most of the grammarians of his time, including his master 'Abû 'Alî, he was a Mu'tazilite and openly professed his adherence to the ideas of this theological school. In his view the study of language may help people to avoid theological errors. Many lay people, for instance, believe that the attributes of God mentioned in the *Qur'ân* are real, physical attributes: this is abhorrent to the strictly monotheist theology of the Mu'tazila, and according to Ibn Jinnî the linguist may help people to understand that when these attributes are mentioned they are meant metaphorically. The discussion of the origin of speech falls within the same realm of Mu'tazilite interest, in particular because of the important question of the status of the *Qur'ân*.

In almost all linguistic traditions the origin of speech is one of the fundamental questions. Even lay people confronted by the first babbling of their children, or traders having to deal with peoples speaking different tongues, or teachers attempting to instruct children with different linguistic backgrounds cannot but wonder about the origin and development of the instrument of speech. As soon as linguists introduce a diachronic dimension in their investigations, they, too, start asking questions about the origin of the words and phrases that constitute their object of study. Yet, one of the most conspicuous features of the Arabic linguistic tradition is the almost total absence of any serious discussion of this issue. On the whole the Arabic tradition was curiously reluctant to tackle the question of where language comes from. Ibn Jinnî's theories demonstrate that some scholars at least did concern themselves with the question of the origin of speech.

Before we go into the contents of the quotation from Ibn Jinnî we need to discuss the place of diachrony in Arabic linguistics. In chapter 3 we have seen that the task of the grammarian was not primarily to describe or prescribe linguistic norms but to explain its structure. The grammarian's point of departure was a fixed corpus of linguistic utterances consisting of the text of the *Qur'ân*, the pre-Islamic poems, and the idealized speech of the Bedouin. Once the Bedouin had become affected by the speech of the urban population they could no longer be trusted as guardians of the pure Arabic language, so that the grammarians could rely only on texts that had been codified for all times. No grammarian could fail to notice, however, that ordinary people spoke quite differently from the language analysed in the linguistic treatises, but, rather than concluding that the language itself was changing, the grammarians categorized these changes as linguistic errors and concluded that most people were unable to speak Arabic correctly. By definition the language itself could not change: it had been used by God in His last revelation, and this meant that it was sacrilege to allow for the possibility of any changes.

From the beginning of Islamic civilization (cf. chapter 1) scholars were aware of the tension between what is said and what is meant by a speaker. In the course of the development of the Arabic linguistic tradition this tension was interpreted in the sense that speakers have the right and the freedom to use speech creatively, that is to say, they are not bound by the rules of the language but may modify their speech according to their communicational needs. Thus, for instance, speakers may change the order of the words in the sentence, saying things like *'amran ḍaraba zaydun* "'Amr hit Zayd", i.e., "it was 'Amr that Zayd hit". This does not invalidate the rule that the grammarians deduced from their corpus, according to which the word order of Arabic is Verb–Agent–Object, since on an underlying level the actual word order reappears: *ḍaraba zaydun 'amran*. In this way the grammarians found a way out of the confusing variation in actual speech utterances and could maintain their rule system without in any way constraining the freedom (*ittisâ'*) of the speakers.

Likewise the grammarians acknowledged the existence of factors such as the frequency of usage (*kathrat al-isti'mâl*) or the aversion of heaviness in speech, i.e., the avoidance of consonant clusters and certain combinations of vowels and glides. These factors operated synchronically at the surface level of speech and facilitated the fluency of speech that the Arabs admired above all other things, while at the same time the underlying level took care of the ordered symmetry of the system of language. In other words, they exploited these factors as discourse phenomena without giving them any diachronic status as principles of historical change. In their framework, frequency of usage does not erode the language but leads to more fluent pronunciation whenever speakers use an expression frequently.

In many linguistic traditions the difference between chronologically distant varieties of speech is one of the main incentives for the emergence of a linguistic discipline. In Greek civilization, for instance, the manifest differences between the language of the Homeric epic poems and the language of Classical Attic prose cried out for an explanation in terms of a diachronic development of language. Unlike the Greek grammarians, however, the Arabs did not recognize any change in their language, and, consequently, such a motive was lacking in their tradition: the language in the grammarians' corpus remained the same for all eternity.

A second motive for a diachronic preoccupation may be the awareness of other languages. But in this respect the Arabs resemble the Greeks in their stubborn refusal to acknowledge any other language than their own as a "real" language. For the Greeks the speakers of other languages than Greek were barbarians, that is, people who stammer. In Arab civilization all languages of the conquered peoples were viewed with equal distaste. From the earliest period of the conquests languages such as Hebrew, Syriac, Greek, Persian, Coptic, and Berber were regarded as far inferior to the language of the Arabs. Arabic was the language of prestige, being the language preferred by God and by the specialists in verbal prowess, the Bedouin. Where other peoples' prophets excelled in miracles in the form of magical tricks or medical wonders, the Arab prophet Muḥammad had brought only one miracle, a text that was of inimitable beauty, in the literal sense of a text that could not be emulated by anybody.

With very few exceptions, such as the Andalusian grammarian 'Abû Ḥayyân (cf. below, chapter 13), the Arabic grammarians were not in the slightest interested in other languages. Either the other languages had the same structure as Arabic, in which case it was unnecessary to study them, or their structure was different, in which case they were by definition inferior to Arabic and not worthy of any attention at all. Even those grammarians who themselves were native speakers of other languages – and there were quite a few of these, starting with Sîbawayhi – were convinced of the superior qualities of the Arabic language. Thus, for instance, Ibn Jinnî used to ask scholars of Arabic who were of Persian extraction – among them his main teacher 'Abû 'Alî al-Fârisî – about the relative value of the two languages, Arabic and Persian. He reports (*Khaṣâ'iṣ* I, p. 143.1–5) that they all preferred Arabic, both rationally and aesthetically, and even resented his asking them such a flippant question.

In the absence of the two main motives for a diachronic dimension to linguistics – developmental change in the language and the variety of languages – the grammarians could devote their exclusive attention to the study and explanation of their immutable linguistic system, and this they did with great fervour. Seen from this perspective it is actually quite astonishing that there was a period in which the Arabs hotly debated the origin of speech. This debate coincided with a growing interest in Greek logic and philosophy, and the two developments were no doubt connected. The confrontation with Greek philosophy not only provoked a discussion about the universal value of linguistic knowledge and the relationship between thought and speech (cf. chapter 4) but it also raised the question of the origin of language, with all its concomitant theological implications in a society imbued with the spirit of Islam and the belief in divine omnipotence.

As far as we know, the discussion about the origin of speech started in the circles of the Mu'tazilite theologians, whose apogee was in the first half of the ninth century CE (cf. above, chapter 4). The Mu'tazila's main tenets were God's unity and His justice, both of which had a bearing on their views on language. The first tenet, the unity of God, precluded the existence of any other eternal entity, and this forced the Mu'tazila to clarify the status of the *Qur'ân* as a part of God's creation. Until then, the ordinary believers' reverence for the revealed text had assigned to the Book a sacred status that was tantamount to eternity. This belief in the eternity of the *Qur'ân* had never been part of any official creed, but the Mu'tazilites' emphasis on the created character of the *Qur'ân* stirred up a storm of protest among the orthodox believers, which increased when the Caliph al-Ma'mûn raised the dogma of the createdness of the *Qur'ân* to the status of state doctrine in 833. A board of inquisition (*miḥna*) investigated all public servants in order to certify their adherence to the official doctrine. When the *miḥna* was dissolved a few years later the doctrine of the created *Qur'ân* had been discredited entirely.

In itself the createdness of the *Qur'ân* does not say anything about the nature or status of the language in which it was revealed. Yet there was a marked tendency on the part of the adherents to this doctrine to emphasize the human nature and origin of speech, especially when coupled with the second tenet of Mu'tazilite theology, the belief in God's justice. This belief implied for them that man has a free will; otherwise, he could not be taken to account for his sins. When human beings are responsible for their own acts, then they are the sole agents of these acts, and, contrary to the orthodox belief of Islam, not God but man himself may then be said to bring his own acts into existence. In connection with language this means that the one who speaks is the one who brings speech into being. This may seem like a rather trivial conclusion, but to mainstream Islam in the ninth century it was a revolutionary idea, precisely because of its implications for theology. In one passage Ibn Jinnî talks about the Qur'ânic verse 4/164 "and God spoke to Moses" and says that this is not metaphorical but real. The attribute *mutakallim* "speaking" can be given only to someone who actually produces speech. This verse therefore means that God is speaking and consequently that the *Qur'ân* is created.

Only within such an ideological framework could a discussion about the status of speech and language originate. We know that in the period in question many grammarians adhered to the school of the Muʻtazila, and this was probably not a coincidence. The Muʻtazilites had been discredited as theologians by the public failure of the inquisition. Their only chance of spiritual survival lay in scholarly activities that had nothing to do with theology directly. Because of their known interest in linguistic arguments there is reason to believe that they found a new home in disciplines like linguistics. The number of grammarians associated by the biographers with Muʻtazilite sympathies is considerable, indeed, among them were Ibn Jinnî, al-Fârisî, az-Zajjâjî, Quṭrub and many others (cf. also below, chapter 10, on the "principles of law").

The rising popularity of the Muʻtazila among intellectuals in the ninth century was also related to the introduction of Greek knowledge. The Muʻtazilites established the primacy of reason over revelation: one cannot invoke the authority of the text of the *Qur'ân* unless one has established first by logical and rational means that Islam is the true religion. They were therefore strongly attracted by the technical devices Greek logic and philosophy had to offer to this debate. In the confrontation between logicians and grammarians (cf. above, chapter 4) the grammarians opposed the logicians' claims about the status of meaning, but in accordance with their Muʻtazilite leanings they did not object to the use of logical methods as such. Most scholars in the period in question enthusiastically endorsed the application of new scientific tools.

It is not clear to what extent the introduction of Greek knowledge brought to the Islamic world detailed information about the Greek debate about the origin of speech. Greek discussions on this issue centred on two key words, *phúsis* and *thésis*, highly ambiguous notions that were responsible for a lot of confusion. The central issue of the Greek discussion had been the epistemological value of language. Since the days of the Sophists and the discussion in Plato's *Kratylos* philosophers had debated the possibility of deriving knowledge from the names of objects. According to some philosophers words signify "by nature", that is to say there is a correlation between the physical world and language (*phúsei*). According to their opponents words are arbitrary symbols of meaning (*thései*) and do not tell us anything about the natural world. In the course of time the debate became muddled by later interpretations of the two key words, until in Hellenistic times some philosophers came to interpret them as terms for the creation of speech. In this new context *phúsei* referred to a creation of language by natural causes, as for instance in the philosophy of Epicurus and Lucretius, whereas *thései* referred to a (human or divine) initiative in the process of creation.

Islamic discussions about the origin of speech operated with two sets of terms. On the one hand, speech was said by some to have originated by *waḥy* or *tawqîf* "revelation", on the other hand there were those who said that the origin of speech had been a process of *iṣṭilâḥ* or *tawâḍu'* (*waḍ'*) "agreement, convention". It is immediately obvious that the discussion in the Islamic world was concerned with one thing only, the question of who had created speech, God or man. Almost all participants in the discussion were convinced of the arbitrary nature of speech, so that its epistemological value was not at issue. In this respect the Arabic linguistic tradition differs fundamentally from the Greek and seems to have developed autonomously. In philosophical writing some influence may have taken place. The literal sense of the Arabic term *waḍ'* "placement, institution", which is frequently used in discussions of the topic, suggests a connection with the Greek term *thésis*, which has exactly the same lexical meaning, in particular in the context of the theory of the first and the second imposition of speech.

As is clear from the text of Ibn Jinnî, the basis for the discussion about the origin of speech was the Qur'ânic verse 2/31 "He taught Adam all the names". This Qur'ânic evidence remained the primary argument for the partisans of the divine creation of speech. There were two more verses from the *Qur'ân* that were often adduced in this connection. In one verse (Q. 53/23) God warns the believers that the names of the idols revered in Mecca are just names, invented by them or their ancestors without any authorization from God, and in another (Q. 30/22) He alludes to the creation of *'alsina* "tongues, languages". As a logical counter-argument to the conventionalist thesis the partisans of the creation of language by God also pointed out that any convention presupposes another convention in which it is agreed upon, which leads to an infinite regress.

The main arguments of the conventionalists were twofold. In the first place they stated that language must precede the revelation, since no revelation is possible without a prior language in which it can be revealed. In the second place, they claimed in a passage that is reported by the later compiler as-Suyûṭî, the creation of speech by God would lead to a theologically incorrect position. For if God had created speech, He would have to create also in man the knowledge about the connection between speech and meaning, which would mean that man would know God necessarily. This runs counter to the Mu'tazilite belief in free will and their views on man as a free agent. Here we see again the connection between the conventionalist thesis and Mu'tazilite theology. As for the evidentiary value of the Qur'ânic verses that were adduced by the creationists they argued that other interpretations were possible. At first view the verse about Adam would seem to clinch the matter, since it explicitly assigns the initiative of the creation of language to God. But the combined ingenuity of the commentators produced so many interpretations of this one single verse that the matter was hardly decided. One could, for instance, say that this verse meant that God enabled Adam to invent language or to initiate a convention with his children. Others asserted that the names in question were the names of the angels or the names of all created beings. The verse about the creation of "tongues" could apply to tongues as a part of anatomy rather than to language, and the verse about false names was directed against idolatry.

The arguments as summarized above remained the standard arguments in a discussion that after a period of no more than 150 years had become completely sterile. If authors mentioned the two positions at all they simply copied their predecessors' arguments and, as a general rule, refused to take sides themselves. The debate had lost its relevance almost immediately after it had started. Before the real discussion had started, dissenting opinions with a fresh view on the issue had been ventilated, but these never became popular. The Mu'tazilite theologian 'Abbâd ibn Sulaymân, who died in 864, claimed that there was a natural relationship (*munâsaba ṭabî'iyya*) between words and things. We know about his theory only from later sources (as-Suyûṭî, *Muzhir*, ed. by Muḥammad 'Aḥmad Jâr al-Mawlâ *et al.*, 2 vols, Cairo, n.d., I, p. 47.3), but Ibn Jinnî alludes to it when he says:

> Some people believe that the origin of the languages lies in sounds that are heard, for instance, the howling of the wind, the

roaring of the thunder, the murmuring of the water, the braying of the donkey, the croaking of the raven, the neighing of the horse, the belling of the deer, and so on. From these sounds the languages originated. In my view this is a correct point of view and an acceptable opinion.

(Ibn Jinnî, *Khaṣâ'iṣ* I, pp. 46–7)

Even though 'Abbâd's views were regarded by most scholars as heterodox, they inspired another line of research followed by Ibn Jinnî: the relationship between sound and meaning. Ibn Jinnî's interest in this matter is clear from two chapters he dedicated to the question of sound symbolism in his *Khaṣâ'iṣ* (II, pp. 145–68). About the possibility of *'imsâs al-'alfâẓ 'ashbâh al-ma'ânî* "words imitating meaning" he says that it is "a famous and attractive topic" (*mawḍi' sharîf laṭîf*). The examples he adduces are simple onomatopoeic words such as *ṣarṣara* "to cry [woodpecker]", *qa'qa'a* "to rattle", but also more complicated examples, such as the general use in Arabic of the second stem with reduplication for iterative or intensive actions (e.g., *kasara* "to break"/*kassara* "to shatter"). One of the most vivid examples is that of the difference between the two verbs *khaḍima* and *qaḍima*, which both mean "to crunch" but which are used for different kinds of food, the former for fresh fruits like melons or cucumbers, the latter for dry food, like fodder for animals.

A quite logical sequel to this theory was his attempt to detect the inner harmony in the Arabic lexicon by a peculiar theory on the etymology of Arabic roots, called *al-ishtiqâq al-kabîr* "great etymology". Normally etymology in Arabic grammar stood for a method to find out by morphological or phonological means the derivates of one root. Thus, for instance, the grammarians demonstrated that from the root (*'aṣl*) *k-t-b* a host of nouns and verbs were derived, with a common semantic load (cf. above, chapter 2, p. 26). We have seen that in al-Khalîl's dictionary roots were arranged by permutations, too, but without any hint of a common meaning. Ibn Jinnî went one step further: he maintained that all permutations of a certain set of radicals carry a common semantic load. One of the examples adduced by him is that of the radicals *k-l-m* which in their different permutations produce words with the semantic load of "force, intensity", e.g., *kalm* "wound" (because it is the result of force), *kalâm* "speech" (because it is the cause of evil and violence), *kamula* "to be perfect" (because what is perfect is strongest), *lakama* "to punch" (because it is an act of violence), *makûl* "having little water [a well]" (because this is a disaster), *malik* "king" (because he is a forceful person), and so on. Themain reason for this exercise in etymology seems to be a desire to find out what the essential meaning of words is.

Both 'Abbâd's theory and Ibn Jinnî's etymological method remained incidents in the history of ideas in Islam, not because they ran counter to orthodox beliefs or Mu'tazilite theology but simply because they did not touch the real issue. What was at stake was not the process in which human civilization, including language, originated: most Muslims had no problems with what was essentially an Aristotelian view on the mutual agreement between humans as the basis of ordered civilization. The alternative of a natural origin of speech was not controversial, either. But the central question was the status of the Arabic language. It shared in the reverence of the believers for the revealed Book, and in the mind of pious believers both the *Qur'ân* and the Arabic language belonged to the realm of the sacred. This view was supported by the apparent meaning of the Qur'ânic verse about God's dealings with Adam and His mysterious intervention in the development of humankind.

Once the Mu'tazilites had started to question the status of the *Qur'ân* as an eternal document and in order to safeguard God's unity had reduced its status to that of a part of His creation, the question of the origin of speech turned into a more trivial question, that of the actual authorship of the names. Since the position of extreme *tawqîf* seems to have been abandoned in the course of the debate and apparently no one continued to believe in a mysterious infusion of language *in toto* in the ears of the first people, there was room for intermediate positions: the meaning of the Qur'ânic verse could be that God had inspired Adam to create names for all the objects, or God had taught him the names of the angels only and left him at his own wits to create the rest of speech. In the meantime, the question of the origin of speech had lost its theological relevance for the theologians, and since there was no conclusive evidence for either position anyway, most of them decided that it was not worth their while to discuss it any further. This became more or less the orthodox point of view when the famous theologian al-Ghazzâlî (d. 1111) stated that both positions were equally well possible from a rational point of view.

For the grammarians the issue of the origin of speech had never held much attraction anyway. One looks in vain in linguistic treatises for references to this issue. Ibn Jinnî and the orthodox grammarian Ibn Fâris (d. 1004) seem to have been the only exceptions to this rule. Ibn Jinnî was probably driven by his Mu'tazilite ideas to dedicate an entire chapter to the problems surrounding the discussion. Ibn Fâris may have been stimulated in a like manner to defend his orthodox position and persuade his readers not to believe in any Mu'tazilite rationalist nonsense about man's own initiative in this matter. His chapter on this topic starts simply with "I say: the language of the Arabs is revelation, and the evidence for this is the words of God 'He taught Adam all the names'". Apart from references to the text of the *Qur'ân* he also strikes back at his fellow grammarians with the following argument:

> The proof for the correctness of our point of view is the unanimous agreement of the scholars about arguments based on the language of the Bedouin, whether they agree or disagree about something, and on their poems. If language were really an institution and a convention, they would have no more rights to argue on the basis of their language than we would have to argue on the basis of contemporary speech.
>
> (Ibn Fâris, *Ṣâḥibî*, ed. by Moustafa Chouémi, Beirut, 1964, p. 6.3–6)

Most grammarians regarded Arabic as a given fact, which it was their task to explain as best they could. The absence of diachronic thinking in Arabic linguistics is partly responsible for this lack of interest. The grammarians dealt with a fixed corpus and maintained that this language never changed. The question of its origin was of no importance to them.

There is one development of the debate that must be mentioned here: when the theologians had decided that the actual authorship of the creation of speech did not endanger the basic tenets of Islam one way or the other, they continued to be intrigued by the conventional character of language. Since there were no adherents to a belief in the epistemological quality of language, the system of language was accepted as an established body of words. This view was developed further in the discipline of the *'uṣûl al-fiqh* "principles, fundamentals of law", another place besides linguistics where homeless Mu'tazilites could find a refuge from a world that was increasingly opposed to rationalist theologians. In this disguise they continued to dedicate themselves to the study of the implications of language in a special sub-discipline, called *waḍʿ al-lugha* (cf. below, chapter 10).

Chapter 9

A new semantic approach to linguistics

Al-Jurjânî and as-Sakkâkî on meaning

Know that fronting of a constituent occurs in two ways. In the first place, fronting with the underlying intention of postposing. This takes place with every constituent that you decide to maintain in its status and category, even when it is fronted, for instance when you front the predicate of the topic, or the direct object before the agent. E.g., when you say *munṭaliqun zaydun* "leaving is Zayd" and *ḍaraba ʿamran zaydun* "Zayd ʿAmr hit" [i.e., "Zayd hit ʿAmr"], it is obvious that by fronting *munṭaliqun* and *ʿamran* you do not shift them from their syntactic position in the sense that the former remains the predicate of the topic, in the nominative, and the latter remains direct object, in the accusative, just as they were before fronting.

The other kind of fronting is when there is no underlying postposing, but you shift the constituent from its former status to a new and different status, and a new and different declension. An example of this is when you have two nouns, either of which can be topic, the other being its predicate. In that case you can front either one, for instance when you sometimes say *zaydun al-munṭaliqu* "Zayd is the one who is leaving" and at other times *al-munṭaliqu zaydun* "the one who is leaving is Zayd". In this example you do not front *al-munṭaliqu* while leaving it in its former status as predicate of the topic of the sentence, but you shift it from its position as predicate to become the topic; likewise you do not postpose *zaydun* while maintaining it as topic, but you shift it from its syntactic position as topic, and it becomes the predicate. Even clearer is the expression *ḍarabtu zaydan* "I hit Zayd" and *zaydun ḍarabtuhu* "Zayd, I hit him". In the latter sentence *zaydun* is fronted, but does not continue to be the direct object that is governed in the accusative by the verb; on the contrary, it receives the nominative since it has become the topic of the sentence, and the verb is occupied by the pronoun [-*hu*] and becomes the predicate [of *zaydun*]. When you understand this distinction, I shall continue with the rest of my commentary.

Know that we have not found any fundamental discussion of this issue, except for the notion of "attention and concern". The author of the *Kitâb* [i.e., Sîbawayhi] says in his discussion of the agent and the direct object: "It is as if [the Arabs] front the constituent whose presence is most important to them and about which they are most concerned". Yet, both constituents are equally relevant and important to them, and he does not give any example of this. According to the grammarians the meaning of this is that sometimes people are more concerned about the person to whom an action occurs and they do not care about the one who made it occur. For instance in the case of a Khârijite [i.e., a member of the Khârijite sect] who goes out and mocks and corrupts and does a lot of harm. They want to kill him but do not care and are not concerned by whom he is killed. When he is killed and someone wants to announce this, he fronts the Khârijite in the sentence and says *qatala l-khârijiyya zaydun* "the Khârijite Zayd killed" [i.e., Zayd killed the Khârijite]; he does not say *qatala zaydun al-khârijiyya* "Zayd killed the Khârijite", because he knows that there is no gain for the people in knowing that Zayd was the killer, so that he should mention that fact in order for them to be concerned by it and rejoicing in it. He knows from their situation that what they are expecting and what they want to know is, when the killing of the heinous Khârijite took place, and that they are redeemed from this evil.

But if there is a man who has absolutely no wickedness and of whom people did not believe that he was capable of killing someone and he kills someone, and somebody wishes to inform people of this, he fronts the mention of the killer and says: *qatala zaydun rajulan* "Zayd killed a man". This is because what interests him and what concerns other people about this killing is its singular character, its rareness and its unexpectedness. Obviously, what makes this event rare and unexpected is not the person to which it happens but the person by whom it happens. In itself this is a correct principle, but he [i.e., Sîbawayhi] should have recognized something like this meaning

> in every instance of fronting in speech and explained in which way concern played a role. This led people to believe that it suffices to say that something was fronted because of a concern [on the part of the speaker] and because [the speaker] regarded it as more important, without mentioning the modality of this concern and why it was more important. Because of this neglect the issue of fronting has never occupied an important role in their minds, and they have neglected to address it properly, so that you find that most people follow him [i.e., Sîbawayhi] and pay only lip service to it and there is nothing more shameful than that. In the same way they deal with other issues, so that they do not investigate elision and repetition, overt and covert separation and junction, nor any other phenomenon.
>
> (al-Jurjânî, *Dalâ'il al-'i'jâz*, ed. by Muḥammad Rashîd Riḍâ, 6th ed., Cairo, 1960, pp. 82–3)

In our sketch of Sîbawayhi's linguistic theory (chapter 3) we have referred to the fact that his criteria for explaining language structure were predominantly formal. Sîbawayhi mentions semantic differences between constructions as a motive for syntactic differences and he uses the judgment of the native speaker as an important factor in the distinction between sentences, but the semantic differences in themselves are not the subject of his research. This approach to linguistic analysis remained the model for most of the subsequent tradition. In the eleventh century a major shift in linguistic approach took place, which emphasized the role of semantics in linguistic studies. The theologian, grammarian, and literary critic 'Abd al-Qâhir al-Jurjânî, who died in 1078, was one of the driving forces behind this shift. For most of his life al-Jurjânî lived in the Persian province of Jurjân; his only teacher in grammar was a nephew of the famous grammarian 'Abû 'Alî al-Fârisî (cf. above, chapter 8). In spite of the fact that he worked somewhat outside the mainstream of linguistics and never even visited Basra or Baghdad, he managed to found his own circle of pupils in this outpost of Arabic civilization and to establish a reputation as a linguist and rhetorician all over the Islamic world. His most famous works are two treatises that deal with rhetoric: the *Dalâ'il al-'i'jâz* "Arguments of the inimitability [of Qur'ânic style]" and the *'Asrâr al-balâgha* "Secrets of eloquence". Apart from these books he also wrote a highly interesting commentary on al-Fârisî's introduction to linguistics *al-'Îḍâḥ*, and a textbook on the governing words in language.

The central theme of al-Jurjânî's writings is the neglect of semantics by most scholars. The main targets of his reproach are not the linguists, however, but the theologians. Why they are the ones to blame becomes obvious when we consider the fact that in his major works al-Jurjânî deals with the religious theme of the *'i'jâz al-Qur'ân* "the inimitability of the *Qur'ân*". From the ninth century onwards this theme had been treated by theologians in the context of their theories about prophethood. It was generally believed by Muslims that the Prophet Muḥammad had not performed any miracle except one: even though he could not read or write he had brought a revelation whose style was superior to any human writing. The dogma of the *'i'jâz al-Qur'ân* had a special relevance for Mu'tazilite theologians: since they held that the *Qur'ân* was created (cf. above, chapter 8, p. 107) they were particularly interested in showing its superior qualities as part of God's creation.

Al-Jurjânî's publications constituted a major contribution to the discussion about the *'i'jâz al-Qur'ân*, but he was not the first author to investigate the inimitable style of the revealed text. In the ninth/tenth centuries theologians and literary critics, many of whom were Mu'tazilites, had attempted to define what exactly were the superior properties of the *Qur'ân*. This discussion coincided with a debate among literary critics about the evaluation of literary works. The central notions in this debate were *ma'nâ* "meaning" and *lafẓ* "expression", a dichotomy that also played a fundamental role in the history of Arabic grammar. We have seen above that in the discussions between the logicians and the grammarians (cf. above, chapter 4) the inherent ambiguity of the terms *ma'nâ* and *lafẓ* was the main stumbling block for an understanding between the two parties. For the logicians the meanings were the logical ideas that were signified by the expressions, for the grammarians they were identical with the functions of the words. Some confusion was created by the fact that the grammarians continued to use the word *ma'ânî* also in the sense it had possessed in the earliest commentaries on the *Qur'ân*, namely the intentions of the speakers (cf. above, chapter 1).

In the discussions among literary critics the general trend seems to have been to regard the *ma'ânî* as the ideas or the topics of a poem or a literary text. These ideas are available to everyone, whereas the selection of the *'alfâẓ*, the expression of these ideas in language, determines the quality of the literary work.

Al-Jurjânî decidedly rejected this attitude towards literary criticism. In his view the concentration on the expression of the text, whether it was a literary work or the *Qur'ân* itself, was the main reason for what he calls "the corruption of taste and language". In his view *ma'nâ* was what determined the quality of the style, and it would be absurd to attribute qualities of eloquence to the expression as such:

> Know that whenever you look into this [corruption of taste and language] you find that it has only one cause, namely their view about the expression and the fact that they assign to the expression attributes . . . without properly distinguishing between those attributes that belong to the expression as such and attributes that they assign to them because of something that belongs to its meaning.
>
> [Al-Jurjânî then explains that eloquence does not reside in the correct application of grammatical rules or the avoidance of soloecisms; these are only necessary, not sufficient conditions for the quality of a text; he then concludes:]
>
> When we look at declension we find that it cannot possibly play a role in the assignment of superior quality, since it is inconceivable that the nominative or the accusative in one utterance could have an advantage over that in another utterance. What we can imagine is that we have two utterances in which mistakes against the rules of declension are made; in such a case one may be more correct than the other. Alternatively, we may have two utterances, one of which continues to be correct, whereas the other does not. But this does not constitute a different degree of superiority [in the expression], but quite simply negligence [of the speakers] in one instance and correct use of the declension in the other.
>
> (al-Jurjânî, *Dalâ'il al-'i'jâz*, p. 256)

The originality of al-Jurjânî as a rhetorician is that he linked his view on meaning as the determining factor in the quality of a text to a linguistic dimension by considering it not in isolation but always as it is realized within a coherent text. Composition or cohesion (*naẓm*) is the key notion of both the *Dalâ'il* and the *'Asrâr*, and in both works he attempted to define this principle in linguistic terms. Since he was probably writing mainly for a

Mu'tazilite audience, he wished to impress them with the need to study not only theology but also the minutiae of grammar and literary theory precisely in order to improve their understanding of the inimitability of the *Qur'ân*. What he proposed to do was to support this doctrine with arguments taken from linguistic theory. His main point was that it was not enough simply to say that the *Qur'ân* was inimitable because of its style or composition, but all particular aspects of this style had to be pointed out.

For this programme the discipline of grammar had to be reformed first: instead of the usual emphasis on the formal properties of syntactic constructions grammarians had to shift their attention to the true source of excellence and eloquence, which was the meaning of the text. In order to look at language from this perspective it was necessary to go beyond the level of the individual word. Words cannot be eloquent in themselves, but they need a context. Only when the context is properly ordered (*naẓm*) can there be eloquence and superiority of style. In this context proper ordering refers to a correspondence between the meanings in the mind and the words in the sentence. In this respect he disagreed absolutely with the Mu'tazilites who separated meaning as inner speech from meaning as a property of a linguistic utterance. Al-Jurjânî differed from most other writers on eloquence in another point as well: he made the correspondence between meaning and expression conditional on the proper application of the rules of grammar. Hence his attention for the details of word order, which is supposed to reflect the hierarchy of the elements in the mind; this principle is amply illustrated in the quotation at the beginning of this chapter.

In his analysis of style al-Jurjânî does not hesitate to criticize Sîbawayhi for his almost exclusive concentration on syntactic criteria. Some of the examples in the quotation above have been mentioned in earlier chapters as examples of the way Arabic grammarians relied on formal criteria in their syntactic analysis of the language. Semantic preoccupations did not determine their analysis, although, to be sure, these were of course not absent. In the example of the fronting of constituents Sîbawayhi already knew that there was a semantic difference between the sentence *ḍarabtu zaydan* and *zaydun ḍarabtuhu*. The point is that this semantic difference was of no great interest to him: he regarded it as self-evident and as something the native speaker would immediately recognize. For him the difference in word order was a sign of the *'inâya* and *ihtimâm* "interest and concern" of the speaker, who indicated with the position of the constituents in the sentence their relative interest in the mind of the speaker. For the grammarian the important thing was to analyse the formal differences that made this semantic difference possible.

When there are two syntactic variants of a construction Sîbawayhi attempts to explain the difference in case endings, but does not show any interest in the difference in semantics. On the other hand, when for instance a particle does not affect the case endings of the other words in the sentence, such a particle is not deemed worthy of any detailed treatment, for instance, the particle *'innamâ* "but, only", which has a complicated semantic scope but does not exercise any governance on the other constituents of the sentence. Another example is that of the conjunctions *wa-* and *fa-*, which are both co-ordinating conjunctions, but with subtle differences in the degree of connectivity between the clauses they join. In the work of al-Jurjânî such topics are of prime importance and he devotes a long passage to the various functions of *'innamâ*.

Whenever there is a formal difference between two constructions, al-Jurjânî's main premise is that it always entails a difference in meaning. He explicitly distances himself from "the grammarians" – including Sîbawayhi – who have neglected this aspect of language use. As an example we may quote here the case of the two variants of the predicative construction:

> *'inna zaydan la-yaf'alu*/ *'inna zaydan la-fâ'ilun*
> "Zayd really does"/"Zayd is really doing"

In this construction the first variant uses the imperfect verb, the second the active participle to express the notion of predication. Sîbawayhi regards them as synonymous and uses this synonymy as one of the arguments for the right of the imperfect verb to receive declensional endings (cf. above, chapter 3): both the imperfect and the (nominal) participle perform the same function. Al-Jurjânî on the other hand, maintains that there is a large semantic difference between the two sentences: the verb always expresses movement, whereas the nominal form of the participle expresses a state:

> The next division [in the nuances of the predicate] is that between an assertion in the form of a noun and that in the form of a verb. This is a subtle distinction, which is indispensable in the science of rhetoric. The explanation is that the semantic role

> of the noun is to assert a meaning about something without implying its constant renewal, whereas the verb's semantic role is to imply the constant renewal of the meaning that is asserted of something. When you say *zaydun munṭaliqun* "Zayd is leaving", you assert his actual departure without making this departing something he constantly renews and produces. Its meaning is just like in the expression *zaydun ṭawîlun* "Zayd is large" and *'amrun qaṣîrun* "'Amr is short". You do not make length and shortness of stature something that is renewed and produced, but just assert these properties and imply their existence in general. In the same way you do not intend in the expression *zaydun munṭaliqun* "Zayd is leaving" anything more than that this is asserted of Zayd.
>
> (*Dalâ'il*, pp. 121-2)

Another example, as already mentioned above, is that of word order. According to Sîbawayhi, in a nominal sentence, composed of a definite and an indefinite word, the definite word becomes the topic (*mubtada'*) and the indefinite word the predicate (*khabar*), as in

zaydun munṭaliqun
mubtada' khabar
"Zayd is leaving"

But when there are two definite words he asserts that it is up to the speaker to front the one or the other, so that

al-munṭaliqu zaydun/zaydun al-munṭaliqu
"the one who leaves is Zayd"/"Zayd is the one who leaves"

are identical in status. Here again al-Jurjânî believes that the grammarians have not understood and analysed actual usage, because both sentences have a different intentional meaning. In the quotation given above, the position of the object is discussed by him in the same way: the sentence with the word order Verb–Object–Agent expresses a different intention from the one with the word order Verb–Agent–Object.

We have seen above (chapter 3, p. 49) that the most fundamental distinction in Arabic syntax is that between two sentence types: nominal sentences and verbal sentences. The nominal sentence consists of a topic and a predicate, whereas the verbal sentence has a verb and an agent. In Sîbawayhi's *Kitâb* this distinction was introduced on the basis of the difference in syntactic behaviour between the two types: in *zaydun ḍaraba* "Zayd, he hit" and *ḍaraba zaydun* "Zayd hit" only the former exhibits agreement between the noun and the verb (cf. the plural sentences *az-zaydûna ḍarabû/ḍaraba z-zaydûna*). This is why the word *zayd* in the first sentence is regarded as topic (*mubtada'*), whereas the word *zayd* in the second sentence is analysed as the agent (*fâ'il*) of the sentence. In the framework of logical analysis, for instance in al-Fârâbî's writings (cf. above, chapter 6, p. 87) both sentences are analysed as propositions, containing the same two constituents: subject and predicate. For these two notions al-Fârâbî translates the Greek terms (*hupokeímenon* "subject" becomes *mawḍû'*; *katêgoroúmenon* "predicate" becomes *maḥmûl*) and does not pay any attention at all to the syntactic differences between them in Arabic.

In al-Jurjânî's analysis the role of the *mubtada'*, the topic of the sentence, is analysed in much greater detail. The speaker uses the noun in fronted position because he wishes to draw the attention to it as the focus of the sentence. The syntactic consequences of this position are just the mark of this difference, not the focus of the grammatical analysis.

Al-Jurjânî's plea for the inclusion of semantics in linguistics was taken up by later writers who aimed at a new systematization of the sciences. The most famous of these writers was as-Sakkâkî (d. 1229), who wrote a *Miftâḥ al-'ulûm* "Key of the sciences" in which he introduced the term *'ilm al-'adab* as the name for a new science, which was to embrace all sciences that in one way or another dealt with language. The word *'adab* in Arabic culture indicated the combination of qualities that an intellectual needed to possess in order to be able to function as an intellectual (*'adîb*). In Modern Arabic the word has come to be used as an equivalent for the Western concept of "literature", but in Classical Arabic culture it was a much more wide-ranging concept that included among other things knowledge of poetry, knowledge of the history of the Arabs, the ability to talk eloquently and correctly and to use a refined vocabulary, the ability to participate in witty conversations, and in general the good manners that were expected from an intellectual, something like a cross between an English gentleman and a French *homme de lettres*.

In as-Sakkâkî's classification of the sciences *'adab* was the term chosen to indicate the new science, the *'ilm al-'adab*, which was to include the following sub-sections: morphology (*'ilm aṣ-ṣarf*);

syntax (*'ilm an-naḥw*); and the two sciences of meanings (*'ilm al-ma'ânî*) and clarity (*'ilm al-bayân*). The first two sciences are the traditional domain of linguistics as they had been established by Sîbawayhi (cf. above, chapter 3). The innovation is constituted by the third section that about meanings and clarity. In his introduction to this third section as-Sakkâkî explains the purpose of these two sciences as follows:

> Know that the science of meanings follows the properties of the constructions of the language in conveying information, and the connected problem of approving and disapproving these, in order to avoid mistakes in the application of speech to what the situation dictates by paying close attention to this.
>
> (as-Sakkâkî, *Miftâḥ al-'ulûm*, ed. by Nu'aym Zarzûr, Beirut, 1983, p. 161)

He then gives examples of the kind of constructions that are studied by the science of the meanings. When you hear someone say *'inna zaydan munṭaliqun* "indeed, Zayd is leaving" you know that the speaker wishes to deny any doubt or reject any denial about the fact that Zayd is leaving. On the other hand, when he says *zaydun munṭaliqun* "Zayd is leaving", he just wishes to make an assertion about Zayd's departure. In other words, the kind of meanings that are studied in this science are connected with the way the intention of the speaker is translated in his choice of construction, the pragmatic function of language and the situational context being the important factors dictating the choice of construction.

The *'ilm al-bayân* is the companion science of the science of meanings. It is defined by as-Sakkâkî as follows:

> It is the knowledge of the expression of one meaning in different ways, by referring to it more or less clearly, which serves to avoid mistakes in the application of speech to the full expression of what one wishes to say. Our remarks here indicate that whoever wishes to understand the full intention of the words of God Almighty urgently needs these two sciences. Woe to those who dabble in exegesis without proper attention to these two sciences!
>
> (as-Sakkâkî, *Miftâḥ*, p. 162)

The science of *bayân* is the finishing touch to the conveying of information and cannot be separated from the science of meaning. As we have seen in earlier chapters, *bayân* was often used to indicate the "plain meaning" of the text, or its explication by the exegetes. But in the context of as-Sakkâkî's new classification of sciences *bayân* has come to mean metaphorical usage of the language. In this section of his work he deals with subjects such as similes, metaphors, figurative speech, anaphora.

Later writers on grammar, even when they continued to follow the methods of technical grammar as they had been laid down by Sîbawayhi, could never avoid completely the new trend that had been initiated by al-Jurjânî. Among the works of Ibn Hishâm (d. 1360), for instance, who wrote a number of conventional treatises of grammar and a commentary on the *'Alfiyya* of Ibn Mâlik, as so many other writers had done, we also find a work entitled *Mughnî l-labîb 'an kutub al-'a'ârîb*. In this book, whose title may roughly be translated as "The treatise that makes the books of the true Bedouin redundant for intelligent people" Ibn Hishâm presents a picture of a completely changed discipline of linguistics. In the introduction to the *Mughnî* he tells the reader that after having studied many books on declension he found that they all had in common one thing: their immoderate length. In his view this was caused by three things: they tended to repeat themselves unnecessarily, they included topics that had nothing to do with declension, and they belaboured the obvious. It is certainly true that his own treatment of declension in Arabic and of the functions/meanings of the particles is strikingly original in its inclusion of the kind of semantic issues that had been discussed by writers such as al-Jurjânî and as-Sakkâkî.

The introduction or reintroduction of semantic elements in discussions on language corresponded to a deeply felt need to liberate grammar from the straitjacket of technicality. In this sense the ideas of al-Jurjânî were just one expression of a feeling of dissatisfaction with the way linguistics was developing that was expressed also by Ibn Maḍâ', who complained about useless morphological exercises and theoretical discussions that had nothing to do with the living language (cf. below, chapter 11). Another way of expressing this is Ibn Khaldûn's complaint about the lack of interest in literature he found in many grammatical writers. In the beginning grammar had been a combination of expertise about poetry, and a grammarian was an *'adîb*, an intellectual and cultured person who could be expected at the caliphal court to entertain people with his cultured conversation. But in later centuries grammar had become the dry discipline of schoolmasters. Ibn Khaldûn compares the *Kitâb Sîbawayhi*, which does not restrict itself to grammatical rules but is filled with quotations from the poetry and the proverbs of the pre-Islamic Arab tribes, with the writings of later grammarians, who are interested only in formulating rules. A fortunate exception are the grammarians in his own region of the Islamic world, Islamic Spain, who had preserved some of the old love for language as a living receptacle of literature rather than a collection of rules.

Chapter 10

The conventional character of language

The science of the "institution of speech"

The universal rules of languages

Know that the investigation is either about the essence of language, or about the quality of its signification. Since the signification is conventional, the investigation has to be either about the one who establishes speech, or about that which is established, or about that for which it is established, or about the way to know the establishment.

The investigation of the essence of language

Know that according to the experts the term "language" is used homonymously for the meaning that resides in the mind and for the articulated sounds that are heard. In the science of the principles of law there is no need to investigate the first meaning; the only thing we shall talk about here is the second meaning.

'Abû l-Ḥusayn [al-Baṣrî] says: "Speech is what is composed of the sounds that are heard, that are distinct and conventional". Sometimes it is added to this: "which are produced by one speaker".

[Ar-Râzî then discusses this definition of language and proceeds with the investigation about the author of the establishment of language; he concludes that there are no decisive arguments for either human or divine institution of speech, so that the only solution is to refrain from any judgment in this matter.]

Investigation of that which is established

Know that one human being is unable to procure independently everything he needs. It is indispensable for them to assemble with other people in a community, in which they help each other, so that each one of them acquires what he needs. For this purpose they all need to be able to communicate to their fellow human beings what they have in mind. This communication needs a medium; they could have instituted something else than language to communicate what was in their mind, such as special movements by special members of the body, in order to indicate the categories of substances. But they found that the most convenient medium for this was that of the articulated sounds. . . .

Investigation of that for which it is established

. . . It is obvious that there need not be for every meaning an expression signifying it. This is even impossible, since the number of intelligible meanings is infinite; if it were necessary to have an expression to signify each meaning, this would be either a one-to-one relationship or a shared relationship. The first option is invalid, since it would lead to the existence of an infinite number of expressions. The second option is also invalid, since among the shared expressions there would either be some that would be used for infinite meanings, or there would not be among them such expressions. The first option is invalid, since the institution of words cannot take place until after rational insight, and rational insight of infinite things one by one is impossible for us. This being so, we must exclude the possibility of communication with such expressions.

The second option would imply that the things signified by the expressions would be finite, because then the expressions would be finite and the signification of each expression would also be finite. Adding finite things to finite things a finite number of times can result only in finiteness, so that the total number would always be finite. The collection of infinite things would then not be signified by the expressions.

Now that this principle is firmly established, we say that meanings are of two kinds: those that need to be expressed, and those that do not need to be expressed. Language cannot bc without expressions to denote meanings of the first category, since when they are needed intensely the motives to express them are abundant and there are no impediments to expressing them. When the motives are abundant and there are no impediments, it becomes inevitable. With regard to the things that do not need to be expressed intensely, language may lack expressions to signify them. . . .

The expressions have not been established to signify the external objects, but they have been established to signify the conceptual meanings. The proof for this is that when we see a body from afar and assume that it is a stone, we call it by that name. But if we come near and find out that it is an animal, which we assume to be a bird, we call it by that name. If we come still nearer and find out that it is a human being, we call it by that name. The fact that the difference of names correlates with the differencc of concepts demonstrates that the expression can signify only the latter. Likewise in the compound expressions, when you say *qâma zaydun* "Zayd stood up", your words do not convey Zayd's standing up, but your judgment about Zayd's standing up, and your predicating this about him. When we then find out that this judgment is not mistaken, we infer from it its physical existence. But the expression itself does not signify the external state of affairs. God knows best!

(ar-Râzî, *al-Maḥṣûl fî 'ilm 'uṣûl al-fiqh*, ed. by Ṭâhâ Jâbir Fayyâḍ al-'Ulwânî, 6 vols, Riyadh, 1979, I, pp. 233–6; 261; 265–7; 269–71)

The title of the work by the great Qur'ânic commentator ar-Râzî (d. 1209) from which the above quotation has been taken means "The result in the science of the principles of law". It is one of the large compendia on this science that have become available in the last few decades and that have enabled us to become acquainted with this science. Its author, Fakhr ad-Dîn Muḥammad ibn 'Umar ar-Râzî, is known chiefly for his large commentary on the *Qur'ân*, entitled *Mafâtîḥ al-ghayb* "The keys to the hidden things", which is one of the most instructive bodies of knowledge in Islamic exegesis. The introduction to the commentary contains a large section on linguistics in which he deals with the same kind of topics that were discussed by Mu'tazilite grammarians such as az-Zajjâjî (cf. above, chapter 5) and Ibn Jinnî (cf. above, chapter 8). His compendium on the principles of law (*'uṣûl al-fiqh*) also contains a large section on linguistics, but here he restricts himself to those linguistic subjects that are of direct relevance to legal thinking.

From the name of the science, "principles of law", one would certainly not expect it to give any special attention to language. Yet one look at the table of contents of the *Maḥṣûl* suffices to show that a large part of the theoretical considerations of the *'Uṣûliyyûn* (i.e., those who deal with the *'uṣûl al-fiqh*) was directed towards the study of language. In table 10.1 we have listed the subjects of the nine chapters that make up the section on language, which amounts to more than 340 pages in the printed edition.

The relationship between the principles of law and the study of language becomes clear when we look at the development of this science. We have seen above (cf. chapter 8) that in the ninth century for some time the theological school of the Mu'tazila held the supremacy in Islamic theology. After the failure of the *miḥna*, the inquisition instigated by the Caliph al-Ma'mûn, they lost their power and became very unpopular, both in official theology, where they were branded as heretics, and with the general public. They were not allowed to teach in academies of theology, and there were several incidents of scholars accused of Mu'tazilite leanings being threatened by a mob when they tried to preach in the mosque.

This is not to say that the Mu'tazila became a forbidden sect, but in some places it was certainly not wise to advertise one's adherence

Table 10.1 Topics in the section on language in ar-Râzî's *Maḥṣûl*

Chapter	*Topic*
1	general principles of languages (the origin of the establishment of language, subject of establishment, object of establishment)
2	classification of words
3	compound words
4	synonymy
5	homonymy
6	literal and metaphoric usage
7	conflicting interpretations of words (literal/metaphoric, particular/general, etc.)
8	explanation of particles whose knowledge is indispensable in law (e.g., *wa-* "and", *fî* "in", etc.)
9	modalities of argumentation on a scriptural basis

to the principles of Mu'tazilism, above all, the createdness of the *Qur'ân*. When Mu'tazilites became unwelcome in theology they found other ways to promote their ideas. In grammar many Mu'tazilites found a new channel for their theories: in the ninth and tenth centuries many famous grammarians held Mu'tazilite ideas. Their influence was even greater in the new science that was developed in the tenth century, that of the *'uṣûl al-fiqh*. We do not know exactly when the first treatises on this science were published; the most important works on the principles of law were written in the second half of the tenth and in the eleventh century.

In other disciplines the term *'uṣûl* had also come to be used as a technical term at about the same time; in the *'Îḍâḥ* az-Zajjâjî (cf. above, chapter 5) uses it for the primary rules of language, as they are set out in empirical treatises of grammar. Ibn as-Sarrâj calls *'uṣûl* the first tier of linguistic explanation; his main work was entitled simply *Kitâb al-'uṣûl* "Book of principles". In theology the *'uṣûl al-kalâm* "principles of theology", and in later grammatical treatises the *'uṣûl an-naḥw*, held a similar position as the principles of the science of law: in these contexts the term came to mean the epistemological principles or criteria of knowledge in science. The usual canon of criteria included the methods of analogical reasoning, consensus among the scholars, textual evidence, and accepted usage.

Although Mu'tazilite influence was manifest in most treatises on the *'uṣûl al-fiqh*, not all *'uṣûlîs* were Mu'tazilite; the author of the *Maḥṣûl* was certainly not a Mu'tazilite. None the less, the emphasis on linguistic issues, which the Mu'tazilites introduced in the study of legal principles, to a large degree changed its perspective. The central notion in the theoretical considerations of the legal scholars became *waḍ'*, literally "institution" or "imposition", a term derived from the discussions about the origin of speech (cf. above, chapter 8), but which had lost its diachronic connotation and had come to mean the established character of language. This established character or conventionality of language was what the legal scholars needed for their programme of deriving all legal rules by accepted methods from the texts. The conventionality of language was connected with the ideas about the origin of speech, but the exact modality of that origin had become irrelevant. In the compendia this issue is usually treated summarily and then dismissed as of no consequence, for instance by ar-Râzî. At the beginning of the second chapter of the section on linguistic issues in the *Maḥṣûl* ("investigation about the one who established speech") he explains that words can signify meanings either by themselves or by convention; in either case the act of institution may be of human or divine origin or both. In the discussion he wholly concentrates on the epistemological issue. At the end of this chapter he concludes that with regard to the identity of the author of the institution, which is irrelevant for the science of law anyway, it is impossible to decide in favour of either position. Therefore, he prefers to leave the matter undecided.

What was of interest to the legal scholars who worked in this discipline was not so much the historical development and origin of speech as the relationship between words and their denotata. It is not hard to see why this shift in emphasis took place. For the legal scholars the single most relevant question was to know the exact domain of the instructions in the *Qur'ân* and in the collections of sayings of the Prophet. In the ninth century the founder of the Shâfi'ite school of law, ash-Shâfi'î (d. 820), had written a *Risâla* "Treatise" in which he dealt with the various ways things are expressed in the *Qur'ân*; he did not use the term *waḍ'* yet, but laid the basis for a new approach to the text. In the first chapter of his treatise ash-Shâfi'î introduces the notion of *bayân* "explanation, plain meaning" and then says:

> Explanation is a word that encompasses the meanings whose principles are united but whose branches are separated. The minimum of these united, separated principles is that they are an explanation for those who were addressed by it among the people in whose language the *Qur'ân* was revealed. All of it was alike for him, even though some of it was more emphatically clear than other parts; all of it was different for those who did not know the Arabic language.
>
> (ash-Shâfi'î, *Risâla*, ed. by 'Aḥmad Muḥammad Shâkir, 2nd ed., Cairo, 1979, p. 21)

With this complicated formulation ash-Shâfi'î probably intends to say that the text of the *Qur'ân* in itself possesses a plain meaning, but that there are various degrees of clarity: some of it is self-evident from the text of the *Qur'ân*, for instance the prohibition to drink wine or to eat pork; some of it is prescribed in the *Qur'ân* as a general duty, but the details were given by the Prophet orally, for instance the exact details of the ritual prayer; still other commandments derive entirely from the teaching of the Prophet.

Finally, there is a category in which human beings are enjoined to exercise their own *ijtihâd*, i.e., their mental effort to understand. With this division in categories of religious knowledge ash-Shâfi'î legitimizes the work of the legal scholar, which must be a combination of textual evidence and accepted methods of elucidation. In the rest of the *Risâla* he discusses such points as general versus particular meaning, abrogation within the text, and the use of the analogical method (*qiyâs*) to find out the rules of application of God's commands.

In the tenth century the Mu'tazilites adopted the term *waḍ'* to indicate the established character of language. In their legal-linguistic investigations they applied themselves to the same topics as ash-Shâfi'î had studied, such as particular versus general meaning, homonymy versus synonymy, and metaphoric versus literal usage. The relevance of these topics for a lawyer is clear: they were concerned with the precise relationship between words and their denotata, not because of an interest in the structure of language itself, nor because of an interest in the relationship between speech and thought, but simply because they wished to build their deduction of rules on a firm theoretical basis.

The discussion of metaphorical usage of language illustrates the kind of problems that the legal theorists faced. It was an accepted fact in Arabic linguistics that words are sometimes used in a derived meaning, for instance when we call a man "lion". This *majâz* is defined as "an expression that is used to signify a meaning other than the meaning for which it has been established" ('Abû l-Ḥusayn al-Baṣrî, *Mu'tamad* p. 17). Such a definition soon leads to theoretical problems: if we assume that the *Qur'ân* contains metaphorical usage, we also have to assume that God sometimes uses words to signify a meaning other than the meaning for which He Himself has established them. For this reason, some theologians absolutely refused to accept metaphorical usage in the *Qur'ân*. Others tried to find a solution by stating that these words had originally been established for two meanings: "man" and "lion" are therefore homonymous meanings of the word *'asad*. But such an interpretation ignores the fact that the meaning "man" is actually a derived, a marked use of the word and clearly has a different status from the meaning "lion". The solution chosen by 'Abû l-Ḥusayn al-Baṣrî is to say that the word is indeed used in a different meaning than the usual one, but this deviation from the usual meaning itself is a conventional property of language (*muwâḍa'a* "agreement, convention", from the same root as the term *waḍ'*). Al-Baṣrî's treatment of this topic became the basis for the later compendia of the legal theorists such as al-Ghazzâlî (d. 1111) and also for ar-Râzî.

The structure of the treatises on the principles of law is basically an attempt to discuss theology and law in terms of Aristotelian logic. This is apparent from the very beginning of each treatise in which the scope of the science is determined with the help of the Aristotelian questions about aim, subject, and means. Each science aims at the establishment of certain theorems (*masâ'il*), which are applied to the subject matter (*mawḍû'*) of that science with the help of premises (*mabâdi'*), notions that have been established independently from that science. In the case of the science of the principles of law, the premises that are needed are those of theology and linguistics. Therefore, any book on the principles of law starts with a discussion of these premises.

An essential question in the discussion of *waḍ' al-lughah* is that of the legitimation of the established language. Since the legal theorists are not concerned with the process of creation of speech, what they mean by "legitimation" is the transmission of knowledge about the meaning of words (*tawâtur*): how do we know that words signify what they signify? This is a purely conventional legitimation, since they are not concerned with establishing a link between language and physical reality. The theorists deal with the transmission in the same way in which the traditionists deal with the legitimation of the sayings from the Prophet (*ḥadîth*): for each assertion there must always be an authority. In the case of linguistics there had been a long history of this kind of legitimation. Since the days of Sîbawayhi grammarians had been forced to adduce sources for the rules and meanings they quoted. Just as the traditionists could not be content with only one authority for a given saying by the Prophet, the lexicographers could not establish the meaning of a word on the basis of only one poetic line or one informant. It is interesting to see how the legal theorists attempt to formulate a policy for finding out what the correct meaning of a word is. In this connection they develop a set of criteria to which the linguistic transmission must obey, as in Ibn al-'Anbârî's (d. 1181) *Luma' al-'adilla*, which reads like a legal treatise on the science of language. The most pressing problem was the question in how far analogy (*qiyâs*), which we have come to know as an instrument of linguistic explanation, may be used as a means of finding out what words mean. Most theorists rejected this use, just as Sîbawayhi, centuries earlier, had rejected the use of analogy as a way of producing words and rules, and correcting the *Qur'ân*. In the *Maḥṣûl* ar-Râzî distinguishes between two kinds of linguistic knowledge:

> The first kind is the current and generally known; about such expressions we know without any doubt that they were established some time in the past for these meanings. We find, for instance, that we are convinced that the words *samâ'* "heaven" and *'arḍ* "earth" were used in the time of the Prophet – may God protect him! – for these two nominata. . . . The second kind are the rare expressions, which can be known only on the basis of a single tradition. If you acknowledge this, we say that most words in the *Qur'ân* as well as their syntactic and morphological properties belong to the first kind and may, therefore, without any problem be used as evidence. There are only very few words of the second kind; these cannot be used in decisive arguments, but only in speculation.
>
> (ar-Râzî, *Maḥṣûl* I, pp. 294–6)

Leaving aside the matter of the rare words, the meaning of the words used in the *Qur'ân* and the traditions of the Prophet is, therefore, clear. The main concern of the legal theorists is to develop a method of ascertaining the intention of the text. In this they distinguished between the explicit meaning of the text, and the implicit meaning. The explicit meaning is equal to the literal meaning, the *ẓâhir*, which for people like Ibn Ḥazm was the exclusive source of information about the meaning and purpose of the text (cf. below, chapter 11). But very often the intention of the text is not clear since words are not used only in a particular but also in a general sense, which is a potential source for ambiguity and confusion. It is the task of the theorist to find out what the real intention is by linking the general sense to the individual context. He is authorized to do so because the general sense is an established factor in language, too, as is metaphorical usage. In order to avoid arbitrariness the theorists had to be very careful with the application of their methods, otherwise they would lay themselves wide open to the objections of the Ẓâhirîs, who claimed that the only sense of a text is the sense that is immediately available to the average native speaker.

In the "linguistic premises" of the writings of the legal theorists the givenness or established character of language was studied for the sake of its role in legal arguments. Later these introductions grew into a separate science, the "science of the institution of speech" (*waḍ'*), which studied the relationship between words and their denotata for its own sake. If language is an established given, each and every element of language must have its own established meaning, not only lexical words but also what we would call morphemes and suffixes. In this framework each element is regarded as the name of something, and the task the scholars of the science of *waḍ'* set themselves was to determine for each element of what it was the name, i.e., what it stood for. The theorists in this science were not concerned with the link between names and physical reality, since they believed that the names in language stood for concepts residing in the mind. The first to engage in this kind of study in a systematic way was the fourteenth century scholar 'Aḍud ad-Dîn al-'Îjî (d. 1355) in his *ar-Risâla al-waḍ'iyya*. His work gave rise to a series of treatises in this science which reached its apogee in the eighteenth century, well outside the Classical period of the study of Arabic, and remained popular until well into the twentieth century.

The difference between earlier approaches to language and the approach of the *waḍ' al-lugha* becomes clear when we look at the category of words that includes the definite nouns and the demonstrative, personal, and relative pronouns. Since the introduction of logic in the Arabic world such words had been regarded by the grammarians as universal, since their meaning was universal: they were applicable to all members of a certain species, but their meaning did not include each and every individual to which they were applied. In the science of the *waḍ' al-lugha* these words were treated as particular because in actual usage they were applied to only one particular member of the species. For those who developed this science "meaning" was that for which a certain expression had been established: words such as "he" or "this" had been established to be applied to particular instances of this category, therefore they could not be called universal. In the way of thinking of al-'Îjî, the "author" of the language (*wâḍi' al-lugha*), whether it was a human being or God, established words like "he" or "the man" not for a class of individuals but for application to each member of that category. This innovation was crucial for the authors of the treatises on the *waḍ' al-lugha*: if they were to assume that the author of language established these words for a universal idea, there would be no link with the actual application of the word to one particular instance. The case of the pronouns illustrates the need they felt to demonstrate the givenness of language not only in its general meaning but also in its actual use. Since the hearer understands the meaning of the expression "he" in a given instance, although the meaning of the word does not include all these particular instances, the context of the word must be an identifying factor: for a personal pronoun the discourse situation provides such an identification, for demonstratives a physical context is needed, to which the speaker can point.

The demonstrative and personal pronouns form one category of establishment: universal expressions for particular ideas. Two other categories of establishment were distinguished: particular expressions for a particular idea and universal expressions for a universal idea. The first category contains the proper names, which are said by al-'Îjî to have been established as a particular expression for a particular idea. The second category is that of expressions such as "man", which have been established as expressions for the universal idea of "man", rather than expressions that are applied to particular instances of men.

The categorization of the modes of establishment was important for another purpose as well. Since the givenness of every single element in speech had to be demonstrated, even particles must be the names of ideas. In the case of a particle such as *fî* "in", the idea for which this expression has been established is the notion of "being in" or "in-ness"; in Arabic such abstract notions are indicated by abstract nouns, for instance in the case of the preposition *fî* by the noun *ẓarfiyya* (*ẓarf* is a container, thus *ẓarfiyya* is something like "containment"). In the theory of the *waḍ' al-lugha* this again is a case of an universal establishment for a particular instance: in each sentence in which *fî* is used, a particular instance of "in-ness" is intended, which the author of the language of course did not know, just as in the case of the demonstrative pronouns he established an expression that could be used for particular instances. The difference between the demonstrative pronouns and particles such as *fî* is that the latter have been established to denote an idea in something else. In his *Kitâb* Sîbawayhi (cf. above, chapter 3, p. 36) had stated that the particle *jâ'a li-ma'nan* "came for a meaning"; later grammarians had added that this meant that the particle contributed to the meaning of something else. For authors such as al-'Îjî the particle *fî* indicated the "in" relation between other ideas. In the sentence *zayd fî d-dâr* "Zayd is in the house", for instance, it indicated a particular instance of one idea finding itself within another.

In order to account for the distinction between lexical and grammatical categories, or between lexical and morphological meaning, the authors of the *waḍ' al-lugha* introduced another distinction, that between the establishment of expressions that existed independently (*waḍ' shakhṣî* "individual institution"), for instance, words such as *rajul* "man" or *zayd* "Zayd", and the dependent establishment of expressions that could exist only in other expressions (*waḍ' naw'î* "categorial institution"), for instance, morphological patterns like *fâ'il* "active participle"; the latter are realized in words such as *ḍârib* "hitting", *kâtib* "writing", and so on. In grammatical treatises both categories of expressions were said to have a "meaning" (*ma'nâ*): the lexical meaning was the domain of the lexicographers, and the categorial meaning was the exclusive domain of the grammarians (cf. above, chapter 3).

In the theory of the *waḍ' al-lugha* only the categories of the verbal nouns, the isolated nouns (nouns that are not derived from a verbal noun), the pronouns, and the particles belong to the "individual institution" (*waḍ' shakhṣî*); all other elements of the language have been derived from this establishment by combining them with an expression of the "categorial institution" (*waḍ' naw'î*), i.e., by morphological derivation. Some disagreement existed among the representatives of the *waḍ' al-lugha* concerning the lexical material, i.e., the radicals that form the lexical words. The majority view held that the word *ḍarb* had been established individually for the idea of "hitting"; by applying to it various expressions of the "categorial institution" (*waḍ' naw'î*) the rest of the words containing the radicals *ḍ-r-b* were established, e.g., *ḍârib* "hitting", *ḍaraba* "he hit", etc. But there were some authors who believed that the establishment of an expression for the notion of "hitting", too, belonged to the domain of the "categorial institution": the author of the language had established the form *ḍ-r-b* for all expressions that derived from these radicals, including the word *ḍarb*.

What connects the treatises of the *waḍ' al-lugha* with the Mu'tazilite authors of the *'uṣûl al-fiqh* at the beginning of this chapter is their emphasis on the conventionality of speech. For the Mu'tazilite legal theorists this point was relevant because they needed the premise of the conventional character of language in order to legitimize their deduction of legal rules from the texts in a methodical and acceptable way. For the authors of the *waḍ' al-lugha* the analysis of the establishment of speech became an exercise in its own right. Starting from the premise that if language is established each of its element should stand for an idea, they developed a complicated system of establishment rules. This developed into a separate science of its own without a direct connection with practical applications.

Chapter 11

Ibn Maḍâ' and the refutation of the grammarians

My purpose in this book is to eliminate from grammar that what the grammarian can do without, and to draw attention to the common errors they make. One instance of this is their claim that the accusative, the genitive, and the jussive always occur with an overt governor, whereas the nominative occurs both with an overt and a covert governor. They speculate that in the sentence *ḍaraba zaydun 'amran* "Zayd hit 'Amr" the nominative in *zaydun* and the accusative in *'amran* are produced by *ḍaraba*. Don't you see that Sîbawayhi – may he rest in peace! – says at the beginning of his book "The reason I call them eight endings is to distinguish between, on the one hand, those words that receive one member of these four pairs because it is produced by a governor; those endings are never permanent with the word; and, on the other hand, those words whose last consonant has a permanent ending that never disappears as the result of the action of another word'? The obvious implication is that the governor causes the declension, and this is manifestly wrong.

'Abû l-Fatḥ Ibn Jinnî and others propose a different explanation. After an exposition on the overt and covert governors 'Abû l-Fatḥ says in his *Khaṣâ'iṣ*: "In reality and in actual speech the government of the nominative, accusative, genitive, and jussive is exercised by the speaker himself, not by anything else". He emphasizes the role of the speaker himself in order to eliminate any ambiguity. Then he further emphasizes this by adding "not by anything else". This is Mu'tazilite talk. The orthodox point of view is that these sounds can be only the work of God Almighty. They are attributed only to man like the rest of his voluntary actions.

Concerning the statement that words produce each other, this is false on both rational and religious grounds. Nobody in his right mind says such things, for different reasons. It would take too much time to mention all of them, since we aim at conciseness. One of these reasons is that the agent must necessarily exist when he performs his action. But declension is not produced until after the governor has disappeared: *zaydan* is not put in the accusative after *'inna* in the phrase *'inna zaydan* "indeed, Zayd" until after the disappearance of *'inna*.

Someone might ask: "How can we refute those who believe that it is the meanings of these expressions that govern?" The answer is as follows: "According to their theory agents act either by will, like the animals, or by nature, like the burning of fire and the cooling of water. But according to the orthodox believers there is no agent but God. The acts of human beings and animals are an act of God Almighty, and likewise those of fire and water and all other acts. This has been demonstrated elsewhere. No person in his right mind would maintain that linguistic governors can govern, either by their form or by their meaning, because they cannot act by will, nor can they act by nature."

Someone might object: "But they use these expressions only metaphorically and as an approximation. When the words to which they attribute the governing action disappear, the declensional endings that are attributed to them disappear as well, and when they are present, the declension is present as well. This is what some theories call the active causes." The answer is: "If their theory of governors did not lead them to alter the speech of the Arabs, to pull it down from the heights of eloquence to the depths of stammering, to claim the defectiveness of what is perfect, and to distort the real purpose of meanings, they would be perfectly free to do so. But since their belief in the function of words as governors leads to just such things, it is not allowed to follow them in this."

(Ibn Maḍâ', *Kitâb ar-radd 'alâ n-nuḥât*, ed. by Shawqî Ḍayf, Cairo, 1982, pp. 76–8)

It is clear that the author of the above lines did not have much sympathy for grammarians as a breed. From the title of his book, *The Book on the Refutation of the Grammarians*, we may deduce that he was not enthusiastic about their theories, either. His full name was 'Abû l-'Abbâs 'Aḥmad ibn 'Abd ar-Raḥmân Ibn Maḍâ', a grammarian from Cordova in Islamic Spain, whose fame rests mainly on this small book – no more than seventy pages in the printed edition – in which he sets out to destroy the entire building of linguistic theory as it had been practised from the days of Sîbawayhi. Not much is known about Ibn Maḍâ''s life. He was born in 1119 in Cordova and died in 1195 in Seville. At an early age he left his native city and travelled to other places in Islamic Spain and North Africa in his search for knowledge; according to his biographers he was well-versed in grammar, medicine, theology, geometry, and Islamic law. Because of his adherence to the principles of the Ẓâhirite school of theology he was appointed chief judge by the Almohad emir Yûsuf ibn 'Abd al-Mu'min and in this position, which he held until his death, he assisted the authorities in banning the writings of all other theological schools.

Ibn Maḍâ''s theological opinions are not known in detail, but we do know from his career that he fanatically supported the Ẓâhiriyya. This school had been established in Islamic Spain by the famous theologian Ibn Ḥazm of Cordova (d. 1064). According to Ibn Ḥazm the basis of theological knowledge is what God Himself has told us in the revelation. This in itself is, of course, not very remarkable since most Muslims would agree that the *Qur'ân* constitutes the basis of Islam. But, as we have seen in chapter 1, there was an old tradition of interpreting the *Qur'ân* in order to elucidate the intention of the speaker. Most commentators attempted to reconstruct the "actual" meaning of the text in order to find out what God had meant with His instructions. In the study of Islamic law (*fiqh*) an entire methodological apparatus had been set up for the construction of a legal system on the basis of the instructions in the *Qur'ân*. The most important, and at the same time the most controversial, instrument to extrapolate from the Qur'ânic commands and regulations to general laws for all aspects of Islamic society was the *qiyâs*, the analogical reasoning that was also invoked frequently by grammarians in their explanations of grammatical phenomena (cf. above, chapter 3, p. 47). It is this instrument that Ibn Ḥazm attacks most fiercely, since in his view it represents the worst instance of human arrogance of God's power.

In his critique of analogy Ibn Ḥazm frequently touches on questions that are connected with language, for instance in the classification of things in genus and species. Most people believe that we know that things belong to a certain species because they resemble each other: when we find out that one individual belongs to a species, we deduce on the basis of our knowledge and sensory information that other individuals that resemble it belong to this species too. This is what could be called "analogy by resemblance". For Ibn Ḥazm even such a use of analogical reasoning is excluded because only God knows which things are really alike. The only conclusion one can draw is that those things belong to one species that are called by the same name; we possess this knowledge by virtue of our being native speakers of the language. Thus, when the *Qur'ân* forbids the eating of pork or the drinking of wine, this applies to all objects that in our experience are called by this name.

It is even worse when people introduce the principle of "cause" (*'illa*) to their arguments. According to Ibn Ḥazm what we call causes, exist in nature because God has created them there: fire, for instance, always burns, and there are no instances where fire does not burn, nor are there instances of burning without fire. This means that God has created a natural law (or rather, a "habit of nature"), which may be observed by human beings. There is nothing within the fire that causes it to burn. For, were we to draw this conclusion, we would also be forced to admit that in the things that God forbids there is something which makes them forbidden by themselves, independently from God's judgment. This is tantamount to positing the existence of another eternal principle next to God.

It is not in our power, either, to find out why God forbids certain things and permits other things. The only thing we can do is take to the letter the instructions in the *Qur'ân* that we as native speakers can understand by virtue of our knowledge of the language. For instance, when God determines that it is forbidden to drink wine (*khamr*), the manifest meaning is that we are not allowed to drink any object to which the name of *khamr* is applied. This is the only correct way of obeying God's commands. It would be wrong to apply our rational arguments to the text and reason that we are not allowed to drink *khamr* because it is intoxicating and that therefore all intoxicating beverages are forbidden. It would be equally wrong to attribute the cause of the prohibition of the drinking of *khamr* to some property of the wine, for instance, the fact that it is made from grapes, so that every beverage that is not made of grapes would become admissible even though it was called *khamr*. In both cases we arrogate God's power and meddle in things that are not within our human domain.

Ibn Ḥazm's reasoning on the basis of the manifest meaning of the text of the *Qur'ân* sometimes leads to unexpected conclusions. In some respects his opinions are those of the ultra-orthodox in so far as the strict application of the Qur'ânic rules are concerned. But in other instances he sounds remarkably "liberal", for instance when he says that there is no reason why Arabic should be regarded as a superior language:

> Some people believe that their own language is superior to all other languages. This is meaningless, because the aspects of superiority are known: things are superior either by their work or by selection. But languages do not work, and there is no scriptural testimony about the selection of one language rather than another. God Almighty says: "We have sent each prophet in the language of his community so that he can explain things to them", and the Almighty also says: "We revealed it only in your language in order that they may remember it". With these words He informs us that the only reason He revealed the *Qur'ân* in Arabic was to make the Prophet's community understand the message. In this respect Galen was mistaken when he said: "The language of the Greek is the most superior language, because the rest of the languages resembles the barking of dogs or the croaking of frogs". This is absolute nonsense because anyone who hears a language other than his own and does not understand it, regards it in the same way as Galen does other languages.
>
> (Ibn Ḥazm, *al-'Iḥkâm fî 'uṣûl al-'aḥkâm*, ed. by 'Aḥmad Shâkir, Cairo, n.d., I, p. 32)

The contradiction between the two attitudes is, of course, only apparent: Ibn Ḥazm follows the letter of the text, but only when it tells us something explicitly. In the absence of scriptural testimony, it is not allowed to draw any conclusions: specifically, there is no proof that God regarded the Arabic language as superior, hence Ibn Ḥazm's rejection of a special status for Arabic. Just like any other language it was created by God, without whose divine inspiration human beings are unable to invent anything, be it language or science or art.

Ibn Ḥazm's rigorous application of *ẓâhirî* reasoning was followed enthusiastically by Ibn Maḍâ' and applied by him to the writings of the grammarians, with which he had become familiar during his study of the *Kitâb* of Sîbawayhi. The thrust of his argument is directed against three principles that constituted the basis of linguistic theory: that of the governor (*'âmil*); that of *'iḍmâr* "suppression" and the reconstruction by the grammarian (*taqdîr*); and the theory of grammatical analogy (*qiyâs*). We have seen above (especially chapter 3) that these principles represent the basis of linguistic theory in the Arabic tradition and any attack on them is aimed therefore at the very core of the theory.

The first principle of linguistic theory that he attacks is that of government (*'amal*). His criticism of the grammarians' use of the term *'awâmil* subtly modifies the meaning of this concept as it is used in grammatical reasoning. In the passage he quotes from Sîbawayhi's *Kitâb* the presence and absence of declensional endings is correlated with the presence and absence of a governing word in the sentence. We have seen above (chapter 3, p. 45) that this was the starting point of Sîbawayhi's distinction between declensional endings and endings without a syntactic function. The correlation of declensional endings and governors in linguistic theory is interpreted by Ibn Maḍâ' in the sense that the grammarians regard the governors as the physical cause of the declensional endings. This is an interpretation the grammarians themselves had already rejected a long time ago. There are, in fact, many texts in which they explain that it is naive to regard the governors as anything else than theoretical constructs. In his *Khaṣâ'iṣ* Ibn Jinnî states quite explicitly that the real cause of the declensional endings is the speaker who pronounces the endings. To be truc, such a solution would not have satisfied Ibn Maḍâ', since as a Ẓâhirî theologian he did not believe in free will and regarded God as the Creator of all things in this world. But other grammarians, too, who did not have Ibn Jinnî's Mu'tazilite leanings, did their best to explain that *'amal*, the operative force of the governor, is not a physical phenomenon but an abstract notion introduced by the grammarians. Ibn al-'Anbârî (d. 1181), for instance, the author of a large collection of controversial questions that were discussed by the Basran and the Kufan grammarians, explains the abstract nature of the principle of *'amal* in the following way. According to most grammarians, in a nominal sentence such as:

muḥammadun nabiyyun
"Muḥammad is a prophet"

the nominative of the predicate *nabiyyun* is caused by the governor *muḥammadun*, which is the topic of the sentence (cf. above, chapter 3). But about the governor of the topic itself scholars disagreed. The theory followed by Ibn al-'Anbârî states that the nominative of the topic is an abstract principle, called *ibtidâ'*, i.e., "the being used as topic", which in his view is the same as saying that there are no overt governors. When people object that the absence of governors cannot be a governor itself he retorts:

> The only reason why we say that the governor is the *ibtidâ'*, even though the *ibtidâ'* is nothing else than the absence of overt governors, is that governors in this discipline are not physical, effective causes like the burning of fire, the drowning in water or the cutting of a sword, but signs and abstract constructs. Since there is unanimous agreement that they are signs and abstract constructs, they can consist just like all other signs both in the presence and in the absence of something. If you have two cloaks and you wish to distinguish between them, you can dye one of them and leave the other without dye. Then the absence of dye in the one cloak has the same distinctive force as the presence of dye in the other.
>
> (Ibn al-'Anbârî, *al-'Inṣâf fî masâ'il al-khilâf bayna n-naḥwiyyîna l-Baṣriyyîn wa-l-Kûfiyyîn*, ed. by Gotthold Weil, Leiden, 1913, pp. 22–3)

We do not know whether Ibn Maḍâ' really believed that grammarians regarded governors as physical causes, or was perfectly aware of such explanations as the one by Ibn al-'Anbârî and simply equated government with physical cause as a polemical trick in his refutation of the grammarians. But his arguments against this straw man were certainly effective.

The second principle that was attacked forcefully by Ibn Maḍâ' is that of suppression as an explanatory principle in linguistic theory. From the very beginning grammarians had recourse to an underlying level of language in order to explain the syntactic relations between constituents in the surface sentence. The difference between the two levels was explained by them as a natural tendency on the part of the native speaker to suppress (*'iḍmâr*) or, as Ibn Maḍâ' calls it, delete (*ḥadhf*) elements in their speech in order to be as concise as possible. The Arabs, as they say, are averse to longwindedness in speaking and therefore take the liberty of leaving out parts of their message. From the point of view of a Ẓâhirî grammarian the problem is, of course, that the reconstruction by the grammarian harbours an element of arbitrariness. This is particularly risky when the text of the *Qur'ân* is involved: it is very tempting for human beings to reconstruct the intention of the text by inserting elements, but in this way they threaten to distort the manifest meaning (*ẓâhir*) of the text, which every native speaker recognizes immediately.

In his discussion of suppression Ibn Maḍâ' distinguishes between three kinds of deletion of elements from the surface structure. In the first place, there is the suppression of an element, without which the message cannot be understood properly, but which is left out by the speaker because it is obvious to the hearer. This category of deletions includes cases such as *zaydan* "Zayd [accusative]", said to someone who is distributing money. In that case the addressed person understands that the complete message is *'a'ṭi zaydan* "give Zayd". This is a common phenomenon in speech, which occurs in the *Qur'ân* as well, e.g., Q. 16/30 *wa-qîla lilladhîna ttaqaw mâdhâ 'anzala rabbukum qâlû khayran* "It was said to those who fear God: what did your Lord reveal? They said: something good", i.e., "He revealed something good". The reason such parts of the message may be left out is that the addressed person already knows the omitted parts, and it is more eloquent to be concise in your message.

The second category of suppressions in linguistic theory concerns cases where the element that is supposed to have been suppressed does not add anything to the message. In the sentence:

'a-zaydan ḍarabta-hu
[interrogative article]-zayd [accusative] you hit him
"Zayd, did you hit him?"

the fronted object *zaydan* has an accusative ending. The grammarians claim that at the underlying level there must be a suppressed verb:

**'a-ḍarabta zaydan ḍarabta-hu*
"*did you hit Zayd, did you hit him?"

They argue that the accusative of *zaydan* can be explained only in this way, since the verb in the surface sentence is already "occupied" with an object (*-hu* "him"), and the accusative still needs a governor. For Ibn Maḍâ' this is a good example of the unwarranted way in which grammarians posit underlying levels, which are completely unnecessary once one abandons the position that each accusative in the sentence must have a governor. In the example given here the speakers put *zaydan* in the accusative simply because that is the rule in their language, not because they are forced to do so by a hidden governor. Ibn Maḍâ' cleverly points out that when the verb has a prepositional object as in

mararta bi-zaydin
"you passed by Zayd [genitive]"

fronting the object also leads to an accusative:

'a-zaydan mararta bi-hi
"Zayd [accusative], did you pass by him?"

He challenges the grammarians to explain this accusative: they cannot posit a suppressed verb *mararta* in this case, since in that case *zayd* would have to be preceded by a preposition *bi-*, that would put it in the genitive.

Even worse are the speculations of the grammarians in instances of suppression of the third category, since these change the meaning of the sentence. In Arabic, for instance, the vocative particle *yâ* "O!" is sometimes followed by an accusative as in

yâ 'abda llâhi
"O servant [accusative] of God"

Many grammarians posit an underlying verb in this construction in order to explain the accusative, for instance:

**yâ 'unâdî 'abda llâhi*
"*O, I call the servant of God"

According to Ibn Maḍâ' not only is this insertion of a suppressed verb unnecessary, but it also changes the meaning of the surface sentence: instead of a vocative sentence it has become a propositional sentence, which may be true or false.

The third principle for which the grammarians incurred Ibn Maḍâ''s wrath is that of grammatical analogy (*qiyâs*). We have seen above that Ibn Ḥazm strongly objected to the use of analogical reasoning because it leads to conclusions that human beings are not allowed to draw. In linguistic theory the consequences are perhaps not as dire, but the underlying reasoning implies the same human arrogance vis-à-vis God's omnipotence. In az-Zajjâjî's *'Îḍâḥ* three different levels of explanations of grammatical phenomena were distinguished (cf. above, chapter 5): the primary causes, which are the rules of grammar as the native speaker knows them; the secondary causes, which operate with the principle of resemblance between elements of the system; finally, the highest level is constituted by the *'ilal naẓariyya wa-jadaliyya*, i.e., by causes that may be discovered through speculative thinking. By reasoning rationally the grammarian is able to find out why grammatical phenomena are as they are. From Ibn Maḍâ''s point of view such an approach to God's creation amounts to blasphemy. Just as human beings have to obey the rules God has laid down in the *Qur'ân* without asking why these rules are as they are, but simply accepting them as God's commands, the speaker has to accept the rules of grammar, without speculating about the reasons behind these rules:

> One of the things that have to be removed from grammar is the theory of the secondary and tertiary causes. An instance of this is when someone wants to know about the word *zaydun* in the expression *qâma zaydun* "Zayd stood up", why it is in the nominative. The answer is that this is because it is the agent, and agents are always in the nominative. He may then say: "And why is the agent in the nominative?" The correct answer is to say to him: "This is how the Arabs speak, as we know for sure by a continuous transmission from them. There is no difference between such an example and that of someone who knows that something is forbidden by a Qur'ânic text. There is no need to know the reason behind this in order to transfer it to similar cases, and to ask why it is forbidden. A legal expert does not have to answer such a question."
>
> (Ibn Maḍâ', *Radd*, p. 130)

This quotation shows the immediate theological relevance of Ibn Maḍâ''s arguments against linguistic theory. He is not against the study of language as such (as a matter of fact, he intersperses his arguments with quotations from grammatical writings in order to show that he knows what he is talking about), but he wishes to rid linguistic theory of harmful elements that are of no use for a better understanding of language and constitute a threat for the orthodox believer.

In his discussion of grammatical argumentation Ibn Maḍâ' accepts only the primary causes; from his perspective these are not causes at all, but facts which the native speaker may observe.

Once you have noticed that the agent of a sentence is put in the nominative, you know that you have to put every agent in the nominative because this is a rule of the Arabic language. No further explanation is needed beyond this observation, which is based on empirical fact. In one of the last sections of his treatise Ibn Maḍâ' gives examples of useless exercises to which grammarians subject their pupils precisely because they wish to train them in inventing ever more complicated explanations for linguistic phenomena. We know from other sources that grammarians sometimes invented hypothetical forms in order to interrogate their pupils about the phonological rules. In one extreme example a grammarian asks his students what the various derived forms would be for a verb consisting of three glottal stops. On one such exercise Ibn Maḍâ' comments:

> They apply all these theories to one single issue, so how will it be if it is applied to many more issues? Disagreement will reign, the tent-ropes of speech will be stretched to no advantage and for no sensible reason. People are unable to memorize the pure Arabic language, so how could they memorize such needless conjectures? What we musț remove from grammar is arguments about matters that do not help us to speak correctly.
>
> (*Radd*, p. 140)

In the Classical period of Islam not many grammarians showed any interest in the *Kitâb ar-radd*. This is hardly surprising, since accepting the point of departure of the treatise would have been tantamount to abandoning most of the things grammarians held dear. But when the manuscript was rediscovered in the twentieth century, it went through a curious renaissance. Its edition by the Egyptian scholar Shawqî Ḍayf in 1947 caused a minor shockwave. The book had been unknown for a long time in the Arab world and its publication came at the height of a debate about education in general and linguistic education in particular in the Arab world. Many people were dissatisfied with the way the Arabic language was taught in the schools: the curriculum consisted largely of the old grammatical texts, such as the *'Alfiyya* of Ibn Mâlik (d. 1273), an elementary treatise on grammar in one thousand verses, which served as an introduction to grammar. During the Classical period scores of commentaries had been written on this treatise, which was one of the most popular textbooks of grammar all over the Islamic world. As a result the material was obsolete and the standards of teaching were very low. As in most diglossic societies almost nobody was able to talk freely in the high variety of the language and schoolchildren generally hated the rigour of grammar training in Classical Arabic which was felt to be nothing more than learning by rote and lacking any practical use.

Some people attributed the lack of success of the school system to the language itself and demanded a simplification of the language (*tabsîṭ al-lugha*), for instance, by abolishing categories that were no longer current in Modern Standard Arabic but were still repeated by all grammar books, such as the category of the dual and various constructions with the verbal noun. Others felt that the grammatical system was at fault and called for a reform of grammar (*tabsîṭ an-naḥw*). To the proponents of a reform of the school system, and in particular the methods of language teaching, Ibn Maḍâ''s ideas were a gift from heaven, since they amply demonstrated what was wrong in grammatical education, even in modern times. As an example Ḍayf quotes the distinction between words with declensional endings and those with permanent endings. The two groups are identical in form; the only reason why the grammarians distinguish between them is that they are forced to work within the framework of government. It is much easier, he asserts, simply to concentrate on the form of the word without bothering with the identification of governors.

Significantly, such a plea for reform needed a medieval alibi to be acceptable. Shawqî Ḍayf constantly repeats that the reforms he has in mind ("a new approach to grammar") do not constitute a threat to the structure of Arabic and he quotes Ibn Maḍâ''s respect for the native speaker as the best possible approach to the study of Arabic. Grammarians, he says, have made things unnecessarily difficult in order to make themselves indispensable. In connection with this he quotes an anecdote about al-Jâḥiẓ who complained to the grammarian al-'Akhfash about the fact that for the average reader his books were only partly comprehensible; to which al-'Akhfash responded by pointing out that this was his way of earning money: if people always understood grammar books, they would not need a grammarian to explain them, and he would be out of a job. With this anecdote Shawqî Ḍayf no doubt hinted at the approach of some of his fellow professors at the University of Cairo and the Azhar University, who made a livelihood out of the instruction in a grammatical system they themselves had complicated needlessly. No doubt the rediscovery of Ibn Maḍâ''s book was a great help to linguists such as Shawqî Ḍayf, who could refer to this venerable example when people reproached them with their attack on the old-fashioned methods of grammar. In the book he published jointly with another proponent of the reform movement in Arabic linguistics, 'Ibrâhîm Muṣṭafâ, *Taḥrîr an-naḥw al-'arabî* "Liberating Arabic grammar" (Cairo, 1958), the new ideas were put into practice: among other things all references to government were abolished from grammar. This publication, which was sponsored by the Egyptian Ministry of Education, caused such an outcry that no attempts were made to introduce the new concepts in the curriculum.

Chapter 12

Ibn Khaldûn on the history of Arabic

Know that technically speaking language is the expression of an intention by a speaker. This expression is an articulatory activity and by necessity it becomes a habit in the active organ, which is the tongue. In each community this habit corresponds to their conventions. The habit which became current with the Bedouin is the most beautiful habit and the clearest in the explanation of their intentions. . . . They use this without having recourse to any theoretical knowledge: it is only a habit of their tongue, which they transmit from one another, just like to this day children take over our language.

But when Islam came, and they left the Ḥijâz in order to conquer the empires that were in the hands of the nations and states and when they mingled with the non-Arabs, their habit started to change as the result of the different ways of speaking they heard from those who attempted to learn Arabic, for hearing is the source of linguistic habits. Arabic became corrupted by the deviating forms, because they started to get used to what they heard. Their scholars began to fear lest the language become completely corrupted and people grow accustomed to it, so that the *Qur'ân* and the Tradition would become incomprehensible. Consequently, they deduced rules from their [sc., the Bedouin's] way of speaking that were universally valid, like the universals and rules [of philosophy]. They used these rules as a canon for the rest of speech, comparing like with like. They found, for instance, that the agent is put in the nominative, the object in the accusative and the topic in the nominative. They became aware that the meaning changes with the changes in the vowels of these words. As a technical term for this phenomenon they introduced the word *'i'râb* "declension" and for the element that is responsible for the change the word *'âmil* "governor", and so on. All these words became technical terms for them. They put them down in writing and made it into a special discipline, which they called *'ilm an-naḥw* "science of grammar".

(Ibn Khaldûn, *Muqaddima*, ed. Beirut, 1967, p. 546)

The great historian Ibn Khaldûn (d. 1356) is chiefly known for the introduction (*Muqaddima*) to his world history. This introduction (some six hundred pages in the printed edition) is an essay in social history, in which Ibn Khaldûn discusses the origin and development of civilization, taking as his point of departure the dichotomy of Bedouin and sedentary life. According to his view of history civilization develops from a nomadic way of life towards a sedentary one. One of the differences between the two lifestyles is the amount of free time that is left to the citizens of sedentary states. Since they do not have to spend all their time trying to find food and shelter, they develop new pastimes, among them the crafts and the sciences. Therefore, Ibn Khaldûn includes in his sketch of the development of civilization a discussion of the origin of the discipline of linguistics. He says that the Bedouin spoke Arabic according to their natural disposition and did not need grammarians to tell them how to speak. But in sedentary civilization things changed: decadence set in and the language threatened to become corrupted. In Ibn Khaldûn's account this process of corruption is connected with the "invention" of grammar.

Ibn Khaldûn's views on the historical development of the Arabic language are an important testimony of the way the Arabs themselves regarded the history of their language. In order to understand the development of this linguistic attitude in the Arab world, we need to take a look at the Arabs' ideas about the development of their own language. Their history of the language starts in the period before Islam. In this period, commonly called the *Jâhiliyya* "the period of ignorance", when the Bedouin had not yet received the message of Islam, all tribes spoke one language, *al-'Arabiyya*. In the grammarians' writings we find many references to linguistic differences between the tribes, the so-called *lughât*, but these differences did not destroy the essential unity of the language.

As an example of a much-quoted tribal difference we may mention the pronunciation of the glottal stop (*hamza*). According to the Arab grammarians the Eastern tribes in the Arabian peninsula pronounced this sound, whereas the Western tribes, including the tribe of the Prophet Muḥammad, Quraysh, ignored it. Thus, where the Bedouin in the East said *qâ'im* "standing", the Western Bedouin pronounced this word as *qâyim*. Similar differences are reported about other sounds and about lexical items, but the grammarians explicitly maintain that anything said by a "real" Arab counts as correct Arabic.

The consensus among Western Arabists about the linguistic situation on the Arabian peninsula before Islam differs rather sharply from this point of view. According to most Western Arabists there was a distinction in the *Jâhiliyya* between the everyday speech of the tribes and the language of poetry and the *Qur'ân*. The latter variety is usually called the pre-Islamic or poetico-Qur'ânic koine, whereas the colloquial varieties of the Arab tribes are referred to as the pre-Islamic dialects. In this view the dialects of the tribes had already started to lose some of the characteristics of the Classical Arabic language, in particular the use of case endings.

According to Ibn Khaldûn's account the pure language of the Bedouin remained unaltered until the Arabs came in contact with other peoples during the period of the conquests when they conquered a large area of the inhabited world, that stretched from Central Asia to Islamic Spain. In the interaction between the Arabs and the conquered peoples the Arabic language was used, but since these peoples had a lot of trouble in learning the complicated structure of the Arabic language they made mistakes and thus corrupted the Arabic language. The central theme in the account by Ibn Khaldûn is this corruption of the language. Translated into modern terminology his account would seem to describe a process in which imperfect learning of a second language takes place. In the context of the Arabic-speaking world this means that the colloquial forms of the language that originated during the period of the conquests were actually imperfect varieties of Arabic. Since the grammarians focused on the *'Arabiyya*, they found nothing of interest in such "corrupted" versions of their language. This opposition between grammatical Classical language and ungrammatical colloquial speech has remained intact in the Arab world to this day.

Western accounts of the history of Arabic sometimes acknowledge the existence of imperfect varieties in the contact between the conquered peoples and the Arab conquerors but they maintain that these disappeared when arabicization set in, and all inhabitants of the empire took over the native version of the language. In this view there was no break in the transmission from the pre-Islamic colloquial variety to the modern dialects, and any development there may have been was a gradual, natural process of language change. The Arabic dialects are then seen as the language of the conquerors, with the inhabitants of the conquered territories in the role of passive learners of the language of the new masters. Some attempts have been made to link regional differences between the dialects with substratal influence from the languages of the conquered territories (Coptic, Syriac, Berber, Persian, South Arabian) but according to recent research it is hard to demonstrate beyond any doubt traces of substratal influence.

It is important to realize that in their description of the language the grammarians left out a large part of linguistic reality. Actual speech differed considerably from the idealized construct that we find in the grammatical literature. In the fourth century of Islam (tenth century of the common era) nobody spoke the Classical language any more, and the mother tongue of all speakers was a colloquial variety that was largely identical with the modern dialects. The Arabic speech community was a diglossic one and, in order to understand the Arabs' attitude towards language, we need to go into the nature of diglossia in somewhat greater detail. In a diglossic society there are two varieties of the language, since the seminal article on this phenomenon by Ferguson (1959) usually referred to as the high and the low variety, each with its own domain. The high variety is used only for writing and formal speaking, for instance in lectures or public speeches, whereas the low variety is used for informal speech situations, between friends and relatives. A second difference is that the high variety is learnt at school as an artificial norm, whereas the low variety is the mother tongue of all speakers.

In such a situation it is not uncommon for the members of the community to believe that the high variety is the actual mother tongue of all speakers, and although in ordinary speech nobody uses the high variety, everyone still feels they are native speakers of that variety in spite of the fact that at most it is a variety learnt at school, and therefore hardly attainable for the entire community. Some people even go so far as to deny the existence of the low variety, and there is a general tendency to regard those forms that belong to the vernacular as nothing more than linguistic errors or, alternatively, as a form of the language used by women, children, and other non-intellectuals.

This situation is not unlike the one that obtained in Hellenistic Greece and in the Romance countries in the medieval period. In both cases the Classical language, Greek or Latin, was regarded as the real language, whereas the popular form of the language, in Greece the precursor of Modern Greek and in the Roman empire the Romance dialects, was not recognized and thus was irrelevant for linguistic purposes. When Latin grammarians discuss popular errors in speaking, they do not talk about the actual Romance dialects but about the mistakes people make when they try to use Classical Latin for which they lack the education. Historical linguists sometimes refer to this "faulty Latin" as Vulgar Latin, but in spite of its name it is certainly not identical with the actual colloquial language.

Similarly, in the Arab world there were many grammarians who wrote treatises about errors in speech (the so-called *laḥn al-'âmma* "mistakes of the common people"), but they are not concerned with a comparison between the low and the high variety, let alone with a description of colloquial speech. These treatises are concerned with those errors which semi-literate people make when they attempt to write in Classical Arabic. They are not our only source for "faulty" Arabic, since we know how uneducated people wrote from a wide range of documents, ranging from papyri to technical treatises about veterinary medicine. The term usually applied to this category of texts is Middle Arabic, just as Vulgar Latin is the name for the documents in "faulty" Classical Latin. The idiom of these texts is a mixture of Classical Arabic with vernacular elements and hypercorrections. It is not a language in its own right, and certainly not identical with the earliest Arabic vernaculars.

Without specifying details the Arab grammarians referred to the process that had led to the emergence of such "faults" in the Arabic language as a "corruption of the language" (*fasâd al-lugha*). They were certainly not unique in their application of such a concept to the development of language. Actually, it is a common notion in situations in which there is a standard language alongside vernaculars that are derived from it. For the medieval Western grammarians of the sixth/seventh centuries CE the Romance dialects were nothing but a corrupted form of Latin. Typically, grammarians in such a situation concentrate on various markers of the high variety that are absent in colloquial speech. Such markers may, for instance, be the declensional endings. Anyone unable to use the declensional endings correctly is then said to be illiterate. Obviously, from this point of view it would be downright ridiculous to assign to the colloquial varieties a grammatical structure of their own. Here the similarity between the two areas ends, since the political development in the Romance-speaking area diverged sharply from that in the Arab world. After the fall of the Roman empire the various areas in which Romance dialects were spoken became independent, and in the newly established nations the colloquial variety served as one of the binding factors. This facilitated the acceptance of the colloquial varieties, such as French and Italian, as languages in their own right. The Latin language remained in force, however, for a long time as the language of scholarship and religion.

In the Arabic-speaking world no such development took place. Although several areas gained independence at a rather early date, for instance the caliphate of Cordova and several petty kingdoms in North Africa and Central Asia, the cultural and intellectual ties, and in particular the religious ties, with the core areas of the Arabo-Islamic world remained intact. All inhabitants of the various Islamic empires regarded themselves as belonging to one community, that of Islam, of which Arabic, i.e., the Classical Arabic language of the *Qur'ân*, was the most powerful symbol. This explains why the colloquial language continued to be regarded as a debased form of the Classical language, a view that even nowadays is still current. One quite often hears Arab intellectuals assert that the colloquial language as such does not exist. They explain away the very obvious differences between the Classical Arabic language and the current colloquial variety as mistakes that are to be avoided. Traditional Islamic universities shun the study of dialects, which is regarded as detrimental to Arab unity and sometimes even as an attempt on the part of the colonial powers to break up this unity and set up the Arab countries one against the other.

This neglect of the dialects is closely linked with the absence of the concept of "diachrony" in the Arabic linguistic tradition. We have seen above (chapter 8) that in Arabic linguistics the notion of "diachrony" was largely absent. In the early period of Arabic grammar the grammarians, many of whom were non-Arabs themselves, could still rely on their Bedouin informants for information about the Classical language, i.e., the language of poetry and the

Qur'ân. Very soon, however, and certainly within the first centuries of the Islamic era, they were forced to admit that most Bedouin tribes had been affected by sedentary speech. From now on the language of the Bedouin (*kalâm al-'Arab*) became an idealized construct. The grammarians' analysis of the language was therefore by necessity based on sources that, once they had been selected, were fixed for all eternity, viz. the pre-Islamic poems and the text of the *Qur'ân*. These sources continued to be legitimized by reference to Bedouin speech, even when the pure Arabic-speaking Bedouin were no longer around. In the view of the grammarians, however, authenticity of the sources could never become an issue: the native speakers of Arabic had had a perfect knowledge of their own language, and the reference to these idealized speakers sufficed for the grammarians' purposes. At the same time, the immutable nature of the sources and the absence of any monitoring device made it impossible to accept any development in the language.

The second noteworthy element in Ibn Khaldûn's account concerns the link he sees between the corruption of the language and the origin of the discipline of linguistics. In Chapter 1 we have seen that in the Arab world exegetical comments constituted the earliest manifestation of the study of language. Scholars set out to explain the text of the Holy Book and its sometimes obsolete vocabulary. As we have seen in the introduction the indigenous accounts of the origin of the grammatical tradition, on the other hand, all stress the connection with the frequency of speech errors made by non-Arab converts in early Islam. The most popular account is that about 'Abû l-'Aswad ad-Du'alî (d. 688), which we have quoted above (p. 3). If we combine the story about ' Abû l-'Aswad with the data in Ibn Khaldûn and with the many anecdotes about grammatical mistakes in the mouths of recent converts to Islam in the first century of the Islamic era, it becomes clear that in early Islamic society some people were acutely concerned about the correctness of speech, and as a result the protection of the language against corruption became a serious issue. But very soon the focus of linguistic study shifted from a struggle against illiteracy towards an exclusive interest in the structure of the Arabic language, with no attention for any deviations. Not surprisingly, in the exegetical treatises there is no mention at all of any mistakes, since the commentators restricted themselves to commenting on the text of the Holy Book and did not deal with the structure of the language as such. When the first grammatical treatises were written the situation of diglossia in the speech community had already crystallized and the colloquial variety was no longer regarded as a relevant factor. Thanks to the efforts of people like 'Abû l-'Aswad, though not necessarily by him personally, a school system had been established, in which the sons of the nobility were educated. The ordinary Muslims listened to the recitation of the text of the *Qur'ân*, but were not expected to speak the Classical language. As soon as there was a school system, this took care of the dangers that threatened the Arabic language and ensured that the important people, the elite, received a training in the high variety, which became known as "the correct language" (*al-lugha al-fuṣḥâ*).

When the uninterrupted transmission of the Classical language had been safeguarded, references to the changes in the language became exceedingly rare. Not only did grammarians hasten to warn their readers for any change in the fixed norms of the language, they even explicitly rejected any diachronic interpretation of the underlying levels in speech that were adduced by them in their linguistic reasoning, for instance in reference to phonological cycles. We have seen above (chapter 5) that linguistic explanations could be given at various levels. Az-Zajjâjî defined the highest level of explanation as the one in which external causes are brought in to legitimize the grammarians' arguments. In the case of *qawama* the rule is applied because of an external principle that is formulated by the grammarians in terms of a tendency on the part of the speakers to avoid combining heavy sounds: the combination of the glide *w* with two vowels is too heavy for the speakers, which is why they change this combination into *â*. Such an explanation could, of course, easily be interpreted in a diachronic fashion: in the course of time speakers applied certain euphonic principles to the language and changed it. But Ibn Jinnî (d. 1002) explains that when the grammarians say that the verbal form *qâma* derives from *qawama* this does not mean that at any time people used the form *qawama*: the grammarian does not describe a historical process but a synchronic rule that takes place between underlying phonological structures and the surface realization.

> The underlying form of *qâma* "stood up" is *qawama*. . . . This has led some people to believe that such forms, in which the underlying level is not identical with the surface form, at one

> time were current, in the sense that people once used to say instead of *qâma zaydun: qawama zaydun*. . . . This is not the case, on the contrary: these words have always had the form that you can see and hear now.
>
> (Ibn Jinnî, *Khaṣâ'iṣ*, ed. by Muḥammad 'Alî an-Najjâr, 3 vols, Cairo, 1952–6, I, p. 257)

Other grammarians, too, explicitly deny that any account they give of the hierarchical relations between the elements of the language could be interpreted diachronically. Az-Zajjâjî, for instance, explains that nouns are prior to verbs, but he adds:

> Analogous to this, we also say that nouns come before verbs, because verbs are the events of the noun. But it has never been true that for some time there was only speech with nouns, and only afterwards people started to use verbs in their speech as well. On the contrary, people always used the two of them together, and each one of them has its own rights and its own position.
>
> (az-Zajjâjî, *'Îḍâḥ*, ed. by Mâzin al-Mubârak, Cairo, 1959, p. 68)

This emphasis on the ahistorical character of the phonological rules and the relations between the categories of the language serves, of course, to underline the permanence and continuity of the Arabic language. In Western linguistics a historical perspective has been present since the nineteenth century with its emphasis on the historical-comparative nature of linguistics, but even long before that the awareness of the relationship between Latin and the vernacular languages quite naturally led to a view of language growth and language development in which linguistic change was regarded as a natural phenomenon.

In the Arabic-speaking community nobody could fail to be aware of the difference between actual speech and the language of the *Qur'ân* or the presumed language of the Bedouin. Still, this did not lead to a developmental view of the relationship between both. Language, Ibn Khaldûn says, is a habit that is transmitted from generation to generation without any change. Since the tranmission has been uninterrupted from the time of the *Jâhiliyya* to his own time, and since the native speakers can never be at fault, the correctness of the language is guaranteed and there is no room for any change. As far as the grammarians are concerned, their duty is to explain the rules of this language, rather than impose grammatical laws. After all, they operated on the assumption that there were native speakers, who knew perfectly well how to speak Arabic and did not need any grammarian to tell them what was linguistically correct or incorrect.

Ibn Khaldûn's description of the development of grammar focuses on the use of grammar for establishing linguistic norms and standards, and this may seem to contradict the above remarks about the non-normative character of grammar. According to his account grammar was "invented" as a set of rules to fight incorrect language. We must keep in mind, however, that Ibn Khaldûn was not a grammarian and that he was much more interested in the general development of culture than in the methodological presuppositions of the linguists. For him it must have been apparent that the grammarians' a-normative attitude could not apply to the whole of society, but only to the idealized construct of the native speaker. He believed that at all levels of culture there had been a general deterioration, and language formed no exception to this rule. Therefore, he felt that the individual native speaker could not be trusted, hence it was safer to use the testimony of the texts as final authority. Besides, in his time, and particularly in his part of the world, North Africa, there were hardly any Bedouin tribes that by any standard could be regarded as native speakers of the Classical language. There may therefore very well have been a normative streak in the kind of grammar that was practised in this region. One could even speculate that the discrepancy between standard language and colloquial speech was even more acute in the Maghrebine area of the Arabic-speaking world with its highly idiosyncratic dialects.

Ibn Khaldûn's attitude towards the development of language is also visible in his remarks about linguistic variation. In the *Muqaddima* he notes that there are regional variations in the vocabulary. People from different regions use different words to indicate even quite familiar objects in daily life, such as bread or kitchen utensils. This is an observation by a non-linguist, who is simply interested in the variety of human culture. Similar observations are made by Arab geographers, who brought back from their travels descriptions of the different customs, including the linguistic ones, among the peoples of the Islamic empire. The grammarians do not offer any explanation for this phenomenon: what is more, most of them do not even mention it. One would expect the lexicographers to devote at least some attention to regional variants, but they, too, cling to the accepted vocabulary that is found in their sources. It is true that in the pre-Islamic period variants are reported from the Bedouin tribes, but these variants had become accepted as different manifestations of the *'Arabiyya* and were, so to speak, canonized as part of the closed corpus of the language. The grammarians merely note that the Arab tribes who roamed the desert in the Arabian peninsula used different forms and different words. Since all Bedouin are to be regarded as native speakers, all variants are in principle acceptable, even though they are no longer productive. That is to say, it is not allowed to use them in our own speech or base our linguistic explanations upon them. In other words, variation had been there from the beginning and had to be accepted as part of the genius of the Arabic language, just as this language contains a large number of synonyms and homonyms. Contemporary regional variation in the lexicon, on the other hand, was not regarded as a relevant problem the grammarians had to explain.

In some cases the accepted language contained mixed variants from different pre-Islamic dialects, a phenomenon called by the grammarians *tadâkhul al-lughât* "the interpenetration of dialectal forms". As an example we may quote the case of the verb *ḥasiba* whose imperfect is irregular: instead of the expected *yaḥsabu* for all verbs with vowels *a-i-a*, it is *yaḥsibu*. One would expect such a phenomenon to provoke a diachronic explanation: one tribe used the verb *ḥasiba/yaḥsabu*, another tribe had the forms *ḥasaba/yaḥsibu*, and afterwards people started to use the perfect form of the one, and the imperfect form of the other tribe. Yet this kind of explanation, which we would be tempted to call diachronic, was a synchronic matter for the grammarians: all variants belong to the general vocabulary of the *'Arabiyya*, from which the speakers are free to select items in their production of speech. In the case quoted here they conventionally choose the incongruent forms.

Another seemingly diachronic development in the language is connected with the influence of changing circumstances on the vocabulary. The most famous example is, of course, that of the advent of Islam. With the message of the new religion a host of new notions entered pre-Islamic society. The Bedouin started to use existing words in a new, religious sense. As an example we may quote the word *'islâm* itself, which means "surrender", but in the new context came to denote the surrender to God and, hence, the new religion. In a sense, the new meaning had already been latent in the word and one could say that there was no real change even in this case. After all, creativity was always characteristic of the truly eloquent speakers of Arabic, the Bedouin. Unlike al-Fârâbî (cf. above, chapter 6) Ibn Khaldûn attributes the new meanings of the religious vocabulary to internal developments in Arabic.

A final word must be said in this chapter about the relationship between Arabic and other languages in the entirely a-diachronic framework of the Arab grammarians. In chapter 8 we have seen that Islamic society as a whole tended to regard language as something that had been given or, at the very least, inspired by God, who had chosen the Arabic language for His revelation and thereby made clear that the Arabic language was superior to all other languages. The Arab grammarians knew, of course, that some languages resemble each other more than others, but since they were not interested in any development, the relationship between languages was seen as a something static. Unlike the Hebrew grammarians (cf. chapter 13) they were not interested in finding out the reasons for this relationship. In the standard view of the distribution of humankind over the world, people after the Flood had split into various groups and each of these groups had possessed its own language, its own habit as Ibn Khaldûn calls it. Quite naturally, the more directly related these groups are, the more related their languages. The attempts of the logicians to study different languages, especially Greek and Syriac, as realizations of a universal structure had failed (cf. above, chapter 4); as a result we hardly find any reference to other languages in the treatises of the grammarians. There is one important exception, that of 'Abû Ḥayyân (d. 1344). As we shall see in chapter 13, he broke away from this convention and did study the structure of other languages, such as Turkic, Berber, Ethiopian, and Mongolian, albeit with the help of the model of Arabic grammar. But 'Abû Ḥayyân was an exception: for most grammarians the other languages simply did not exist.

Ibn Khaldûn was not a grammarian, but precisely because of his interest in the growth of human civilization and culture he could take an open view of the phenomenon of language and study its role in society. Unlike the professional grammarians he took into account the actual linguistic situation and, although he did not break away completely from the fiction about the existence of only one ideal language, he showed himself to be well aware of the tension between the two varieties of the language, the Classical language and the colloquial variety.

Chapter 13

The Arabic model and other languages

The description of Turkic and Hebrew

The verb [in Turkic] is divided into three parts: imperative, past, and resembling. The imperative is the root; the past verb, the resembling verb, the active participle, the passive participle, the verbal noun, the noun of place, the noun of manner, and the noun of instrument are secondary forms, derived from the imperative.

Imperatives are addressed either to a third person or a second person or a first person. If the imperative is addressed to a third person, it must have one of the consonants of the imperative, e.g. *sanjar kalsun*, i.e., "let Sanjar come!", or in the third person plural *sanjar kalsunlâr*, i.e., "let them come!". *Sug* is the particle of the imperative that is equivalent to the particle *li-* in Arabic.

If the imperative is addressed to a second person, it is either singular or non-singular. If it is singular, the most correct form is the imperative without any addition, but it is possible to add at the end *ghil* or *gil* with a Bedouin *g*. If the word is velarized it is *ghil*; if it is palatalized *gil*. The source of velarization and palatalization is the actual usage (this is something we have already dealt with in the Book of the Verbs that we have compiled about this language). If the imperative has a vowel *u* in the beginning, there is an *u* in the ending, unless it contains a vowel *a*. For instance, *ṭurghul*, *kulgul*, *kustargil*, *'urghul*. If it has a vowel *a* or *i* in the beginning, there is an *i* in the ending, unless it contains a vowel *u*. For instance, *barghil*, *'ishtgil*, *takturghil*. If [the imperative of the second person] is singular, you add one *n* and say *ṭurun*; if you wish, you may add a *z*, which indicates respect, and say *ṭurunuz*. This *z* is what remains of *siz*; you may also add *siz*, saying *ṭurunsiz*, which is used for emphasis.

If the imperative is addressed to a first person, it is either singular or non-singular. If it is singular, you say *barġâyim* and *kalkâyim*, i.e., "let me go!", "let me come!"; if it is not singular you say *barġâlim* and *kalkâlim*, i.e., "let us go!", "let us come!". The imperative of the first person is rarely used in Arabic, but in this language it is very frequent.

The characteristics and features of the past and the resembling verb have already been discussed in the chapter about morphology. The consonant before the *r*, that is the marker of the resembling verb is either with or without a vowel. If it has a vowel, you add the *r* without change; if it is without a vowel, you provide it with *u* or *a*, according to what you hear. We have clarified this in the Book of the Verbs. This applies to those verbs that do not end in *lâ*, which is used for the causative. *Lâ* changes its *'alif* into *yu*, and you say *suzlâyuz* and *bashlâyuz*. It may also be deleted, so that you say *suzlâz* and *bashlâz*. Underlyingly it is a *y*.

The predicative future verb, if it is velarized, has as particle *ghâ*, e.g., *ṭurghâ*, i.e. "he will stand up"; if it is palatalized, its particle is *kâ*, e.g., *kalkâ*, i.e., "he will come". We shall come to talk about positive and negative and interrogative and prohibitive verbs in the chapter on the verb and the participle, if God Almighty permits.

('Abû Ḥayyân, *Kitâb al-'idrâk li-lisân al-'Atrâk*, ed. by Ahmet Caferoğlu, Istanbul, 1931, pp. 120–1)

The extract from the description of Turkic translated here is one of the very few examples of a description of a foreign language in Arabic grammatical literature. In the preceding chapters we have repeatedly stressed the fact that the Arabic grammarians were interested solely in the analysis of their own language. Except for the Greek language in the writings of the philosophers (cf. above, chapter 6) other languages than Arabic, if they are mentioned at all, are usually viewed in a negative light. The linguistic pride and chauvinism of the Arabs goes back to pre-Islamic roots, but was reinforced by the *Qur'ân*, which the Muslims regarded as a miracle of verbal superiority and excellence. The admiration of the Arabic language was taken over by all conquered peoples. Even when Ottoman Turkish replaced Arabic in the role of administrative language in the Seljuk and later in the Ottoman empire, and even when Persian became the new cultural language of the Islamic East, Arabic remained the language of religion, and all languages in the sphere of influence of Islam borrowed extensively from it.

Persian became a language with its own tradition of literature and scholarship; it was the language in which Islam was exported to most countries in the East, such as India and Malaysia. But if we look at the technical terms for grammatical categories in Modern Persian, we find that most of them are Arabic loans. This means that probably Arabic was the medium through which the Persians started to describe their own language. Unfortunately, the Persian linguistic tradition is largely unexplored territory. Before Islam there must have been some kind of lexicographical tradition about which nothing much is known. After Islam there were Persian treatises on literary theory, as well as a large body of literature on philosophical topics, but grammatical writings on the Persian language have not been preserved.

We are somewhat better informed about the grammatical literature on Turkic. The quotation at the beginning of this chapter was taken from the work of an Arabic grammarian, who gave a description of Turkic according to the model of the Arabic linguistic tradition. His name was 'Abû Ḥayyân al-Gharnâṭî; he was born in 1256 in Granada and died in 1345 in Cairo. 'Abû Ḥayyân was a grammarian of note with famous works such as a commentary on the *'Alfiyya* of Ibn Mâlik. His commentary, entitled *Manhaj as-sâlik ilâ 'Alfiyyat Ibn Mâlik* "The way of the traveller to the *'Alfiyya* of Ibn Mâlik" became one of the most popular commentaries on this treatise. He wrote several books on grammatical theory and a large Qur'ânic commentary, entitled *al-Baḥr al-muḥîṭ* "The all-embracing ocean".

For the general history of linguistics 'Abû Ḥayyân's fame rests mainly in the fact that unlike all of his colleagues he was interested in other languages than Arabic alone and wrote a series of books on them. Among his works were descriptions of Ethiopian, Mongolian, and Turkic. Only some of his treatises on Turkic have been preserved, among them the famous *Kitâb al-'idrâk li-lisân al-'Atrâk* "The book of understanding the language of the Turks". This book, consisting of a grammar and a dictionary, constitutes one of the best historical sources for the Turkic language.

The Turkic language described by 'Abû Ḥayyân was a recent

arrival in the Islamic world. From the ninth century onwards Turkic-speaking slaves had been imported by the Islamic caliphs from Central Asia to serve in their personal guard. In the thirteenth century a slave dynasty of Turkic soldiers settled in Egypt under the name of Mamluks. They reigned there for about three hundred years, constituting a Turkic-speaking elite, with scant knowledge of Arabic. During their reign 'Abû Ḥayyân arrived in Egypt, where he worked as a teacher of grammar, and it is their variety of Turkic that he describes as the *lugha turkiyya*, the model of Turkic that was regarded by the native speakers as the best linguistic model. Other varieties he mentions, such as Qipchaq and Turcomanian, are presented as less prestigious variants of Turkic. The term *lugha turkiyya* parallels exactly the Arabic custom of speaking about the *lugha 'arabiyya*, an ideal standard of the language. We do not know how the Mamluk speakers themselves evaluated the varieties of speech they knew. But apparently, 'Abû Ḥayyân adapted his own concept of a standard language to the concept of a standard Turkic language, with varieties that were designated as less eloquent.

Since 'Abû Ḥayyân knew no other linguistic model than that of the Arabic grammarians, he never felt the need to question the validity of this model for all other languages. This does not mean that he did not recognize differences between languages. In the quotation above he clearly describes some phenomena that are different in Turkic, and his book abounds with remarks about the differences between Turkic and Arabic. He mentions these differences without any evaluative remarks and does not give the impression that he regarded Turkic as a barbaric language. Because of his adherence to the Arabic model 'Abû Ḥayyân sometimes had to adapt Arabic grammatical terminology to the structure of Turkic. One of the most remarkable phonological phenomena in the Turkic languages is that of vowel harmony. It consists in a rule specifying that all vowels in the word are either front (*i, ü, e, ö*) or back (*ı, u, a, o*). For an Arabic grammarian it was difficult to give general rules for this phenomenon. In the first place, Arabic grammar had only three vowels, *a*, *i*, and *u*. In the second place, the vowels of Turkic are different in number and quality from the Arabic inventory.

The solution chosen by 'Abû Ḥayyân took advantage of the fact that the vowels of Turkic are similar in phonetic realization to the allophones of Arabic vowels. In Arabic /a/, for instance, is realized as a fronted vowel tending towards [e] in the neighbourhood of palatalized, and as a backed vowel tending towards [o] in the neighbourhood of velarized consonants. In the Arabic tradition these features are seen as the result of the quality of the adjacent consonant. In this way the Arabic grammarian could accommodate the Turkic system by assigning the front or back quality of the vowel to the adjacent consonant. This solution was not perfect: in the first place, the rounded vowels of Turkic (/ü/, /ö/) could not be represented in this way; and in the second place, not all Arabic consonants have the opposition velarized/palatalized. Thc latter problem could be solved by using the term *mufakhkham* "emphatic, velarized". Likewise, consonants of Turkic that were unknown in Arabic could sometimes be described by the terms that Arabic grammarians used for allophonic variants or dialectal variants. In the quotation above the consonant g is called the Bedouin *k*, since in Bedouin dialects of Arabic the consonant /q/ is realized as [g]. Another consonant of Turkic, /ch/, is called *al-jîm al-mashûba bi-sh-shîn* "the *j* that is mixed with the *sh*", i.e., /j/ with the feature "voiceless" of /sh/.

The phonological structure of Turkic words is analysed by 'Abû Ḥayyân with the same formalism as Arabic words. We have seen above (chapter 2) that at a very early period Arabic grammarians introduced the device of the consonants *f-'-l* to represent the structure of Arabic words. Since in Arabic many words consist of three radicals, this device works well in that language. If words contain more than three radicals additional *ls* are used, e.g., *tarjama* has the pattern *fa'lala*, because all four consonants are radicals (cf. for instance *takattaba* which is *tafa''ala*, because the *t* is not a radical but an auxiliary consonant). In the first chapter of his *'Idrâk* 'Abû Ḥayyân deals with the *taṣrîf*, i.e., the morphology of the Turkic language; according to him Turkic words have either two, three, four, or five radicals, and he enumerates all the different patterns in which these may occur, e.g., with the five-radical words he has *fa'illal*, like *'aghinghaj*, *fa'lalil*, like *qaṣṭaliq*, *fu'lulul*, like *mushtuluq*, etc. For an Arabic speaker this was probably the only way to familiarize oneself with the shapes of Turkic words, which otherwise would not be transparent.

When he comes to words with more than five radicals, such as *salkinjak* of the pattern *fa'lillal*, 'Abû Ḥayyân says that such words need to be analysed further since they are often compounds from simpler words. *Qilquyruq*, for instance, does not have the pattern *fi'lullul* because it is derived from *qil* "hair" and *quyruq* "tail". In this way he shows that he is interested in the etymology of words, but on an Arabic basis. Just as the Arabic grammarians regard the extraction of the radicals and the auxiliary consonants of a word as the main task of morphology, 'Abû Ḥayyân tries to determine what the original Turkic words are. In the same way he finds a method of identifying loanwords in Turkic by considering their consonants: *firishtilâr*, for instance, cannot be Turkic because it contains the consonant /f/, which does not exist in Turkic.

The structure of Turkic differs considerably from that of Arabic, and it is instructive to see how 'Abû Ḥayyân handled these differences. A good example is that of the verb *'a'ṭâ* "to give" in Arabic, which is construed with two direct objects, e.g., *'a'ṭaytu zayd-an kitâb-an* "I gave Zayd a book". The equivalent verb in Turkic has only one direct object, marked by the accusative suffix, whereas the recipient is marked by what is called in Western grammars of Turkic the dative suffix.

> The direct object is either overt or covert. When it is overt, you say for instance for *'akaltu s-samaka* "I ate the fish" *bâliq-ni yadum*: *-ni* is the marker for the accusative. This is the pure direct object, but verbs that are doubly transitive in Arabic, are transitive with one object only, marked with *-ni*, in this language. The other object is marked with *-gha* and *-ka*. You say with the meaning of *'a'ṭaytu sanjara thawban* "I gave Sanjar a cloak" *sanjar-gha ṭu-ni yardum*. The first word, which is the first object in Arabic, receives *-gha*, and the second, which is the second object in Arabic, receives *-ni*, in accordance with the underlying structure. It is not allowed to switch these suffixes.
>
> ('Abû Ḥayyân, *'Idrâk* p. 139.2–7)

In this example 'Abû Ḥayyân demonstrates his awareness of the difference between the two languages. The point is what constituted his reference: did he regard Turkic as a translation of Arabic, or did he regard both languages as the translation of an underlying structure that could have different realizations in the two languages? The expression *'alâ l-'aṣl* "in accordance with the principle, the underlying form" seems to suggest that he followed the latter approach. Another example is that of the possessive construction in Turkic, which differs completely from that of Arabic. In Arabic the possessive relationship is expressed by the annexion of a genitive noun, as in:

mamlûk-u zayd-in
"slave of-Zayd" [genitive]

In the analysis of the early Arabic grammarians the second noun is regarded as being governed by the first, but later grammarians objected to this analysis: in their view, nouns are too weak to govern, so that they proposed a different analysis at the underlying level:

mamlûk-u li-zayd-in
"slave for-Zayd" [genitive]

In this analysis the genitive ending of *zayd-in* is said to be the effect of the governance of the particle *li-*. It is this interpretation which 'Abû Ḥayyân uses in his analysis of the Turkic possessive construction, which may occur in two forms:

sanjar qul-i
"Sanjar slave-his"

or

sanjar-nin qul-i
"Sanjar-of slave-his"

The ending *-nin*, which is called in Western grammars of Turkic a genitive ending, is categorized by 'Abû Ḥayyân as a particle, equivalent to the Arabic particle *li-* "for"; the entire clause is paraphrased by him as:

li-sanjar mamlûku-hu
"to-Sanjar slave-his"

He could not analyse *-nin* as a case ending, since there was no governor to which it could be assigned. In the possessive construction without the particle he correctly identifies the ending *-i* in the second noun as the possessive pronoun "his". In his analysis he clearly starts from a semantic level, on which a certain meaning is formed, which is then expressed in the two languages in different ways. The semantic level is identical with the underlying level that had been reconstructed for the Arabic expression.

Arabic remained the language in which the Turkic language was described. When the Seljuk Turks occupied Anatolia, they adopted Persian as their cultural language, but retained Arabic as their scholarly and religious language. The same situation obtained in the Ottoman empire, which was founded after the conquest of Constantinople by the Seljuk Turks. For the grammatical description of their own language the Ottoman scholars used the Arabic system, and even nowadays most grammatical terms in Turkish are Arabic loanwords.

In the history of Arabic linguistics 'Abû Ḥayyân's work remained an exception. The main reason why grammarians ignored other languages was the prestige of the Arabic language, which precluded any interest in other languages. In a few cases, however, speakers of other languages borrowed the grammatical model of Arabic linguistics in order to describe their own language, much like the Georgians and the Armenians translated the Greek *Téchnè* of Dionysius Thrax for the description of the grammatical structure of their own languages, Georgian and Armenian. Another language into which the Greek *Téchnê* was translated is Syriac; the earliest Syriac grammatical treatises were based on this Greek model. But when the Syriac tradition was integrated in the Islamic world, the grammarians took over the Arabic model and started to use a terminology that had been translated from Arabic.

In Egypt a number of grammars were written of the Coptic language with the help of the Arabic model. Before Islam there had not been any indigenous grammatical description. After the Arab conquests the language itself soon became a dead language, which survived only as a religious language in the Coptic Christian church. In the thirteenth/fourteenth centuries some Coptic scholars felt that something must be done to help their language survive, and wrote a series of works in Arabic written on the structure of Coptic. Somewhat later this system was introduced in Ethiopia, where it served to start an indigenous linguistic tradition.

A special case is that of the Jewish community in the Islamic empire. Like all religious minorities in the Islamic empire the Jews were granted the status of *dhimmî's*, i.e., protected minorities that paid a special tax in order to guarantee them their religious freedom. Throughout the reign of the various caliphal dynasties they were treated well, and there were hardly any pogroms of the type that was current in medieval Europe. Like most Jewish communities all over the world, the Jews in the Islamic empire soon accommodated to the language of the realm and took over the Arabic language: they were among the first people in the conquered territories who started to speak urban varieties of Arabic and they have continued to do so up till the modern age. Jewish dialects of Arabic in Tunis, Algiers, Yemen and Baghdad belong to the oldest varieties of urban Arabic.

The shift to Arabic was complete, since the Jews not only talked in Arabic but also took over the language for literary purposes. Hebrew was preserved and studied by them only as a dead language of the Holy Book, and Aramaic, the language of some of the later portions of the Bible and the current colloquial language of the Jews at the beginning of the common era, remained in use as a colloquial language until the times of the Islamic conquests and as the language of the commentaries on the Hebrew text after that. Since they were less constrained than their Muslim fellow citizens by the norms of the Classical language, their language, like that of the Arab Christians, exhibits a number of features that may be attributed to the influence of the spoken language. Sometimes the name Judaeo-Arabic is used for this variety of the language.

Judaeo-Arabic was used for almost everything by Jewish authors: private letters, contracts, belletristic works, poetry. In the context of our subject it is important to note that it was used even for commentaries on the Jewish Bible and for descriptions of the Hebrew language. Since Hebrew was a learned language, they needed a metalanguage in which to discuss its structure, and Arabic was the perfect choice for this function. Like all intellectuals in the Islamic empire Hebrew linguists and exegetes received a thorough training in Arabic grammatical methods, which provided them with an instrument to study their "own" language.

This is not to say that the Jewish exegetes did not have exegetical methods of their own. It is very well possible that the sophisticated methods which they had developed for Biblical exegesis were instrumental in developing Islamic exegesis. It is certainly probable that for the narrative exegesis of the *Qur'ân* Jewish sources were used (cf. above, chapter 1, p. 14). But the Jewish grammarians do not seem to have possessed a technical grammatical apparatus, since they took over the Arabic linguistic tradition wholesale. In fact, many of the learned works about the Hebrew language were first written in Arabic and then translated into Hebrew.

In one respect the Hebrew grammarians were in a different situation from their Muslim colleagues: for them Arabic served as the metalanguage for the description of Hebrew and Aramaic, whereas the Arabic grammarians had to use Arabic simultaneously as metalanguage and object language. No doubt this difference explains the fact that the Hebrew grammarians were much more sensitive than the Arabic grammarians to differences and resemblances between languages. Because of the relative transparency of the root structure of the Semitic languages the Arabic grammarians must have been aware of the relationship between the languages. Yet the Arabic grammarians never comment on this remarkable phenomenon, although Arabic historians and geographers sometimes remark on the genealogical relationship of the peoples involved. Both Islamic and Judaic traditions knew the story about Shem as the ancestor of the languages currently spoken in the Middle East. The Arab nation was supposed to derive from Abraham's son through Hagar, Ishmael, which made them relatives to the Hebrews as descendants of his son through Sarah, Isaac.

The Andalusian theologian Ibn Ḥazm (cf. above, chapter 11), who did not express a special predilection for any language, not even Arabic, because there was no evidence that God had selected any language, took the relationship between Arabic, Hebrew, and Aramaic for granted and attempted to explain the difference between them as follows:

> What we have found and learned for a fact is that Syriac, Hebrew, and Arabic, the language of Muḍar and Rabî'a . . . , are one language, which changed with the region in which their speakers settled. There occurred in them the same change that is manifested when an Andalusian hears the accent of someone from Kairouan, or when someone from Kairouan hears the accent of an Andalusian, or when someone from Khurasan hears their accent.
>
> (Ibn Ḥazm, *al-'Iḥkâm fî 'uṣûl al-'aḥkâm*, ed. by 'Aḥmad Shâkir, Cairo, n.d., I, p. 31)

This awareness of a special relationship between the three Semitic languages notwithstanding, explicit references to parallel phenomena in the three languages remained almost entirely limited to the pointing out of common lexical stock. Sometimes such words were regarded as loanwords, but the reluctance on the part of some Islamic authors to recognize the existence of loanwords in the *Qur'ân* (cf. above, chapter 1) sometimes made them assign such alleged loanwords to the category of common vocabulary between the three languages, which after all belonged to speakers that had once belonged to one people, before the dispersion of the sons of Noah. In his commentary on the *Qur'ân* aṭ-Ṭabarî states, for instance, that the *Qur'ân* contains words from every language that has words in common with Arabic. When the shape of these words differs in these languages, the Arabic grammarians attribute this to similar processes as those that operate between the pre-Islamic dialects.

The Hebrew grammarians, on the other hand, did occupy themselves with a systematic comparison of the two or, if one counts Aramaic, the three languages. Such a comparison, however, was not a neutral and commonplace enterprise. From the writings of the Hebrew grammarians we can deduce that there was quite some opposition to those who sought proof from the language of the Muslims in order to elucidate difficult points in the language of the Hebrew Bible. Almost all Hebrew grammarians who use arguments taken from Arabic feel the need to defend themselves against such criticism by their fellow Jews. Ibn Janâḥ (d. 1050), for instance, refers to some of his contemporaries, whom he accuses of having weak knowledge and little understanding, and who under the pretext of religion object to the use of Arabic in writings on Hebrew grammar.

The most common argument for the use of Arabic and Aramaic was the assistance these two languages could lend in the study of Hebrew. All three of them derived from the same stock, but only Aramaic and Arabic remained in use as spoken languages, while the active knowledge of Hebrew was for the most part lost. Thus, a comparison with the continuing tradition of Arabic and Aramaic could help in explaining obscure expressions in Hebrew that nobody understood any more. For most grammarians, however, these comparisons took place only on the level of the comparison of lexical material, and there were very few grammarians who were able to formulate somewhat more general rules of correlation between Hebrew and Arabic. In the *Risâla* by Ibn Quraysh (tenth century) there are some observations concerning this relationship: he remarks on the systematic correspondence between some of the Hebrew and Arabic phonemes, the identical function of the prepositions *bi-* and *li-* in both languages, and the identical suffixes and prefixes in the verbal conjugation.

The problem for the Hebrew grammarians in their efforts at a systematic comparison resided partly in the morphological structure of the language. Before they could go into the details of this comparison they needed to adapt their analysis of Hebrew to the Arabic theory of triradicalism. In the Arabic tradition it was clear from the start that words derive from a root of three (or four or five) radicals. This derivation is sometimes obscured by phonological rules that affect roots containing a glide (the so-called weak roots); *qâla* "to say", *sâra* "to travel", for instance, were reanalysed on the basis of other words as **qawala*, **sayara* (compare, for instance, the nouns *qawl* "speech", *sayr* "journey"). The intricate system the Arabic grammarians devised for the analysis of the weak roots took care of all phonological changes and made the morphology of the language even more transparent than it already was. Even for those nouns that have only two radicals the triradical theory by resorting to *taqdîr* found a third radical: words such as *yad* "hand", *'ab* "father", that belong to the primitive lexical stock were provided by them with an extra radical, usually a glide, in order to incorporate them in the system.

In Hebrew things are somewhat more complicated. Because of historical developments in the language the relationship between derivates from the same roots is not always immediately obvious, and it took the Hebrew grammarians until the tenth century to establish the system of triradicalism for their language. In this development they were supported by the system of Arabic grammar. Yet the theory of triradicalism was never completely accepted by Hebrew grammarians. In fact, Ibn Janâḥ refuses to accept that all words in the language are triradical, and maintains that many of the verbal stems are really biradical. For those Hebrew grammarians and lexicographers who did accept the triradical theory it became much easier to compare the two languages, especially in the categories of the weak verbs.

In spite of their comparative results, the efforts of the first comparativists were unable to influence the growth of the tradition. Hebrew grammarians of later generations ignored the achievements of scholars such as Ibn Quraysh and returned to the synchronic type of linguistic analysis that was *de rigueur* in Arabic grammar. Just as the grammarians who described Turkic and Coptic with the help of the Arabic model of linguistics, they took over this model with few modifications, since they regarded it as universally valid.

As in the case of the description of Turkic the dependence on the Arabic model can be illustrated with an example from phonology. One of the most obvious phonological differences between Hebrew and Arabic is the number of vowels. Arabic has only three vowels, /a/, /i/, and /u/, the long vowels /a:/, /i:/, and /u:/ being analysed by the grammarians as combinations of a short vowel and a glide, i.e., /a"/, /iy/, and /uw/ (cf. above, chapter 2, p. 27). The Hebrew grammarians borrowed the Arabic model and stated that Hebrew, too, also has three original vowels, from which the other vowels are derived. Thus, according to Ibn Janâḥ the original vowels were /a/, /i/, and /u/ as in Arabic; open and closed /o/ are derived from /u/, open /e/ is derived from /a/, and closed /e/ is derived from /i/, because in their pronunciation they incline towards them, just as the allophones in Arabic do.

The grammatical theories of grammarians like Ibn Quraysh and Ibn Janâḥ were generally neglected by scholars in Western Europe and did not influence the development of Hebrew studies in Western Europe. In other respects Hebrew studies in Europe developed in close co-operation with Jewish scholars. But the emergence of comparative linguistics in Western Europe was an autonomous development with completely different roots. Comparative Semitic linguistics had to wait until the elaboration of the historical-comparative method for the Indo-European languages in the nineteenth century.

Abbreviations

Ar.	*Arabica. Revue d'études arabes.* Leiden.
AUU	*Acta Universitatis Upsaliensis.* Stockholm.
GAP	*Grundriss der arabischen Philologie.* I. *Sprachwissenschaft*, ed. by Wolfdietrich Fischer. II. *Literaturwissenschaft*, ed. by Helmut Gätje. III. *Supplement*, ed. by Wolfdietrich Fischer. Wiesbaden: L. Reichert, 1983, 1987, 1992.
HEL	*Histoire, Epistémologie, Langage.* Paris.
HIL	*Histoire des idées linguistiques*, I, II, ed. by Sylvain Auroux *et al.* Liège & Brussels: P. Mardaga, 1989, 1992.
HL	*Historiographia Linguistica.* Amsterdam.
HLNE	*The History of Linguistics in the Near East*, ed. by Kees Versteegh, Konrad Koerner, and Hans-Josef Niederehe. Amsterdam: J. Benjamins, 1983 (= *Studies in the History of Linguistics*, 28).
IQ	*The Islamic Quarterly. A review of Islamic culture.* London.
Islam	*Der Islam. Zeitschrift für Geschichte und Kultur des islamischen Orients.* Berlin.
JAOS	*Journal of the American Oriental Society.* New Haven, Conn.
JCS	*Journal of Coptic Studies.*
JHAS	*Journal for the History of Arabic Science.* Aleppo.
JSAI	*Jerusalem Studies in Arabic and Islam.* Jerusalem.
JSS	*Journal of Semitic Studies.* Manchester.
L & C	*Linguistics & Communication.* Oxford.
LG	*Lexicon Grammaticorum: Who's Who in the History of Linguistics*, ed. by Harro Stammerjohann. Tübingen: Niemeyer, 1996.

MW	*The Muslim World*. Hartford, Conn.
REI	*Revue des Etudes Islamiques*. Paris.
SHAG I	*Studies in the History of Arabic Grammar. Proceedings of the First Symposium on the History of Arabic Grammar, held at Nijmegen 16–19 April 1984*, ed. by Hartmut Bobzin and Kees Versteegh. Wiesbaden: O. Harrassowitz, 1985 (= *ZAL 15).*
SHAG II	*Studies in the History of Arabic Grammar II. Proceedings of the 2nd Symposium on the History of Arabic Grammar, Nijmegen, 27 April – 1 May 1987*, ed. by Michael G. Carter and Kees Versteegh. Amsterdam: J. Benjamins (= *Studies in the History of the Language Sciences*, 56).
SI	*Studia Islamica*. Paris.
Word	*Word. Journal of the International Linguistics Association*. New York.
ZAL	*Zeitschrift für arabische Linguistik*. Wiesbaden.
ZDMG	*Zeitschrift der Deutschen Morgenländischen Gesellschaft*. Wiesbaden.
ZGAIW	*Zeitschrift für Geschichte der Arabisch–Islamischen Wissenschaften*. Frankfurt am Main.

Further reading

Introduction

General histories of linguistics usually content themselves with secondary sources and do not quote extensively from the primary sources (cf. e.g. Itkonen 1991, whose section on Arabic is based entirely on a few secondary sources). General handbooks on the history of linguistics usually contain a section on the history of linguistics in the Arabic tradition; as examples we may mention Blanc's (1975) contribution to the volume on the history of linguistics in the *Current Trends*; Versteegh's (1989b) and Bohas, Guillaume, & Kouloughli's (1989) sections on Arabic in the *Histoire des Idées Linguistiques*, and Fleisch's (1994) somewhat outdated sketch in Longman's *History of Linguistics*. The biographies of approximately sixty Arabic grammarians are included in the *Lexicon Grammaticorum* (*LG*) with further references.

For the history of the Arabic language see the articles in the first volume of the German *Grundriss der arabischen Philologie* (*GAP*), as well as the introductory chapters on the history of Arabic in Holes (1995) and those in Versteegh's (1997) history of the Arabic language, especially the chapter on the emergence of the new type of Arabic.

Specialized introductions to the history of the Arabic linguistic tradition are usually concerned with the theoretical aspects of Arabic grammatical theory, for instance the excellent introduction by Bohas, Guillaume, & Kouloughli (1990). Shorter introductions are available in German (Versteegh 1987; Wild 1987), and English (Carter 1990).

For those who wish to become acquainted with the technical aspects of Arabic grammar Carter (1981) is an excellent introduction. It contains a translation with commentary of an Arabic grammatical text, which may serve as a source book for those wishing to pursue their study of this tradition. Carter discusses all aspects of grammatical structure in extensive notes on the introductory text by ash-Shirbînî he has translated. Versteegh (1995) has a similar set-up: it contains the translation of a text by the grammarian az-Zajjâjî with extensive notes, in which the emphasis is on more general linguistic problems such as the hierarchy of linguistic elements and the nature of linguistic reasoning.

The problem of translating the technical terminology of the Arabic linguistic tradition has become the subject of a heated discussion among specialists in this field. For a critical statement see Carter (1994) and the answer by Owens (1995). A careful and valuable comparison of Arabic theoretical principle with Western linguistic theories is given by Owens (1988), in particular his discussion of the parallels between Arabic grammar and dependency grammar (pp. 31-88) and those between Arabic grammar and transformational grammar (pp. 245–8). For some remarks about the notion of "underlying level" see Versteegh (1994); for common problems in Arabic and modern theories on morphological segmentation see Versteegh (1985) and Itkonen (1991: 157).

We shall see that most of Arabic grammar was oriented towards formal criteria, and in technical grammatical treatises the role of semantics remains mostly implicit. For the ideas on semantics in Arabic grammar compared with those in three other linguistic traditions – Sanskrit, Hebrew, and Greek – see van Bekkum *et al.* (1997).

For the history of the discipline with biographical data on the authors and editions of their works we refer to the handbook of Arabic literature by Sezgin; in this handbook volume VIII (1982) deals with lexicography, volume IX (1984) with grammar. There is no literary history of the discipline, but Flügel (1862) is still useful; there is a short sketch in French by Fleisch (1961: 19–49).

A bibliography of grammatical literature was published by Diem (1983). There are several collective volumes with original articles dealing with various aspects of the Arabic linguistic tradition, such as Versteegh, Koerner, & Niederehe (*HLNE*), Bobzin & Versteegh (*SHAG* I), and Carter & Versteegh (*SHAG* II).

Chapter 1

A general introduction to the *Qur'ân* is Watt's (1970) revision of Bell's work on this subject. The state of the art in modern studies on *tafsîr* is presented by Rippin (1982). The development of Qur'ânic commentaries is treated by Abbott (1967) on the basis of the available papyri. An older work is that of Goldziher (1920), whose treatment of the various approaches to the *Qur'ân* is still highly readable, especially on the subject of the mystical, allegorical, and symbolical exegesis of the text. Wansbrough's (1977) attempt to analyse Qur'ânic exegesis in terms of Jewish Talmudic methods is controversial, but contains interesting observations. It should be added that Wansbrough does not believe that the preserved commentaries of the oldest period of Islam, such as the one by Muqâtil, are authentic; according to him, some of the materials may derive ultimately from earlier commentators, but the commentaries themselves were composed in the third century of the Islamic era. Gilliot (1990) is especially relevant for the connection between exegesis and linguistics in the later commentaries. The issue of the words of foreign origin and the influence of religion in lexicography is discussed by Kopf (1956). The connection between exegesis and the origin of Arabic grammar in Basra and Kufa is the subject of Versteegh (1993). On the existence of two distinct grammatical schools see also Baalbaki (1981), Talmon (1985, 1990), and the survey in Bernards (1993: 3–12).

Chapter 2

A general work on Arabic lexicography is Haywood (1965), outdated, but very readable. On the history of modern Western lexicography of Arabic see Gätje (1985); on the revival of Arabic lexicographical studies in Syria and Lebanon in the nineteenth century see Sawaie (1987, 1990).

The structure of the *Kitâb al-'ayn* and its reception in the later lexicographical literature is discussed by Wild (1965). On al-Khalîl's work as a grammarian and his influence on Sîbawayhi see Reuschel (1959) and Humbert (1994). The possibility of Indian influence in al-Khalîl's phonetic ideas and in the arrangement of the *Kitâb al-'ayn* is discussed and rejected by Law (1990).

For an analysis of the phonetic principles of al-Khalîl's classification of Arabic sounds and on the later development of these principles see Bravmann (1934); for the phonological theories of the Arabic grammarians see Bohas & Guillaume (1984).

Chapter 3

Unfortunately there is no up-to-date translation of the *Kitâb*. Jahn (1895–1900) published a German translation, but it is almost as difficult to follow as the Arabic text. There are three Arabic editions of the *Kitâb*, that of Derenbourg (2 vols, Paris: Imprimerie Nationale, 1881–9; repr., Hildesheim: G. Olms, 1970), which was reproduced in the Bulaq edition (2 vols, Bulaq, 1316 AH; repr., Baghdad: Muthanna Library, n.d.) together with extracts from the commentary of as-Sîrâfî; the third edition is that of Hârûn (5 vols, Cairo, 1966–77), which contains a number of marginal notes from other grammarians, but is fundamentally nothing more than a reprint of the two earlier editions. Humbert (1995) studied all manuscripts of Sîbawayhi's *Kitâb* and concluded that the existing editions use only a very small part of the manuscript tradition; as a result the text as it is used nowadays by most scholars is not a representative text and should certainly be revised thoroughly. Her study also deals with the life of Sîbawayhi and the issue of his teachers. Bernards (1993) is a study of the reception of the *Kitâb* and of al-Mubarrad's attempts first to criticize Sîbawayhi and then to canonize him.

The syntactic methods of Sîbawayhi are analysed by Mosel (1975). Carter (1968) is an extensive study of the quotations in the *Kitâb* and the theoretical principles of his linguistic system; see also Carter (1972, 1973). An evaluation of the quotations from al-Khalîl in the *Kitâb* is given by Reuschel (1959), who concludes that in most respects al-Khalîl already formulated the principles with which Sîbawayhi operated. Levin (e.g., 1985 on the distinction between nominal and verbal sentences; 1986 on the notion of *kalima* "word, morpheme") analyses a number of important terms that occur in the *Kitâb*; one article (1994) discusses the role of the native speaker in the *Kitâb*. An index of the technical terminology in the *Kitâb* was compiled by Troupeau (1976).

One of the earliest analyses of the principles of the Arabic grammarians is that of Weil (1915). A careful and valuable comparison of Arabic theoretical principles and Western parallels is given by Owens (1988); his comparison between the Arabic approach towards dependency and modern linguistic models in dependency grammar is especially worth reading, as is his analysis of the parallels and differences between Arabic grammar and transformational linguistics; cf. also Itkonen (1991). For the distinction between nominal and verbal sentences see Ayoub & Bohas (1983) and Levin (1985). The principle of underlying levels is discussed by Versteegh (1995). On the notion of hierarchy in Arabic linguistic theory see Baalbaki (1979).

Our knowledge of the Arabic tradition is still incomplete and there are very few studies about its development and the innovations that were doubtlessly introduced in the course of more than seven centuries. Owens (1990) has studied the terminology in a number of grammatical texts from the first four centuries of the tradition in order to find a method to trace such innovations, in particular those connected with the two schools of Basra and Kufa. Bohas & Guillaume (1984) concentrate on the late grammarians (twelfth to fifteenth centuries); in various instances they point out that there were innovations on the theoretical level between the early and the late grammarians; on this issue see also Versteegh (1989c).

Chaper 4

The general philosophical context of tenth-century Islam is sketched by Kraemer (1986), who also discusses the debate between as-Sîrâfî and Mattâ ibn Yûnus (1986: 143–51).

The text of thc dcbate was discussed extensively by Mahdi (1970), who analysed the arguments step by step, translating the essential passages into English. A German translation was published with an extensive study by Endress (1986: 163–270) and a French translation by Elamrani-Jamal (1983: 149–63) as an appendix to his study of the relations between Aristotelian philosophy and Arabic grammar. On the universalist claims of the Arab logicians see also Versteegh (1980).

Yaḥyâ ibn ʻAdî's treatise was published for the first time by Endress (1978) and discussed by him in (1977a) in Arabic with an English summary; see also Endress (1986: 272–99) for a German translation. A French translation in Elamrani-Jamal (1983: 187–97). On Yaḥyâ ibn ʻAdî's life and work see Endress (1977b).

Chapter 5

The text of the *Kitâb al-'îḍâḥ* is available in English translation (Versteegh 1995) with commentary and references to further literature. Guillaume (n.d.) is a brilliant analysis of the intellectual framework of the treatise and worth reading in particular because of his emphasis on the interrelatedness between grammar and culture at large. About az-Zajjâjî's ideas on the classification of the parts of speech see Suleiman (1990).

For other grammarians of this period see the survey by Troupeau (1962). Since most of the writings of this period (as far as they have been discovered in the libraries in the Middle East) have been edited only recently, or are still in the process of being edited, there still is not much literature on their theories. On Ibn as-Sarrâj and his pivotal function in the history of Arabic grammar see Taha (1995), who analyses the notion of transitivity in Sîbawayhi, al-Mubarrad, and Ibn as-Sarrâj. On ar-Rummânî and his connections with the ideas of the theological school of the Mu'tazila see Carter (1984). A translation into German of a section from ar-Rummânî's commentary on Sîbawayhi's *Kitâb* was published by Ambros (1979). As-Sîrâfî's commentary on the *Kitâb* – the most important commentary in the entire Arabic grammatical tradition – has not yet been published in its entirety, but extracts from this commentary in German translation are available in Jahn's (1895–1900) translation of the *Kitâb* of Sîbawayhi.

Chapter 6

In his English translation of al-Fârâbî's commentary on Aristotle's *De Interpretatione* and in his notes to the translation Zimmermann (1981) gives an extensive sketch of al-Fârâbî's place in the intellectual context of his time (pp. xxi–cxxxix); on al-Fârâbî's technical terminology see Zimmermann (1972). Al-Fârâbî's ideas about language and logic are discussed by Haddad (1969) and by Elamrani-Jamal (1983) who in an appendix gives a French translation of a long passage from al-Fârâbî's commentary on *De Interpretatione* (pp. 177–80). The most recent publication on al-Fârâbî's ideas about the Arabic language is Abed (1991). The connection between the grammatical terms introduced by al-Fârâbî and those of the Greek grammarians is demonstrated by Gätje (1971); cf. also Versteegh (1977: 46–54).

Chapter 7

There is not much literature on the 'Ikhwân aṣ-Ṣafâ''s theories of speech. A general introduction in their doctrine is given by Netton (1982); Diwald-Walzer (1975). In an unpublished MA thesis van den Heuvel (1988) analyses the epistle on language; some of the material in this chapter was taken from this thesis. Many references to the 'Ikhwân are found in the work of Kraus (1942) on Jâbir ibn Ḥayyân's combination of gnostic knowledge, alchemy, and a lively interest in the symbolic values of numbers, sounds, and words. On the mystic interpretations of the *Qur'ân* see Goldziher (1920).

Chapter 8

A detailed discussion of all texts concerning the origin of speech is given in a lengthy article by Loucel (1963–4) with translations of the most important passages; texts from al-Ghazzâlî, Ibn Sîdah and Ibn Ḥazm were translated into Spanish by Asín Palacios (1939); shorter discussions in Weiss (1974) and Versteegh (1996). The passage on the origin of speech in as-Suyûṭî's compilation was translated in English by Czapkiewicz (1988).

Blanc (1979) discusses the diachronic elements in Arabic grammatical thinking. On Ibn Jinnî's life and linguistic activities see Méhiri (1973); on his theoretical views see also Guillaume (n.d.). The theological context of the Mu'tazilite theories on the origin of speech is discussed in Peters' (1976) study of God's speech. The role of the Mu'tazila in grammar is dealt with by Versteegh (1977: 149–61; forthcoming) and Carter (1984).

Chapter 9

About al-Jurjânî's theories of linguistics see Baalbaki (1983); Rammuny (1985). About his commentary on al-Fârisî's *'Îḍâḥ* see Versteegh (1992). A detailed analysis of al-Jurjânî's ideas about language and style and his relations with Mu'tazilite theory is given in Larkin (1995). A German translation of the *'Asrâr al-balâgha* was published by Ritter (1959).

The discussion in Arabic literary theory about the status of meanings and expressions is analysed by Schoeler (1969).

A German translation of as-Sakkâkî's *Miftâḥ* was published by

Simon (1993), with an extensive introduction and notes about the semantic approach of this author and his predecessors such as al-Jurjânî.

The role of semantics in later grammatical theory is dealt with by Gully (1995, on Ibn Hishâm); Larcher published a series of articles about the pragmatic aspects of later grammatical theory (e.g., 1990, 1993).

Chapter 10

The development of the science of the *'uṣûl al-fiqh* and the role of the Mu'tazila is dealt with by Makdisi (1984); the relationship between grammar and *'uṣûl* and the Mu'tazilites' role as link is discussed by Versteegh (forthcoming). On ar-Râzî's role as an exegete see Gilliot (1990).

The best source for the *waḍ' al-lugha* is Weiss (1966), a very lucid analysis of the principles and theories of this science, from which most of the treatment of the subject in this chapter has been derived; in other publications Weiss deals with special problems that are discussed by the *'uṣuliyyûn* and the treatises of the *waḍ' al-lugha*: the origin of speech (1974), the transmission of language (1984), the classification of the parts of speech (1976).

Chapter 11

There is not much literature on Ibn Maḍâ', but Wolfe (1984) has a complete translation into English; in the introduction he presents a detailed outline of Ibn Maḍâ''s theories; the book also contains a large section on the influence of Ibn Maḍâ' in the modern period (see also Wolfe (1990) on the history of the text). On Ibn Ḥazm there is a large study by Arnaldez (1956), who concentrates on Ibn Ḥazm's ideas about logic and language. Ibn Ḥazm's ideas about the origin of speech are discussed by Asín Palacios (1939).

On the ideas about simplification and reform of grammar see Diem (1974: 126–43) and the Arabic introduction to the edition of Ibn Maḍâ''s book by Shawqî Ḍayf.

Chapter 12

The text of the *Muqaddima* is available in a French (Monteil 1967–8) and an English (Rosenthal 1958) translation, both with an introduction about Ibn Khaldûn's theory of civilization. This theory has been very influential even in Western theories of history. There is not much literature about Ibn Khaldûn's specific opinions about language, but see Irving (1960).

Information about the linguistic situation on the Arabian peninsula in the pre-Islamic period is given by Rabin (1951). For a discussion about the development of the Arabic language see Zwettler (1978). A dissenting opinion (Versteegh 1984) looks upon the process of development of Arabic as a process of pidginization followed by creolization (i.e., the pidgin language becomes the mother tongue of the children in mixed marriages, undergoing various phenomena of expansion and grammaticalization).

Blanc (1979) discusses the place of the concept of "diachrony" in the Arabic grammatical tradition. A very interesting analysis of the role of diachrony and the impossibility of interpreting phonological phenomena in a diachronic sense in Arabic grammar is given by Guillaume (1981 and n.d.). His main topic is the analysis by Ibn Jinnî. The treatises about the *laḥn al-'âmma* are discussed by Molan (1978), who concludes that they do not occupy themselves with the structure of the colloquial language, but with the mistakes in writing by semi-literates.

Chapter 13

A systematic and extensive analysis of 'Abû Ḥayyân's methods is given by Ermers (1995), who analyses in detail the effects of the application of the Arabic model; some of the material in this chapter has been derived from his analysis. On the Ottoman tradition of language study see Kerslake (1994).

On the Coptic linguistic tradition see Bauer (1972), who gives a German translation of a Coptic grammar in Arabic from the thirteenth/fourteenth century; for a survey see Sidarus (1993).

On the linguistic situation of the Jews in the Islamic empire and on Judaeo-Arabic see Blau (1981). For the development of Hebrew grammar see Zwiep (1995). On the comparative methods of the Hebrew grammarians and in particular on the *Risâla* by Ibn Quraysh, see van Bekkum (1983); El-Dabousy (1983); Kaplan (1992).

Bibliographical references

Abed, Shukri B. 1991. *Aristotelian Logic and Arabic Language in Alfârâbî*. Albany: State Univ. of New York Press.

Abbott, Nabia. 1967. *Studies in Arabic Literary Papyri*. II. *Qur'ânic Commentaries and Tradition*. Chicago: Univ. of Chicago Press.

Al-Nassir [an-Nâṣir], 'Abd al-Mun'im 'Abd al-'Amîr. 1993. *Sibawayh the Phonologist: A critical study of the phonetic and phonological theory of Sibawayh as presented in his treatise* Al-Kitab. London & New York: Kegan Paul International.

Ambros, Edith. 1979. *Sieben Kapitel des* Šarḥ Kitâb Sîbawaihi *von ar-Rummânî in Edition und Übersetzung*. Vienna: Verlag des Verbandes der wisschenschaftlichen Gesellschaften Österreichs.

Arnaldez, Roger. 1956. *Grammaire et théologie chez Ibn Hazm de Cordoue: Essai sur la structure et les conditions de la pensée musulmane*. Paris: J. Vrin.

Asín Palacios, Miguel. 1939. "El origen del lenguaje y problemas conexos, en Algazel, Ibn Sîda e Ibn Ḥazm". *Al-Andalus* 4: 253–81.

Ayoub, Georgine and Georges Bohas. 1983. "Les grammairiens arabes, la phrase nominale et le bon sens". *HLNE* 31–48.

Baalbaki, Ramzi. 1979. "Some aspects of harmony and hierarchy in Sîbawayhi's grammatical analysis". *ZAL* 2: 7–22.

—— 1981. "Arab grammatical controversies and the extant sources of the second and third centuries A.H.". *Studia Arabica et Islamica. Festschrift for Iḥsân 'Abbâs*, ed. by Wadâd al-Qâḍî, 1–26. Beirut: American Univ.

—— 1983. "The relation between *naḥw and balâġa*: A comparative study of the methods of Sîbawayhi and Ǧurǧânî". *ZAL* 11: 7–23.

Bauer, Gertrud. 1972. *Athanasius von Qus*, Qilâdat at-taḥrîr fî 'ilm at-tafsîr: *Eine koptische Grammatik in arabischer Sprache aus dem 13./14. Jahrhundert*. Freiburg: K. Schwarz.

Bekkum, Wout Jacques van. 1983. "The *Risâla* of Yehuda ibn Quraysh and its place in Hebrew linguistics". *HLNE* 71–91.

——, Jan Houben, Ineke Sluiter, and Kees Versteegh. 1997. *The Emergence of Semantics in Four Linguistic Traditions: Hebrew, Sanskrit, Greek, Arabic*. Amsterdam & Philadelphia: J. Benjamins.

Bernards, Monique. 1993. *Establishing a Reputation: The reception of the* Kitâb Sîbawayh. Diss. Univ. of Nijmegen.

Blanc, Haim. 1975. "Linguistics among the Arabs". *Current Trends in Linguistics*. XIII. *Historiography of Linguistics*, ed. by Thomas Sebeok, 1265–83. The Hague: Mouton.

—— 1979. "Diachronic and synchronic ordering in Medieval Arab grammatical theory". *Studia Orientalia Memoriae D. H. Baneth Dedicata*, 155–80. Jerusalem: Magnes Press.

Blau, Joshua. 1981. *The Emergence and Linguistic Background of Judeo-Arabic: A study of the origins of Middle Arabic*. 2nd ed. Jerusalem: Ben Zwi.

Bohas, Georges. 1981. "Quelques aspects de l'argumentation et de l'explication chez les grammairiens arabes". *Ar.* 28: 204–21.

—— 1985. "L'explication en phonologie arabe". *SHAG* I, 45–52.

—— and Jean-Patrick Guillaume. 1984. *Etude des théories des grammairiens arabes. I. Morphologie et phonologie*. Damascus: Institut Français de Damas.

——, —— and Djamel Eddine Kouloughli. 1989. "L'analyse linguistique dans la tradition arabe". *HIL* I, 260–82.

——, ——, —— 1990. *The Arabic Linguistic Tradition*. New York & London: Routledge.

Bravmann, Max. 1934. *Materialien und Untersuchungen zu den phonetischen Lehren der Araber*. Göttingen: W. F. Kaestner.

Carter, Michael G. 1968. *A Study of Sîbawaihi's Principles of Grammatical Analysis*. Ph.D. Univ. of Oxford.

—— 1972. "Les origines de la grammaire arabe". *REI* 40: 79–97.

—— 1973. "An Arab grammarian of the eighth century A.D.". *JAOS* 93: 146–57.

—— 1981. *Arab Linguistics: An introductory classical text with translation and notes*. Amsterdam: J. Benjamins.

—— 1983. "Language control as people control in Medieval Islam: The aims of the grammarians in their cultural context". *Arab Language and Culture*, ed. by Ramzi Baalbaki, 65–84. Beirut: American Univ. of Beirut.

—— 1984. "Linguistic science and orthodoxy in conflict: The case of al-Rummânî". *ZGAIW* 1: 212–32.

—— 1985. "When did the Arabic word *naḥw* first come to denote grammar?". *L & C* 5: 265–72.

—— 1990. "Arabic grammar". *Cambridge History of Arabic Literature. Religion, Learning and Science in the 'Abbâsid Period*, ed. by M. J. L. Young, J. D. Latham, and R. B. Serjeant, 118–38. Cambridge: Cambridge Univ. Press.

—— 1994. "Writing the history of Arabic grammar". *HL* 21: 385–414.

Czapkiewicz, Andrzej. 1988. *The Views of the Medieval Arab Philologists on Language and its Origin in the Light of as-Suyûti's* al-Muzhir. Cracow: Uniwersytet Jagiellonski.

Diem, Werner. 1974. *Hochsprache und Dialekt im Arabischen: Untersuchungen zur heutigen arabischen Zweisprachigkeit*. Wiesbaden: F. Steiner.

—— 1983. "Bibliographie Sekundärliteratur zur einheimischen arabischen Grammatikschreibung". *HLNE* 195–250.

Diwald-Walzer, Susanne. 1975. *Arabische Philosophie und Wissenschaft in der Enzyklopädie K. Iḫwân aṣ-Ṣafâ': Die Lehre von Seele und Intellekt.* Wiesbaden: F. Steiner.

Elamrani-Jamal, Abdelali. 1983. *Logique aristotélicienne et grammaire arabe: Etude et documents.* Paris: J. Vrin.

El-Dabousy, Salwa. 1983. *Medieval Linguistics: Ibn Janâḥ's comparative structure of Arabic and Hebrew.* Ph.D. Univ. of London.

Endress, Gerhard. 1977a. "The debate between Arabic grammar and Greek logic in Classical Islamic thought". *JHAS* 1: 339–51 [in Arabic; English summary 320–2].

—— 1977b. *The Works of Yaḥyâ ibn 'Adî: An analytical inventory.* Wiesbaden: L. Reichert.

—— 1978. "Yaḥyâ ibn 'Adî's "Treatise on the Difference between the Arts of Philosophical Logic and of Arabic Grammar". A critical edition". *JHAS* 2: 181–93.

—— 1986. "Grammatik und Logik: Arabische Philologie und griechische Philosophie im Widerstreit". *Sprachphilosophie in Antike und Mittelalter*, ed. by Burkhard Mojsisch, 163–299. Amsterdam: B.R. Grüner.

Ermers, Rob. 1995. *Turkic Forms in Arabic Structures: The description of Turkic by Arabic grammarians.* Ph.D. University of Nijmegen.

Ferguson, Charles A. 1959. "Diglossia". *Word* 15: 325–40.

Fleisch, Henri. 1961. *Traité de philologie arabe. I. Préliminaires, phonétique, morphologie nominale.* Beirut: Imprimerie Catholique.

—— 1994. "Arabic linguistics". *History of Linguistics.* I. *The Eastern Traditions*, ed. by Giulio Lepschy, 164–85. London & New York: Longman.

Flügel, Gustav. 1862. *Die grammatischen Schulen der Araber. Erste Abtheilung. Die Schulen von Basra und Kufa und die gemischte Schule.* Leipzig: F. A. Brockhaus.

Frank, Richard. 1981. "Meanings are spoken of in many ways: The earlier Arab grammarians". *Le Muséon* 94: 259–319.

Gätje, Helmut. 1971. "Die Gliederung der sprachlichen Zeichen nach al-Fârâbî". *Der Islam* 47.1–24.

—— 1985. "Arabische Lexikographie: Ein historischer Übersicht". *HL* 12: 105–47.

Gilliot, Claude. 1990. *Exégèse, langue, et théologie en Islam: L'exégèse coranique de Ṭabarî (m. 311/923).* Paris: J. Vrin.

Goldziher, Ignaz. 1920. *Die Richtungen der islamischen Koranauslegung* (2nd repr., Leiden: E. J. Brill, 1970).

Guillaume, Jean-Patrick. 1981. "Le statut des représentations sous-jacentes en morphonologie d'après Ibn Ǧinnî". Ar. 28.222–41.

—— n.d. *La "cause" des grammairiens: Etude sur la notion de* 'illa *dans la tradition grammaticale arabe (fin IIIè/IXè – milieu du IV/X s.).* Thèse de 3ème Cycle, Univ. de Paris-III.

Gully, Adrian. 1995. *Grammar and Semantics in Medieval Arabic: A study of Ibn-Hisham's* "Mughni l-Labib". Richmond: Curzon Press.

Haddad, Fuad. 1969. "Alfârâbi's views on logic and its relation to grammar". *IQ* 13: 192–207.

Haywood, John A. 1965. *Arabic Lexicography: Its history and its place in the general history of lexicography*. 2nd ed. Leiden: E. J. Brill.

Heuvel, Maryem van den. 1988. *De Iḫwân al-Ṣafâ' en hun epistel over de taal*. MA thesis Univ. of Nijmegen.

Holes, Clive. 1995. *Modern Arabic: Structures, functions and varieties*. London & New York: Longman.

Humbert, Geneviève. 1995. *Les voies de la transmission du* Kitâb *de Sîbawayhi*. Leiden: E. J. Brill.

Irving, T. B. 1960. "A fourteenth century view of language". *The World of Islam. Studies in Honour of Philip K. Hitti*, ed. by James Kritzeck and R. Baily Winder, 185–92. London & New York: Macmillan.

Itkonen, Esa. 1991. *Universal History of Linguistics: India, China, Arabia, Europe*. Amsterdam & Philadelphia: J. Benjamins.

Jahn, Gustav. 1895–1900. *Sîbawaihi's Buch über die Grammatik übersetzt und erklärt*. 2 vols. Berlin: Reuther & Reichard (repr., Hildesheim: G. Olms, 1969).

Kaplan, Roger Jay. 1992. *A Critical Study of the Philological Methods of Yehuda ben David (Ḥayyûj)*. Ph.D. New York Univ.

Kerslake, Celia J. 1994. "Two Ottoman Turkish grammars of the Tanzîmât period". *Proceedings of the VII. Conference of the CIEPO, Held in Pécs, Hungary in 1986*, 133–68. Ankara: Türk Tarih Kurumu.

Kopf, Lothar. 1956. "Religious influences on medieval Arabic philology". *SI* 5: 33–59.

Kraemer, Joel L. 1986. *Philosophy in the Renaissance of Islam: Abû Sulaymân al-Sijistânî and his circle*. Leiden: E.J. Brill.

Kraus, Paul. 1942. *Jabir ibn Hayyan: Contributions à l'histoire des idées scientifiques dans l'Islam*. 2 vols. Cairo (repr., Paris: Les Belles Lettres, 1986).

Larcher, Pierre. 1990. "Eléments pragmatiques dans la théorie grammaticale arabe post-classique". *SHAG* II, 195–214.

—— 1993. "Les arabisants et la catégorie de *'inšâ'*: Histoire d'une 'occultation'". *HL* 20: 259–82.

Larkin, Margaret. 1995. *The Theology of Meaning: 'Abd al-Qâhir al-Jurjânî's theory of discourse*. New Haven, Conn.: American Oriental Society.

Law, Vivien. 1990. "Indian influence on early Arab phonetics: Or coincidence?". *SHAG* II, 215–227.

Levin, Aryeh. 1985. "The distinction between nominal and verbal sentences according to the Arab grammarians". *SHAG* I, 118–27.

—— 1986. "The Mediaeval Arabic term *kalima* and the modern linguistic term morpheme: Similarities and differences". *Studies in Islamic History and Civilization in Honour of Professor David Ayalon*, 423–46. Jerusalem: Cana & Leiden: E. J. Brill.

—— 1994. "Sîbawayhi's attitude to the spoken language". *JSAI* 17: 204–43.

Loucel, Henri. 1963–4. "L'origine du langage d'après les grammairiens arabes". *Ar.* 10: 188–208, 253–81; 11: 57–72, 151–87.

Mahdi, Muhsin. 1970. "Language and logic in Classical Islam". *Logic in Classical Islamic Culture*, ed. by Gustav E. von Grunebaum, 51–83. Wiesbaden: O. Harrassowitz.

Makdisi, George. 1984. "The juridical theology of Shâfi'î: Origins and significance of the *uṣûl al-fiqh*". *SI* 59: 5–47.

Méhiri, Abdelkader. 1973. *Les théories grammaticales d'Ibn Jinnî*. Tunis: Université de Tunis.

Merx, Adalbertus. 1889. *Historia artis grammaticae apud Syros*. Leipzig (repr., Nendeln: Kraus, 1966).

Molan, Peter D. 1978. *Medieval Western Arabic: Reconstructing elements of the dialects of al-Andalus, Sicily, and North Africa from the* laḥn al-'âmma *literature*. Ph.D., Univ. of California, Berkeley.

Monteil, Vincent. 1967–8. *Ibn Khaldûn, Discours sur l'Histoire Universelle* (al-Muqaddima): *Traduction nouvelle, préface, notes et index*. 3 vols. Beirut: Commission Libanaise pour la Traduction des Chefs-d'Oeuvre.

Mosel, Ulrike. 1975. *Die syntaktische Terminologie bei Sîbawaih*. Diss. Universität München.

Netton, Ian R. 1982. *Muslim Neoplatonists: An introduction to the thought of the Brethren of Purity (Ikhwân al-Ṣafâ')*. London.

Owens, Jonathan. 1988. *The Foundations of Grammar: An introduction to medieval Arabic grammatical theory*. Amsterdam & Philadelphia: J. Benjamins.

—— 1989. "The syntactic basis of Arabic word classification". *Ar.* 36: 211–34.

—— 1990. *Early Arabic Grammatical Theory: Heterogeneity and standardization*. Amsterdam & Philadelphia: J. Benjamins.

—— 1995. "The comparative study of Medieval Arabic grammatical theory: A mollusc replies to A. E. Houseman, Jr.". *HL* 22: 425–40.

Peters, Johannes R. T. M. 1976. *God's Created Speech: A study in the speculative theology of the Mu'tazilî Qâḍî l-Quḍât Abû l-Ḥasan 'Abd al-Jabbâr bn. Aḥmad al-Hamaḏânî*. Leiden: E. J. Brill.

Rabin, Chaim. 1951. *Ancient West-Arabian*. London: Taylor's Foreign Press.

Rammuny, Raji M. 1985. "Al-Jurjânî: A pioneer of grammatical and linguistic studies". *HL* 12: 351–71.

Reuschel, Wolfgang. 1959. *Al-Ḫalîl ibn-Aḥmad, der Lehrer Sîbawaihs, als Grammatiker*. Berlin: Akademie-Verlag.

Rippin, Andrew. 1982. "The present status of *tafsîr* studies". *MW* 72: 224–38.

Ritter, Hellmut. 1959. *Die Geheimnisse der Wortkunst (Asrar al-balaga) des Abdalqahir al-Curcani*. Wiesbaden: F. Steiner.

Rosenthal, Franz. 1958. *The* Muqaddima *of Ibn Khaldûn: An Introduction to History*. 3 vols. New York.

Rundgren, Frithiof. 1976. "Über den griechischen Einfluss auf die arabische Nationalgrammatik". *AUU* N.S. 2, 5: 119–44.

Sawaie, Mohammed. 1987. "Jurjî Zaydân (1861–1914): A modernist in Arabic linguistics". *HL* 14: 283–304.

—— 1990. "An aspect of 19th-century Arabic lexicography: The modernizing role and contribution of Faris al-Shidyak (1804?–1887)". *History and Historiography of Linguistics*, ed. by Hans-Josef Niederehe and Konrad Koerner, I, 157–71. Amsterdam & Philadelphia: J. Benjamins.

Schoeler, Gregor. 1969. *Arabische Dichtung und griechische Poetik: Ḥâzim al-Qarṭâǧannîs Grundlegung der Poetik mit Hilfe aristotelischer Begriffe*. Beirut & Wiesbaden: F. Steiner.

Semaan, Khalil. 1968. *Linguistics in the Middle Ages: Phonetic studies in early Islam*. Leiden: E. J. Brill.

Sezgin, Fuat. 1982. *Geschichte des arabischen Schrifttums*. VIII. *Lexikographie bis ca. 430* H. Leiden: E. J. Brill.

—— 1984. *Geschichte des arabischen Schrifttums*. IX. *Grammatik bis ca. 430* H. Leiden: E. J. Brill.

Sidarus, Adel. 1993. "Medieval Coptic grammars in Arabic: The Coptic *muqaddimât*". JCS 3: 1–10.

Simon, Udo Gerald. 1993. *Mittelalterliche arabische Sprachbetrachtung zwischen Grammatik und Rhetorik*: 'ilm al-ma'ânî bei as-Sakkâkî. Heidelberg: Heidelberger Orientverlag.

Stoetzer, Wilhelmus F. G. J. 1986. *Theory and Practice in Arabic Metrics*. Diss. Leiden Univ. [Leiden: The Netherlands Institute for the Near East, 1989].

Suleiman, M. Yassir. 1990. "Sîbawaihi's 'parts of speech' according to Zajjâjî: A new interpretation". *JSS* 35: 245–63.

Taha, Zeinab Ahmed. 1995. *Issues of Syntax and Semantics: A comparative study of Sibawayhi, al-Mubarrad, and Ibn as-Sarraaj*. Ph.D. Georgetown Univ.

Talmon, Rafael. 1985. "Who was the first Arab grammarian?: A new approach to an old problem". *SHAG* I, 128–45.

—— 1988. "'*Al-kalâm mâ kâna muktafiyan bi-nafsihi wa-huwa ǧumla*': A study in the history of sentence concept and the Sîbawaihian legacy in Arabic grammar". *ZDMG* 138: 74–98.

—— 1990. "The philosophizing Farrâ': An interpretation of an obscure saying attributed to the grammarian Ṯa'lab". *SHAG* II, 265–79.

Troupeau, Gérard. 1962. "La grammaire à Bagdad du IXe au XIIIe siècle". *Ar.* 9: 397–405.

—— 1976. *Lexique-index du* Kitâb *de Sîbawayhi*. Paris: Klincksieck.

Versteegh, Kees. 1977. *Greek Elements in Arabic Linguistic Thinking*. Leiden: E. J. Brill.

—— 1980. "Logique et grammaire au dixième siècle". *HEL* 2: 39–52, 67–75.

—— 1983. "A dissenting grammarian: Quṭrub on declension". *HLNE* 167–93.

—— 1984. *Pidginization and Creolization: The case of Arabic*. Amsterdam: J. Benjamins.

—— 1985. "The development of argumentation in Arabic grammar: The declension of the dual and the plural". *SHAG* II, 152–73.

—— 1987. "Arabische Sprachwissenschaft (Grammatik)". *GAP*, II, 148–76.

—— 1989a. "A sociological view of the Arab grammatical tradition: Grammarians and their professions". *Studia Linguistica et Orientalia*

Memoriae Haim Blanc Dedicata, ed. by Paul Wexler *et al.*, 289–302. Wiesbaden: O. Harrassowitz.
—— 1989b. "Le langage, la religion et la raison". *HIL* I, 243–59.
—— 1989c. "Early and late grammarians in the Arab grammatical tradition: The morphonology of the hollow verb". *ZAL* 20: 9–22.
—— 1990. "Freedom of the speaker: The term *ittisâ'* and related notions in Arabic grammar". *SHAG* II, 281–93.
—— 1992. "Grammar and rhetoric: Ǧurǧânî on the verbs of admiration". *JSAI* 15: 113–33.
—— 1993. *Arabic Grammar and Qur'ânic Exegesis in Early Islam*. Leiden: E. J. Brill.
—— 1994. "The notion of 'underlying levels' in the Arabic grammatical tradition", *HL* 21: 271–96.
—— 1995. *The Explanation of Linguistic Causes: Az-Zaǧǧâǧî's theory of grammar, introduction, translation and commentary*. Amsterdam & Philadelphia: J. Benjamins.
—— 1996. "Linguistic attitudes and the origin of speech in the Arab world". *Festschrift Badawi*, ed. by Alaa El-Gibali. Cairo: American University Press.
—— 1997. *The Arabic Language*. Edinburgh: Edinburgh Univ. Press.
—— Forthcoming. "The linguistic introduction to Râzî's *Tafsîr*". *Studies on Near Eastern Languages and Literatures. Memorial Volume Karel Petráček*, ed. by Petr Vavroušek and Petr Zemánek. Prague.
Wansbrough, John. 1977. *Quranic Studies: Sources and methods of scriptural interpretation*. London: Oxford Univ. Press.
Watt, W. Montgomery. 1970. *Bell's Introduction to the* Qur'ân. Revised and enlarged ed. Edinburgh: Edinburgh Univ. Press.
Weil, Gotthold. 1913. *Die grammatischen Fragen der Basrer und Kufer*. Leiden: E. J. Brill.
—— 1915. "Zum Verständnis der Methode der moslemischen Grammatiker". *Festschrift E. Sachau gewidmet*, 380–92. Berlin.
Weiss, Bernard G. 1966. *Language in Orthodox Muslim Thought: A study of* waḍ' al-lughah *and its development*. Ph.D. Princeton Univ.
—— 1974. "The Medieval Muslim discussions of the origin of language". *ZDMG* 125: 33–41.
—— 1976. "A theory of the parts of speech in Arabic (noun, verb and particle): A study in *'ilm al-waḍ'*". Ar 23: 23–36.
—— 1984. "Language and tradition in medieval Islam: The question of *al-Ṭarîq ilâ ma'rifat al-lugha*". *Der Islam* 61: 91–99.
Weiss, Josef. 1910. "Die arabische Nationalgrammatik und die Lateiner". *ZDMG* 64: 349–90.
Wild, Stefan. 1965. *Das* Kitâb al-'ain *und die arabische Lexikographie*. Wiesbaden: O. Harrassowitz.
—— 1987. "Arabische Lexikographie". *GAP* II, 136–47.
Wolfe, Ronald G. 1984. *Ibn Maḍâ' al-Qurṭubî and the Book in Refutation of the Grammarians*. Ph.D. Indiana Univ.
—— 1990. "Ibn Maḍâ' al-Qurṭubî's *Kitâb ar-radd 'alâ n-nuḥât*: An historical misnomer". *SHAG* II, 295–304.
Zimmermann, F. W. 1972. "Some observations on al-Fârâbî and logical

tradition". *Islamic Philosophy and the Classical Tradition. Essays Presented by his Friends and Pupils to Richard Walzer on his seventieth Birthday*, ed. by Samuel M. Stern, Albert Hourani and Vivian Brown, 517–46. Oxford: Cassirer.

—— 1981. *Al-Fârâbî's Commentary and Short Treatise on Aristotle's* De Interpretatione. Oxford: Oxford Univ. Press.

Zwettler, Michael. 1978. *The Oral Tradition of Classical Arabic Poetry: Its character and implications*. Columbus: Ohio State Univ. Press.

Zwiep. Irene E. 1995. *Aristotle, Galen, God: A short history of medieval Jewish linguistic thought*. Ph.D. Univ. of Amsterdam.

Index